D0759834

GENDERED POLITICS IN THE MODERN SOUTH

MAKING THE MODERN SOUTH
David Goldfield, *Series Editor*

GENDERED POLITICS I

The Susan Smith Ca

HE MODERN SOUTH

d the Rise of a New Sexism

KEIRA V. WILLIAMS

LOUISIANA STATE UNIVERSITY PRESS)|(Baton Rouge

Published by Louisiana State University Press
Copyright © 2012 by Louisiana State University Press
All rights reserved
Manufactured in the United States of America
FIRST PRINTING

DESIGNER: Mandy McDonald Scallan
TYPEFACE: Whitman
PRINTER: McNaughton & Gunn, Inc.
BINDER: Dekker Bookbinding

Library of Congress Cataloging-in-Publication Data

Williams, Keira V., 1976–
  Gendered politics in the modern South : the Susan Smith case and
the rise of a new sexism / Keira V. Williams.
      p. cm.— (Making the modern South series)
  Includes bibliographical references and index.
  ISBN 978-0-8071-4768-9 (cloth : alk. paper) — ISBN 978-0-8071-
4769-6 (pdf) — ISBN 978-0-8071-4770-2 (epub) — ISBN 978-0-
8071-4771-9 (mobi)
  1. Smith, Susan (Susan Vaughan) 2. Infanticide—South Carolina—
Union—Case studies. 3. Motherhood—Southern States. 4. Sex
role—Southern States. 5. Sexism--Southern States. 6. Stereotypes
(Social psychology)—Southern States. I. Title. —
  HV6541.U62U568 2012
  364.152'3092—dc23

                                          2012007255

CONTENTS

ACKNOWLEDGMENTS

To quote Hillary Clinton, this one definitely took a village. First of all, thank you to Bryant Simon, my graduate advisor, for fielding countless dumb questions, giving sage advice, reading a million drafts, writing many tedious letters, and being a Tar Heel. Thanks as well to the other members of my dissertation committee (Kathleen Clark, Jim Cobb, Bonnie Dow, and Laura Mason), and to the editors and readers at LSU Press (Rand Dotson, David Goldfield, and Glenda Gilmore). Without all of your able guidance, this would still be an ill-formed lump of clay. All mistakes and bad ideas herein are clearly my own.

Thanks to the University of Georgia History Department and the UGA Graduate School for early funding, to the Newcomb College Center for Research on Women for nurturing me through those first pre-Katrina chapters, and to the Institute for Southern Studies at the University of South Carolina for the financial assistance that got me through the final interviews in Union.

To the people of Union County: you all really made me feel welcome, even though every single one of you knew I was coming to town to ask about something truly awful from your past. Except for the one ill-advised trip on which my sister and I tried to creep around Fair Forest Plantation and got chased out of the driveway by a fleet of cranky Dobermans, Union truly did feel like the "City of Hospitality." From finger foods to full-on meals, from discussions of African American cowboys to *Gone With the Wind*, I am so grateful for your willingness to embrace a complete stranger. Thank you to all interviewees, in alphabetical order: Amy Birnbaum, A.L. Brackett, Rick Bragg, Anna Brown, David Bruck, Bob Cato, Allan Charles, Jules Corriere, Ann Currie, Tom Currie, Twila Decker-Davis, Bob Dotson, Gary Henderson, Phil Hobbs, McElroy Hughes, Bill Howard, Torance Inman, Kevin Kingsmore, Randall Pinkston, Tommy Pope, Alan Raines, Michael Roberts, Thom White, and Toni White. I also wish to thank Susan Smith, who consistently supported this project from afar even though she did not know me and had no idea what I might say. And I wish I knew this guy's name: Thank you to the police officer who pulled me over in Newberry County, just a few miles from the Union County line, for giving me my go-to line about this project instead of a speeding ticket. When I told him that I was racing to Union to do an interview about the Smith case, he leaned against my car, whistled, and said, "Whew, that was some shit, won't it?" I pull out this line whenever I get a weird look about my chosen subject.

Now for the personal stuff: I extend a very sincere appreciation to all the women who hold me up (you know who you are). Lolly, thanks for reading every godforsaken draft of this thing from pathetic little dissertation proposal to full manuscript. Juicy, when you schooled the uptight librarian at our elementary school by telling her that she had to let me read whatever I wanted, whenever I wanted (even though I was only in third grade), you set me on the path to dorkhood. Thank you for making me a reader. And finally, to Dad, who grew up working in the mills of Rock Hill, just one county away from Union. Even though he was Rush Limbaugh's biggest fan, he put me through "bleedin' heart liberal" Carolina and faithfully supported all of my graduate school endeavors, wondering all the while what in the world could be taking me so long. He always joked that he hoped he would live long enough to read this book. Sadly, so very sadly, he did not. This book could not have happened without his unfailing love and encouragement. This one's for you, Big Rodge.

INTRODUCTION

J
UST after eight o'clock on the night of October 25, 1994, the McCloud family of Union County, South Carolina, heard a loud noise outside their lakeside home. Startled, Shirley McCloud opened the door to discover a white woman in her early twenties sobbing on the front porch. The young woman, Susan Smith, blurted out the horrifying information that would hold the entire nation spellbound for the next nine days.

"My kids!" she wailed. "He's got my kids!"

Between gasps and tears, Smith told the McClouds that a stranger had carjacked her Mazda with her two sons, Michael, aged three, and Alex, aged fourteen months, in their car seats in the back. She explained that an African American man jumped into the passenger seat of the car while she was stopped at a red light, telling her, "Shut up and drive or I'll kill you." Smith said she drove about ten miles before the man ordered her to stop the car and get out. She pleaded with the carjacker to let her take the children as he forced her through the passenger door. He replied, "I don't have time. I'll take care of them." The carjacker, now a kidnapper as well, left Smith standing helplessly in the middle of the dark country road screaming, "I love y'all" as he sped off into the night.

For nine days, Smith stayed on message, publicizing her story of the carjacker, a dark South Carolina back road, and her stolen boys through the hundreds of television, newspaper, and magazine reporters who flocked to the small southern town of Union (population nine thousand). The public rallied behind the tragic figure of the young mother who called upon God and the good will of the people to help her find her missing babies. Smith gave television and newspaper interviews daily while her neighbors combed the local woods, double-checked the locks on their doors, and hugged their children close.

On the ninth day of the investigation, the guilt-ridden young mother finally cracked under the police pressure and media scrutiny. Smith's emotional confession revealed how, while reportedly in a suicidal stupor, she rolled her car down a boat ramp into a local lake with her boys strapped safely in the back. The sense of betrayal was palpable throughout the nation as the local sheriff announced the end of the investigation via live feed from all of the major television networks. Veteran reporters shed tears as a cold fall wind blew down Main Street in Union. NBC anchor Tom Brokaw was visibly shaken as the network broke away from the live announcement of Smith's arrest. His voice quavering uncharacteristically, he reminded viewers of Smith's lie: "She appeared just this morning grieving on national TV, saying she could not imagine how anyone might think she was a suspect."[1]

In shock, most observers did not know how to make sense of this anomaly, the supposedly loving mother who killed her own children. But not everyone was at a loss for words. The following Sunday, two days before the historic "Republican Revolution" in which the GOP swept the mid-term congressional elections, Newt Gingrich (R-GA) attempted to sum up the New Right cause at a campaign party in Buckhead, a swanky neighborhood in Atlanta: "I can capture everything we are trying to do in a sense by referring to this weekend's unbelievable tragedy in South Carolina, to getting at the root causes of the decay in our society. I think people want change, and the only way to get change is to vote Republican."[2]

Gingrich made his statement linking the Smith case to the upcoming election just three days after the young mother's appalling confession. This was no random crime, the soon-to-be Speaker of the House argued to his largely white, upper-crust audience: "Susan Smith is an example of what's wrong with America. . . . How a mother could kill her two children, 14 months and 3 years, in hopes that her boyfriend would like her, is just a sign of how sick the system is." Although he later characterized the remarks as "offhand," Gingrich defended his statement to Tom Brokaw in an interview the following night, on the eve of the midterm elections. In fact, he extended Susan Smith's symbolic significance even further: "I do believe there is a direct connection between the general acceptance of violence, the general acceptance of brutality, the general decline of civility in this society, and the patterns of the counterculture when Lyndon Johnson's Great Society began in the late '60s."[3] Some observers criticized Gingrich for crassly capitalizing on disturbing headlines, but the rhetorical link he made between the unknown, mill-town mother and Democratic social programs did not hurt Republican prospects. By the end of the following day, the party controlled Congress, and Republicans had won key statewide elections across the country.

Newt Gingrich presaged the revolution of the New Right, a late-twentieth-century branch of neoconservatism that melded conservative populism and opposition to big government with an authoritarian stance on social issues. Gingrich's messages about perceived social problems and political liberalism, and the subtext of gender, class, and race that undergirded those theories, represent key components of the new conservatism that blossomed in the 1990s. I argue that the Susan Smith case serves as one way to analyze the evolution of the new political culture that characterized the turn of the twenty-first century.

Many scholars have studied the remarkable rise of neoconservatism in the postwar, and especially the post–civil rights movement, era in the United States. There is a general academic consensus that the role of racism in politics changed form during the late 1960s. This "new racism" is distinguished from the old racism by the fact that on the surface it hardly appears to be about race at all. In the new racism, "subtle race appeals," such as references to "law and order," "quota systems," and "personal responsibility," replaced explicit white supremacy. The politics of the new racism relied on this covert language of discrimination to reinstall traditional race and class power dynamics.[4]

The New Right did not function on the new racism alone. Neoconservatism is at root reactionary, galvanized by second-wave feminism as much as by the civil rights movement. Indeed, by 1977, the "International Year of the Woman," feminist successes had begun to "raise a red flag to conservatives," sparking the creation of a broad-based anti-feminist coalition. Within just a few years, the New Right platform rested heavily upon a foundation of gendered assumptions. As the new racism (mostly) replaced the old in politics, sexism ascended, and "being overtly antifeminist became increasingly acceptable."[5]

This antifeminism translated into a rallying cry for the traditional patriarchal family. In the New Right mind, social trends such as working and single motherhood, urban crime, affirmative action, welfare and social services, and reproductive rights, among others, were the hated products of broad changes in the socioeconomic order and in family structures. The response was a politics of nostalgia centered on an idealized nuclear family unit, or what became widely known by the 1990s as "family values" politics. These family-values messages and policies carried with them distinctly hierarchical connotations of race, class, and gender: the fantasy American family was white, middle-class, and patriarchal. The new racism is obvious in some of the new political messages about issues like affirmative action and urban crime. But family-values politics also relied quite heavily on traditional ideas about gender roles. In other words, if neoconservatism is about maintaining traditional hierarchies, then it is not just about white supremacy—it is also about patriarchy. Susan Smith is my case study of these gendered foundations of family-values politics, or what I call the "new sexism." This new sexism, with "family values" as its most recognizable rallying cry, worked in tandem with the new racism, and by the 1990s, both permeated American culture.

Historian Linda Gordon argues that "family crises" have surfaced periodically in American history, and "these fears tend to escalate in times of social stress." She explains that this cultural anxiety generally features an abstract ideal of "the family," or rather "a popular image of what families were supposed to be like, by no means a correct recollection of any actual 'traditional' family." The nuclear family of late-twentieth-century family-values rhetoric is similarly ahistorical. The "modern family" that emerged in the nineteenth century was a product of the industrial economy that separated paid work from housework, turning "men into breadwinners and women into homemakers." The result of sweeping economic changes over the past two centuries, the heterosexual nuclear-family form fluctuated throughout the second half of the twentieth century due to economic instability. Sociologist Judith Stacey argues that the tenuous and impermanent foundation of the male breadwinning wage in post-industrial capitalism doomed the nuclear family structure: "Instability was written into the genetic code of the modern family system (on the 'Y' chromosome), because its sustenance depended upon the wide availability of stable, livable-wage jobs for men." Few "breadwinners" of the working class have ever been able to support full-time housewives, and in the postwar, post-industrial second half of the twentieth century, it became nearly impossible.[6]

At the same time, as a result of the social movements of mid-century, African Americans and women flooded sectors of the job market previously unavailable to them. Timing was clearly key to the family-values debate: opponents of these changes drew a causal link between the changing gendered and racial nature of the workforce and the transformation of the American "family," using that link to explain all manner of socioeconomic problems in the late twentieth century. The apparent "crisis" in American family forms surfaced as a mainstream political concern on the heels of these various movements in the 1970s, even though the "steady erosion of the economic underpinnings" of nuclear families was well in place by this time. As neoconservatives regrouped and recovered from the 1960s, they blamed sociocultural movements and the resulting transformation in the gendered and racial order (such as affirmative action, reproductive rights, sexual permissiveness, gay and lesbian rights, working mothers, single mothers, and lax divorce laws, among others) for destroying the purported foundation of American society, the nuclear family. The results of family-structure changes, they argued, would be no less than complete moral and social decay.[7]

The rise of this new form of political conservatism in the last decades of the twentieth century accordingly featured a dual emphasis on traditional masculinity—the provider and protector—and a retrograde brand of femininity in which "woman" equaled "mother." The growing popularity of the political platform of family values constituted a "cultural counterrevolution" meant to reinstate "traditional places in the pecking order." Family-values politicians thus exaggerated the role of both genders. Conservative pundit Alan Crawford calls neoconservatism "macho politics" that featured John Wayne as its "swaggering, tough-talking" hero. In 1994, this machismo surfaced in national, regional, and local politics: the election results of the midterms led political analysts to dub 1994 the year of the "angry white male" as male voters allegedly tried to regain lost ground with their ballots.[8]

Historian Matt Lassiter argues that a major political coup of the past several decades was not so much the rise of neoconservatism, but rather "that cultural explanations triumphed over economic ones in setting the terms of public debate and determining the direction of public policies." Social and cultural issues became the primary indicator of electability, shifting the entire political spectrum. Despite Clinton's campaign war cry, "It's the economy, stupid," in the early 1990s, the "New Democrats" shifted to the right and joined neoconservatives in spouting the "ubiquitous rhetoric" of family values. Although these politics represented more nostalgic belief than lived reality (studies in the mid-1990s showed no "single culturally dominant family pattern"), the domestic policy wars of the 1990s centered on the American family's ideal "values."[9]

The "revolutionary" midterm election of 1994 clearly signaled change, but there were indications of a resurgence of gender traditionalism outside of formal politics in the 1990s, as well. Various journalists declared the "death of feminism" as the assault on affirmative action gained momentum. A growing cult of idealized motherhood, a "pro-life" movement that had turned violent, a feminized "culture of poverty" created by a "broken" welfare system, rising divorce rates, and cries of "reverse" racism and sexism all belied a severe anxiety over gender at the end of the twentieth century. And it was not just women's roles in society that were under fire; American men had reportedly fallen victim to a "crisis in masculinity" that pervaded the culture.

Gendered Politics in the Modern South uses the Susan Smith case, and the massive publicity surrounding it, as a means of explaining and historicizing the reactionary gender culture of the 1990s. Gingrich's over-reaching argument about Susan Smith is but one well-publicized example. "Angry white male" voters, neoconservatives, "New Democrats" who favored family-values politics, and reporters who trafficked in moral panics represented this distinct kind of conservatism that developed at the end of the twentieth century. Susan Smith's sons "went missing" at a key point in the construction of the new racist and new sexist visions of gender. As a white, married, small-town, God-fearing southern mother, Susan Smith severely tested gendered boundaries with her crime. Although her case spawned many different public narratives, these assorted tales had a singular, underlying cultural logic: Smith became a running cautionary tale about the need for a clear assertion of white paternal power in response to the perceived threats of sociocultural change.[10]

The cultural and political battles over how to fix the so-called "family crisis" were, fundamentally, "debate[s] over gendered identities." Public representations of Susan Smith called upon familiar historical images of woman- and motherhood, many of which now seem to have a timeless quality. American political identities have often relied upon stylized gendered representations; Lady Liberty and Uncle Sam are but two well-known examples. Gail Bederman begins her study of gender and American national identity by stating simply that "every society is known by the fictions it keeps," and she argues that these fictions, many of which rest upon gendered foundations, have very real sociopolitical consequences.[11] In the context of the 1990s, popular gendered images had similarly specific political agendas. In the case of Susan Smith, each public representation supported the unique brand of cultural and political neoconservatism that had developed over the course of the second half of the century. These images, or what I call the "seven Susans," form the structure of this book.

The first of the "seven Susans" was the script provided by Smith herself when she told local law enforcement officers about the alleged carjacking. Smith assumed the seemingly timeless mantle of idealized maternity, and despite the many inconsistencies in her story, the national media generally portrayed Smith throughout those first days as a bereft mother, not the most likely suspect. Mothers have long held a central place in American cultural and political identity, from the revolutionary-era concept of "republican motherhood" to the Cold War suburban ideal of full-time homemaking. In the last two decades of the twentieth century, Americans witnessed the ascendance of a renewed ideal of traditional maternity, known academically as the "mommy myth" or the "new momism." Although the image was, in fact, a new invention, the ideal mothers of family-values culture were based on mythical images from the 1950s: they were white, middle-class, married, stay-at-home, and fully devoted to their children (as opposed to the crassly careerist working mothers—or worse, the selfish and impoverished single mothers—that were allegedly produced by second-wave feminism).[12]

The kind of maternal nostalgia that characterized the "new momism" required a male head of household. Accordingly, David Smith, Susan's husband, played a key role in the early days of the investigation as the primary figure that lent legitimacy to her claims of both maternal and victim status. Other male authority figures, particularly Smith's stepfather and the local sheriff, played supporting roles to Smith's starring one as the ideal, white, middle-class mother in danger. Chapter 1, "Susan Smith and the 'Mommy Myth,'" is an exploration of the maternal images that journalists used to make sense of Susan Smith during the nine harrowing days of the kidnapping investigation.

Although it was a compelling image, the ideal mother enjoyed the shortest reign of all of the "seven Susans." Unlike the hopeful Americans tuning in to the news in the fall of 1994, we all know the awful plot twist in this tale of random kidnapping. After nine days of a nationwide manhunt, Susan Smith confessed to double homicide. Her carjacking lie compounded the horror of her crime, and journalists immediately branded her a classic southern "redneck." According to this line of thinking, Smith's kidnapping cover-up was an example of overt racial profiling that firmly violated the tenets of the more subtle new racism. In public representations, Smith became a southern racist, the second of the "seven Susans."

The criminal described by Smith was a relic of the Jim Crow South—the mythical "black beast" who preyed upon white women—that surfaced often in late-twentieth-century media. This image has a long and distasteful history in the United States, and, like images of motherhood, it played a key role in the maintenance of white supremacy and patriarchy, as many historians have argued. In the late twentieth century, the New Right also relied upon this image, but its use was subtler, in accordance with the new racism. Instead of explicitly racializing the alleged sources of crime, politicians simply paired images of African American men with violence and images of white male Republicans with law and order. In famous examples such as the 1988 Bush campaign's "Willie Horton" advertisement, the implications were clear: a Republican vote was a vote against the "black beast."[13]

As scholars of this recent political rhetoric have shown, the new racism required more covert discrimination than the deliberate racial profiling of a fictional carjacker.[14] The explicitly racist nature of Susan Smith's carjacking lie thus violated the code's rules, and she was outcast as a Jim Crow throwback. In the days following Smith's confession, the connections between whiteness, crime, and regional racial politics hastily realigned into a New Right narrative, one with male heroes—"town fathers" like Union County Sheriff Howard Wells and a coalition of local ministers—at its center. In particular, Wells, the confessor, served as the redeeming white patriarch to Smith, the lone racist (although this ostracization belied the fact that thousands of Americans had readily believed her lie). Positioning Smith as an aberrant, individual racist let all other Americans off the hook and allowed the new sexist narrative of white patriarchy to flourish. In chapter 2, "'A Hard Week to Be Black in Union,'" I chart how the many racial narratives surrounding the Smith case culminated in a simple and familiar tale of white, paternal supremacy redeemed, with the injuries to African Americans during the investigation glossed over and quickly discarded in the weeks after Smith's arrest.

In addition to being branded a racist after her confession, dowdy Susan Smith soon became the unlikely star of a sexy tabloid drama. Feminist scholars and criminologists argue that media narratives of female criminals often feature sexuality as their primary characteristic; indeed, public representations often posit romance or revenge as women's primary motives.[15] Accordingly, Susan Smith became a sexual figure. The arrest ensured her swift fall from Madonna to whore in public narratives. Reporters quickly homed in on Smith's checkered sexual history: her rocky marriage, with evidence of the illicit affairs of both parties; her recent relationship with a wealthy local man, Tom Findlay, son of her boss and known around town as "the Catch"; and repeated molestations by her stepfather in her teens and early twenties. Overnight, Smith became a class-climbing, scheming slut who willingly discarded her status as wife and mother for wealth and sexual gratification. This image, the third of the "seven Susans," was the B-side of the ideal wife and mother, a deviant doppelgänger who also easily fit into New Right narratives of gender, race, and class.

In chapter 3, "The 'Modern-Day Medea,'" I explore this demonized image of Smith following her confession to double homicide. These post-confession public narratives linked Smith's rumored sexual behavior to broader perceived problems of female sexuality in the culture, namely single motherhood and abortion. In this rhetoric, moralizing and sexualization—the refrain of the New Right 1990s—went hand in hand, with Smith serving as a central scapegoat.[16] In this chapter, I use the narrative of Susan Smith's "boyfriend motive" to analyze the sexual politics of family-values morality in the 1990s.

Smith's shifting socioeconomic status was a related theme in the post-confession media coverage. As many historians have shown, the mill towns of the Textile Belt in the South had a distinct class hierarchy.[17] Economic stratification lingered in mill towns even as the region underwent severe transformations due to postwar deindustrialization. The fourth of the "seven Susans" tapped into this history, featuring Smith as a financially struggling single mother and millhand who saw her rich boyfriend as her ticket out of the working class. In these public representations, the downward mobility was chronological: just as she was no longer a wife and a mother after her confession (her husband was estranged and her children were dead), Smith was also automatically working class.

The class-based understanding of Susan Smith's crime found its place in a formal political context. Smith inspired a wealth of negative responses from powerful people such as Newt Gingrich and the old conservative stand-by, William F. Buckley Jr. Susan Smith was a modern young woman loosed from patriarchal protection, a single mother run amok, a working-class millhand trying to sleep, rather than work, her way up the socioeconomic ladder. This image of single mothers who "worked the system" soon became legislated reality in the form of the Personal Responsibility and Work Opportunity Reform Act, part of the welfare reforms championed by Newt Gingrich and the GOP in the mid-1990s. This version of Smith dominated the media coverage as troubling information from her past surfaced continually up to the eve of her July 1995 trial.

As they seized upon the dysfunctional details of Smith's past, reporters stationed in Union used stock images of the South to explain Smith's crime. Scholars agree that images of southern distinctiveness generally serve a scapegoating function, more often than not based on ideas about race, class, religion, and gender.[18] The media used this trope, trafficking widely in "Southern Gothic" stereotypes of rural backwardness, violence, and poverty as they aired

Susan Smith's, and Union's, dirty laundry. Yet the words of Unionites themselves indicate a dialectic between their own analyses of their most famous citizen and the media-constructed, sexy "Southern Gothic" story line that graced the nightly features on the case. In fact, Union was exactly the kind of community in which family-values politics flourished. The Christian Coalition and the Moral Majority both enjoyed a large membership in the South Carolina upstate, including Union County. Politically, Smith's hometown was a microcosm of the nationwide "Republican Revolution": the Tuesday after her confession, Union County voters elected their first Republican representative since Reconstruction.

No one stood for the family-values politics of Union County better than Beverly Russell, Susan Smith's stepfather. Russell was a prominent local business owner, tax consultant, former chairman of the Union County Republican Party, state Republican executive committeeman, and a member of the advisory board of the Christian Coalition. It was, then, front-page news when disturbing allegations against Russell began to surface as both sides of the Smith case prepared for trial. When, in late April (six months after the murders), Russell admitted to repeatedly molesting his stepdaughter over the course of almost eight years, Unionites were truly shocked. Recall that in 1995, Americans had not reached an era in which politicians publicly admitted to sexual misconduct on a frequent basis; thus, the news riveted locals as well as viewers nationwide. Unionites, most of whom believed in the family-values politics that Russell had so ardently espoused, struggled to make sense of this plot twist. In chapter 5, "Union's Family Values," I explore this local narrative.

Their solution was not to reject the false familial rhetoric of the molester in their midst. Rather, they created a new image, the fifth of the "seven Susans": the victimized girl whose recent criminality underscored her lifelong need for a strong father figure. Out of this sordid tale of abused patriarchal privilege, Unionites created a new narrative of the public responsibility to provide a kind of paternal protection so that "lost lambs" like Susan Smith would sin no more. According to extensive interviews I conducted in Union, the local confusion, anger, and shame created by their former celebration of a criminal like Beverly Russell mirrored the broader "crisis in masculinity" of the early 1990s. Union's town fathers, including politicians, business leaders, and ministers, expressed guilt that the system of paternal power in their small community had failed so publicly, but they also expressed a determination to take back that power, starting with Susan Smith. By redeeming this woman (or "girl," as most of them described her), Union could restore patriarchal power and reinstate traditional family values in their troubled community.

This victimized image of Susan Smith was a local creation, but it gradually trickled into national news reports and the American consciousness in the weeks leading up to the trial. In chapter 6, "'In a Lake of Fire,'" I analyze the "sixth Susan": the psychologically damaged woman-child that characterized her legal defense. Although many locals testified during those steamy three weeks in July, the expert witnesses who spent days on the stand and in the headlines dictated the tone of the trial. These experts thoroughly psychologized and infantilized Susan Smith, fleshing out the childlike local image of her through complicated psychiatric diagnoses.[19]

This mentally ill version of Susan Smith more closely resembled the new sexism rather than the kind of legal liberalism derided as the "abuse excuse." As a victim of abuse who was not responsible for her actions, the mentally ill "Susan" fit easily within the patriarchal protection racket of the new sexism. In this narrative, the legal system redeemed patriarchal power by sparing the life of a criminal woman, who had transformed by this point into a victimized, even helpless, girl. The media ran with this logic; by the end of the trial in early August of 1995, Susan Smith, no longer an outrage, had become a tragedy. Pathetic reports detailing her state-issued "paper gown," solitary confinement, and suicide watch accompanied coverage of her sentence of life in prison.[20] This defense would, over the course of just a few years, grow to become a popular one for mothers accused of infanticide.

Susan Smith did not fade from the limelight upon her incarceration in August of 1995. Despite the sympathetic image that characterized Smith's sentencing, one narrative overwhelmed public representations during the decade after her trial: the lying "monster mother" and her "boyfriend motive." Americans remember Smith as the "scheming slut" not because of her own individual attributes, but because of the broader cultural context in which she committed this crime. The shifting notions of power and of public paternal authority discussed herein determined a collectively negative memory of Susan Smith.

Perhaps not surprisingly, given her recurring role as the worst mother in America, it took another sensational case of infanticide to put Smith back on the front pages. Susan Smith endured her most consistent fame since her incarceration during the 2001 and 2006 trials of Andrea Yates, the suburban Houston housewife who drowned her five children while suffering from postpartum psychosis. Until Casey Anthony made headlines in the summer of 2011, Yates was the only violent mother since Susan Smith to have so completely captured the nation's attention. Yates was perfectly suited as an ideal mother: she was white, middle-class, overtly religious, and a homemaker. There was one catch: she had a documented history of severe psychiatric problems reportedly stemming from her relationships with men (the same alleged source of Susan's psychological traumas). Media accounts compared Yates to Smith with the goal of distinguishing between them: Smith was clearly "evil" while Yates was certifiably "insane." Yet the two cases have much in common: despite their vastly different psychological symptoms, Smith's "guilty but mentally ill" defense sounds much like Yates's insanity defense (which won her lifelong psychiatric care rather than life in prison in the summer of 2006).

With Yates's trial, the new image of maternal infanticide made national headlines. Partitioning violent mothers off as mentally ill allows the neoconservative narratives of the previous chapters to flourish unscathed. Andrea Yates, according to this image, was not an extreme example of the inequalities of power that position American mothers as the uncomplaining, sole caretakers of the family-values vision. Rather, as a mentally ill individual, she did not threaten the neo-traditional image of gendered power relations in the slightest. Yates was not representative of the constraints on modern mothers, nor was she a violent woman breaking free from the traditional mold. Rather, she was "crazy," and her psychological disturbance had a uniquely feminine diagnosis: postpartum psychosis. This diagnosis, and particularly its less dangerous counterpart, postpartum depression, became a household phrase with the coverage of the Yates trials.

Although some feminist scholars tout postpartum depression as an important way in which we can acknowledge the difficulties of motherhood in our culture, the diagnosis upholds a distinctly new sexist vision of feminine weakness, dependent motherhood, and the need for a strong paternal figure. In the first decade of the twenty-first century, postpartum depression acquired an aura of cultural common sense, but this diagnosis is in fact a very recent phenomenon, and it has become the primary way in which we now understand maternal violence—a narrative that was not available in the mid-1990s. Feminist criminologists have revisited the Susan Smith case in recent years, arguing that she is best understood as suffering from maternity-based mental illness, the final image of the "seven Susans." In fact, Susan Smith herself reportedly now understands her crime as a function of postpartum hormones.[21]

My explicit intent at the outset of this project was to seek cracks in this gendered discourse; the original idea was to mine the complexity of the contemporary representations of maternal violence. Yet these simplistic, neoconservative narratives constantly overwhelmed me during the course of my research. They often seemed to be vying for my attention, as in snarky headlines like "It's Personal Responsibility, Stupid" or "Feminists Must Unite Behind Susan Smith," in which an editorialist argued sarcastically that Smith was just exercising "her right to control her body" when she murdered her sons.[22] In the end, I concluded that the new sexist narrative functioned, unfortunately, as a hegemonic one. In the "Epilogue," I discuss how this new sexism compares to the vital second-wave critique of motherhood. I also speculate about the function of this narrative in the early twenty-first century.

On the surface, Susan Smith's story is actually fairly simple. This case is about a mother who reacted to the various stressors in her life by killing her two sons. They were defenseless children. She was the primary guardian who murdered them, for whatever reason, and then lied about it. This skeletal plot has little, if anything, to do with changing ideas about gender, race, or class. Hundreds of other mothers do the same, and worse, each year, and they do not make the news. Yet Susan Smith dominated headlines from the fall of 1994 to the late summer of 1995, often trumping even the all-consuming O. J. Simpson case on the nightly news. Feminist Annalee Newitz suggests that Susan Smith fascinated so many Americans for reasons beyond mere sensationalism or bloodlust, and I agree. Each of the "seven Susans" has a specific, if diffuse, political agenda. These images uphold white male patriarchy by prescribing proper authority to correct the behavior of the offending woman, who is clearly ruled by her weak and deviant feminine nature. Susan Smith's violent violation of the accepted boundaries of maternal behavior is thus a unique case study of the neotraditional transformation of gender politics at the turn of the twenty-first century.

SUSAN SMITH AND THE "MOMMY MYTH"

O N TUESDAY, OCTOBER 25, 1994, twenty-three-year old Susan Vaughan Smith awakened early to get ready for her job at a local mill. Although she formerly worked as a weaver at Executive Knits, a textile mill, Susan Smith had made the rare move from mill floor to office: in the fall of 1994, she was the administrative assistant to J. Cary Findlay, owner of Conso Products, the world's top producer of decorative tassels. She also attended school. In the early 1990s, Smith's pregnancy and marriage at nineteen derailed her plans for college after high school, but in the fall of 1994, she was getting back on track by taking literature and physical education at the Union extension of the University of South Carolina. When she was at work or school, her sons, Michael, aged three years, and Alex, aged fourteen months, went to Judy Cathcart's in-home day care, just a few miles from Smith's small home on the outskirts of Union, South Carolina.

Although Smith appeared to be going about her usual routine, it was not a normal day for her. Friends and co-workers who communicated with her that day later reported that she seemed to be an emotional wreck. At the time, Smith was going through a nasty divorce from the father of her children, David Smith. The two had been separated several times, including the ten months between August of 1993 and June of 1994. Susan and David Smith had a brief reconciliation between June and August of 1994, which ended when David Smith moved out and rented an apartment close to their home. In late September, Susan Smith filed for divorce on the grounds of adultery.

The Smiths' three-year troubled marriage involved periodic separations, occasionally physical arguments, and even the organized stalking of Susan by David Smith and his girlfriend, Tiffany Moss. In October of 1994, David Smith had been dating Moss for well over a year; this relationship precipitated the legal separation and divorce proceedings. That September, David Smith moved out of their shared home, but he saw his sons every few days. The estranged couple fought frequently, most recently on Friday, October 21. Although the divorce was shaping up to be a contentious one, Susan and David Smith agreed that it was best for their boys to have regular contact with both of them. There was, however, no formal custody or child support agreement, a problem which added to Susan Smith's stress that October as she struggled to support herself and two young children on her secretary's wage of $6.10 per hour.

Financial stress aside, Susan Smith tried to move on from David after filing for divorce, resuming a relationship with Tom Findlay, the son of her boss at Conso. The two had dated briefly during the Smiths' separation the previous winter; Findlay called it off due to David Smith's aggression and threats. Smith's most recent fling with Findlay ended just the week before, on October 17, 1994, when he wrote her a friendly letter ending their romance. In addition to this unexpected heartache, David's recent discovery of her relationship with Findlay and his resulting threats to counter-charge Susan Smith with adultery left her reeling. David had discovered Findlay's break-up letter in Susan's purse while snooping the previous weekend, and the resulting vicious argument had been plaguing the young mother for five days.

Despite these stressors, Smith's morning at work that fall Tuesday was uneventful. But during the afternoon, her worries rose to the surface. Smith attempted to talk to Tom Findlay three different times. Their conversations were short and upsetting, and she ended up leaving work early. Smith picked the children up from day care, went home, and made her sons a pizza dinner. She later said that she was frantic that evening, and that her sons also began to cry at the sight of her tears. At some point early in the evening, after speaking briefly with David Smith, Susan bundled up the children to protect them from the brisk fall night and strapped them carefully into their car seats. Smith drove aimlessly, stopping once on a bridge over the Broad River, deep in the woods of Union County. She stepped outside and looked at the rushing water, contemplating suicide, but, hearing Michael's cries from the backseat, she returned to the car and kept driving.[1]

Smith drove for a few hours, eventually coming to a stop at the edge of John D. Long Lake, a small fishing lake just off of a country highway about a dozen miles outside of Union. She parked on the boat ramp. What happened next was the subject of much debate over the next ten months. Within hours, the FBI knew her name, and not long after that, Susan Smith made headlines across the nation.

The following night, Wednesday, October 26, 1994, NBC anchor Tom

Brokaw introduced nightly news-watching Americans to Susan Smith. The segment "Where Are My Children?" featured the Union, South Carolina, mother who had been the victim of a carjacking the previous evening. Bob Dotson, the NBC correspondent sent to Union to cover the story, informed shocked viewers that at the time of the crime, Smith's two young sons, Michael and Alex, were in the back seat of the Mazda. The carjacker had taken the boys with the car.

At a morning press conference, Susan Smith tearfully described how the armed man jumped into the passenger side of her car and ordered her to drive. In a voiceover accompanied by a photograph of her sons, NBC quoted Smith: "I just screamed. I said, 'What are you doing?' He said to shut up and drive and he had a gun and he was poking it in my side, you know." Smith sniffed as she told reporters that she pleaded for her sons as the thief forced her out of the car: "I said, 'I'm going to get my children before I go,' and he said 'No, you can't, I don't have time for that,' and just sort of pushed me on out." The two-minute NBC report began and ended with an extreme close-up of a police artist's sketch of the alleged attacker, an African American man in a knit cap.[2]

When Susan Smith implored the alleged kidnapper from television screens across the nation, her media identity relied upon current ideas about what it meant to be a good mother. On camera, she described a physical connection between mother and sons that even a kidnapping could not sever. "I was thinking last night, as a mother, it's only a natural instinct to protect your children from any harm," she explained. The needs of her sons were her own; she was literally sick with worry. The grief-stricken mother had trouble eating, because it reminded her that her boys might be hungry. "It [was] hard to be warm," she told her children via reporters, "because you might be cold."[3]

With these stereotypical maternal lines, Susan Smith emotionally manipulated media-consuming Americans. In doing so, she tapped into a familiar cultural icon that served as the perfect cover for her crime: the nurturing mother. Although Smith deliberately donned this role, she alone did not create her public image. The representations offered by journalists, particularly those working for national media outlets, combined with clips of Smith's own words to create an idealized mother with whom Americans could empathize. During these first few days of coverage, when it was a carjacking/kidnapping investigation rather than a homicide case, the depictions of Susan Smith in the national media adhered to late-twentieth-century prescriptions for ideal motherhood. In televised reports, Smith was solely a mother and a wife—her sons were her entire identity. Journalists supplemented Susan Smith's own version of herself with emotional details, strategic video footage, sound bites, and statistics.

Why were reporters complicit in creating this idealized maternal version of Susan Smith? It is not that her flawless performance duped them. Law enforcement officials questioned her story from the very beginning, and some journalists did, too. Smith's poor acting ability and her probable culpability were the daily focus of many reporters' private conversations with each other, even as they scoured the tiny town of Union for new angles and provided sympathetic coverage each evening. When Smith spoke of her missing boys, she called upon the primary available frame of motherhood in the 1990s, a very difficult script for reporters to challenge without concrete evidence. Academically known as the "mommy myth," this script relied heavily upon the mythical supermoms of 1950s-era sitcoms—think June Cleaver in a perfectly pressed dress, heels, and an apron, beatifically awaiting her children's return from school with a fresh batch of homemade cookies. This nostalgic image of maternity helped to silence other possible readings of the case, ensuring that Smith would be at least temporarily spared public suspicion. Because reporters kept their doubts to themselves, most likely out of concern that they might compromise the investigation, their portrayal of Smith in the first few days constituted an unwilling complicity in her performance of the neotraditional definition of motherhood in the 1990s. This image made up the first of the "seven Susans" that the American public would come to know over the next several months.

This mediated maternal identity reflected the politics of gender that characterized the reactionary neoconservative culture of the late twentieth-century United States. By the 1990s, family-values politics helped to facilitate the meteoric rise of a specific ideal: white, middle-class, married, full-time motherhood. Media studies scholars have deemed this reactionary trend the "new momism," a label that intentionally echoes maternal obsessions of generations past. Women, according to this "mommy myth," were incomplete without children, and Good Mothers devoted their entire beings—body, soul, time, and mind—to their children. This new version of momism was promulgated by sources as varied as panicky news reports on childhood dangers to radio host Dr. Laura Schlesinger to the legislators who authored the mid-decade welfare reform. And there was a clear goal: this "media obsession" with ideal motherhood constituted a "redomestication" campaign that targeted the embattled feminist movement and bolstered the rise of the political right.[4] The cultural politics of gender intertwined with the official politics of family values to push women back into the home and America back to the 1950s.

Like most ideals, the "new momism" mirrored the actual lives of very few, if any, American mothers. Accordingly, the image had a darker side that accounted for these disparate experiences of maternity. There was a clear cultural script for the Bad Mother to complement that of the Good Mother. Narrowly defined, the Good Mother was white, middle-class, chaste, married, the primary caretaker, and not a member of the public workforce. In the words of one psychologist, she was "more like a religious icon than a flesh-and-blood woman." The Bad Mother, then, was all of the things that the Good Mother was not: an ethnic or racial minority, sexual, and/or single. She often worked outside of the home, or worse, she was working-class and therefore a consumer of day care and possibly welfare.[5]

Given the narrow prescriptions of the ideal, the majority of mothers in the United States since the 1980s have been in very real danger of being labeled Bad Mothers. Consider the following statistics: approximately 53 percent of mothers with infants worked for wages outside the home in the 1990s. Over one-third of this same group worked full-time jobs. Almost 55 percent of these working mothers identified themselves as unmarried. Just over one million American women gave birth to children out of wedlock annually in the 1990s. Finally, the incomes of roughly half of these working mothers hovered dangerously close to the federal poverty standards of the mid-1990s. Part- or full-time employment, childbearing or rearing outside of a nuclear family unit, and the reliance of some women on the state for financial assistance are characteristics that describe the norm of modern American motherhood, not a deviation from it. Yet the "new momism" ascended as an ideal, a ubiquitous "siren song blending seduction and accusation."[6] Idealized images of the Good Mother, and demonized images of the millions of Bad Mothers in the United States, served as new sexist code in the family-values 1990s.

The imaginary lines between Good and Bad Mothers were often very fine. Indeed, journalists could have easily labeled Susan Smith a Bad Mother. From the perspective of 2011, the year in which the public virtually executed Casey Anthony for killing her daughter only to be outraged when the jury acquitted her due to an overwhelming lack of physical evidence, the restraint of the media in the initial days of the Susan Smith case seems almost quaint. Hers was no airtight alibi; there were, in fact, plenty of opportunities to question

Smith's story. Although Smith chose the role of the victimized Good Mother, she refused to stay in character. In the very first national report on her story, she suggested that kidnapping might not be the only violent crime endured by her boys. With an exaggerated sniffle, Susan Smith told reporters: "My big thing is, you know, they were screaming, they were crying, and I'm just so scared he lost his patience or something, you know. I don't know." This statement implied the unthinkable: that Smith knew that some kind of harm had come to her children. The NBC report tempered her statement, following it with firm reassurance from Union County Sheriff Howard Wells that the kidnapper's real objective was not to "hurt these children."[7]

In an interview Thursday morning, two days after the carjacking, Susan Smith explicitly offered up the idea that her sons might have been murdered. "I keep trying not to lose hope, but the more time passes, I get scared," she told reporters. "If they are lying somewhere dead, I want them home." That night on the *ABC Evening News,* Smith again indicated her own "failure" as a mother, saying there was more she "could've or should've done" the night of the carjacking. Video footage of the investigative command center accompanied her statement as implicit reassurance that this victimized mother had an army of officials working to restore her family.[8] Smith, of course, did not idly blame herself; in retrospect, it sounds as if she were providing indications of her motive to murder. In her written confession less than a week later, she cited feelings of maternal failure as the primary reason she murdered her sons.

From the outset, Smith struggled to represent herself, offering confusing and contradictory sound bites to the media and to investigators. Those close to her at the time uniformly agree that although she readily portrayed herself as a loving mother to investigators, she tried to resist playing the role for reporters and their camera crews. The morning after the carjacking, she told her estranged husband "she felt she couldn't handle talking to the media." David Smith later said she "appeared overwhelmed with depression," but she relented and the two gave a short press conference. Smith's family urged her daily to "keep talking" to maintain the interest of the media—the more people who knew about the missing boys, the more likely that they would be found. Her mother, Linda Russell, later argued that this pressure from the family forced Smith "deeper" into her lie: "Over and over, we succumbed to the pressure, pushing Susan in front of the cameras, while urging her to try to think of something to help find the babies. We hoped the press could get word to someone, somewhere who would send in a tip. We thought a plea from Susan might soften the heart of the abductor, if he could see how heartbroken she was."[9]

Reporters hounded Smith constantly, and her family pressured her to keep giving them sound bites. David Bruck, her defense attorney, later explained that Susan Smith was not a willing creator of her own media persona during the investigation:

> At the trial, it developed that she was hardly the author of this whole hoax; she was kind of a prop. She was the one that knew what was going on, but she had to be dragged in front of the cameras, she just wanted to sob and howl in a back room at her parents' house. I know that her stepfather, who knew how to put on a political campaign, is the one who got her out in front of the cameras and turned this whole thing into a CNN spectacular, which is no disrespect to him—he thought in good faith that the children really were missing. But people's image is she had cooked this whole thing up like a black widow spider—it's just false. She had to be prodded, pushed every inch of the way, while she just thought, how can I get a gun, how can I kill myself, how can I get out of this?[10]

Over the course of the nine-day investigation, family members constantly had to convince Smith to make statements to the media, and she often tried to back out of promised interviews at the last minute.[11]

Her family may have interpreted Smith's reluctance to talk to strangers as a normal reaction, but many members of the press corps saw it differently. Although their skepticism did not appear in published reports during the first three days of the investigation, many journalists later confessed to some kind of early suspicion of Smith. Initially, the most glaring problem was the behavior of the carjacker. The morning after the carjacking, Gary Henderson of the Spartanburg, South Carolina, newspaper remembers asking his cameraman, in the privacy of their news van, "Why would a black man on the run want two screaming children in the back seat of a car?" Smith's story, Henderson and many others thought, "made no sense at all."[12]

During those first few days of the investigation, law enforcement officials released few details, and no reporters would speculate on the record about something so awful as maternal violence without a clear source (again, a journalistic practice that seems restrained post–Casey Anthony). Instead, they shared their doubts with each other. Randall Pinkston of CBS reportedly "egged the other network correspondents on" by asking, "All right, who's gonna be the first to call bullshit?" Although most did not assume infanticide, some members of the press corps speculated that Smith had hidden her children somewhere because of a domestic dispute. Twila Decker-Davis of the *State* newspaper argued that they all suspected Smith, but they were constrained by the lack of evidence or even basic confirmations of suspicion from authorities. "We tried to reflect our suspicions in our stories," she explained. "However, we were also obligated to report the facts that we could substantiate. We couldn't just call a person a liar or a child killer in print without having something to back up those claims." Reporters thus collectively refrained from publicizing this speculation during the first days of coverage, a silence that ended up helping Smith's admittedly poor performance of maternity.[13]

Their support of Smith's maternal façade was probably unintentional. Gary Henderson, the newspaper reporter from nearby Spartanburg who covered the entire investigation, described the narrative-creation process as almost organic. "A story this big has a life of its own," he explained. "It has as much life as anything alive. It moves and you just hang on."[14] At Sheriff Wells's first press conference the morning after the carjacking, Henderson counted only three other reporters, one photographer, and two cameramen in the room. This number quickly grew into a cast of hundreds. Reporters fed each other leads, and the majority of them called upon the readily available frame of idealized motherhood to make their deadlines in this quickly moving case.

Despite the competitive nature of journalism, the relationship between the local and the national media in the Smith case generally remained congenial. Reporters for national media outlets generally followed the local lead on the Smith case. Twila Decker-Davis of the *State* (Columbia, South Carolina) argued that national correspondents had to rely upon local reporters, because they had access to their "loyal local readers." Indeed, *New York Times* journalist Rick Bragg singularly pinpointed Decker as the "spearhead of the story," especially as public suspicions of Susan Smith began to circulate more freely. Because newspapers and television networks compete for scoops and new angles, they often resort to copying each other. Thirty-six hours into the investigation, Gary Henderson noted the presence of "aggressive," "well-known correspondents" searching for the story in Union by studying the articles he had already written about the case for the *Spartanburg Herald-Journal*. News moves at a rapid pace, and when reporters use each other as their main sources, the result can be a "vicious informational cycle" in which these colleagues "internalize a set of routine story types that are easily reproducible in the time constraints that organize journalistic work."[15]

This cycle appears to have been particularly true of the national coverage of the Susan Smith drama. The collaborative frames that produced the "seven Susans" were not some kind of deliberate media conspiracy. They did not have to be; that is how the news works. With a lack of clues, an ethical unwillingness to speculate on the record, and a young mother who regularly, if reluctantly, supplied stereotypical maternal lines every day or so, reporters did their jobs by forming a narrative out of the incongruous pieces of this story. Yet there were significant details—such as Smith's marital and working status, and the fact that the home from which she gave interviews throughout the entire investigation was her parents' expansive ranch house, rather than her own small home outside of town—that the national news outlets failed to publicize.[16] Journalists stopped short of identifying Susan Smith as the prime suspect on the record during the first three days of coverage, but they also consistently excluded the kind of information that might counteract the image of the idealized mother.

Smith hand-delivered a ready-made Good Mother image to the media, but the sketchy facts and the conflicted emotions of reporters meant that much journalistic legwork went into making the Good Mother narrative work for her. The news relies heavily upon the presentation of a coherent narrative peopled with recognizable characters. Because modern America is an overwhelmingly visual culture, televised accounts of this case had to be especially potent. The immediate, visual nature of televised news makes detailed storytelling difficult. Television journalists and their producers compensate for this fundamental problem of the medium through the strategic use of images, which "personalize a story in ways that cannot be duplicated in print." Each image on television entails a "myth," or an unspoken narrative (such as the "mommy myth") that represents "any belief in a culture that is so ingrained in and pervasive among members of the society that, for the most part, what the belief asserts goes without question."[17] In this case, when media outlets offered sympathetic maternal images of Susan Smith, their agenda perhaps unintentionally dovetailed with hers: both upheld dearly held beliefs about motherhood.

From the moment the news vans arrived and the cameras rolled, the Smith drama was a maternal morality play. Each of the young mother's attributes in the national media coverage constituted a building block of an appropriate maternal image. A twenty-three-year-old, married, white mother of two stolen sons was a useful poster child for the New Right cultural and political program that subtly urged women to retreat from the perilous public sphere. The expansive definition of Bad Motherhood was a cautionary tale that targeted all women. Failure to conform to the narrow ideal meant running the risk of condemnation, or worse.

According to the media and popular culture, there were very real repercussions for children, as well. The close scrutiny of motherhood at the end of the century coupled with another media fixation, one that Susan Smith capitalized on when she reported the "carjacking": stranger violence against children, or "stranger danger." By the final decades of the twentieth century, the theme of endangered children had become a key news peg for everything from imported toys to Halloween candy to household chemicals. Parenting magazines, editorials, and the nightly news cautioned primary caretakers to practice hawk-like vigilance over their children's daily lives.[18]

Kidnapping represented a related public paranoia in the 1980s and 1990s that similarly pointed women and children back to the safe haven of the home. Prior to the late twentieth century, generally only high-profile kidnappings, like the Lindbergh case, made national headlines. By the 1980s, however, kidnappings garnered big headlines. Part of the reason for this lay in the realization that widespread media attention could help parents and law enforcement officials locate missing children. But, as Paula Fass points out in her study of famous American kidnappings, this was not a new tactic; investigators had been skillfully using the press in kidnapping cases since at least the late nineteenth century. The explosion of attention to the crime in the 1980s—daily headlines, pictures on milk cartons and billboards, plots on popular television shows and made-for-television movies—certainly made it seem as if America had an unprecedented epidemic of child-snatching on its hands. The overwhelming media attention turned these relatively rare tragedies into a full-blown public panic. The nation's most trusted news anchors narrated features on "Parents' Fears" and "stranger danger," complete with ominous shots of empty playgrounds. Media reports suggested that as many as two million American children disappeared each year, a misleading statistic that was exponentially wrong. Official crime statistics indicate that in 1988, for example, strangers kidnapped between two and three hundred children, and, of those, fewer than half died as a result.[19]

In this context, Susan Smith's horrifying kidnapping tale actually represented a stock news report about children. As such, it was virtually guaranteed national press. And in the media of the late 1980s and early 1990s, it was not just children who were at risk. Their mothers were endangered, as well. Or rather, some of them were. As Susan Faludi famously pointed out, the falling birth rate and the perceived procreative failure of some women post–second-wave feminism was an enduring myth of the era's cultural politics. This epidemic apparently only afflicted white women. At the same time that these women experienced infertility (or worse, chose not to have children), the birth rates of African American women—Reagan's "welfare queens"—allegedly reached "epidemic proportions" in the 1980s. Anyone who read or saw these reports had only to do the math: if white women were infertile or choosing not to procreate, and their lovely white children were disappearing at a record pace, the nation would surely experience a jolting demographic shift. Author Ben Wattenberg blamed second-wave feminism and cautioned, in quintessential new-racist language, that the "birth dearth" (the title of his alarmist tome on the topic) could spark an international imbalance, causing the "Third World" to "become dominant." Wattenberg's paranoia of international power imbalances due to the postponement of white childbearing is evident even on the cover of his book: the incredible subtitle of *The Birth Dearth* is "What Happens When People in Free Countries Don't Have Enough Babies."[20]

This hysteria added up to a complicated message with a simple answer. White American mothers were putting society at risk by postponing childbearing until too late, selfishly choosing not to procreate, abandoning their children to shifty strangers in day care while they pursued careers, and voluntarily going into perilous public spaces with their children. And anywhere could be dangerous: Etan Patz vanished at his school bus stop in 1979, and Adam Walsh disappeared in a department store in 1981.[21] The solution was the "new momism": mothers who spent every waking moment with their children could easily avoid many of these public dangers. Children would be safer if only America's mothers would stop trying to be anything else—although the danger still lurked, as Susan Smith's case revealed.

In this context, the hysterical, crying, young Susan Smith was, it seemed, a Good Mother straight out of central casting. The first night of national news coverage revealed to the public all that they needed to know about Smith. "I just feel hopeless," she sobbed in her first press conference, a supportive David

Smith by her side. "I can't do enough. My children wanted me. They needed me. . . . I can't do anything but think about them."[22] Reporters and producers skillfully filled in the details not provided by the "victim" herself. Footage of Susan Smith with her husband silently underscored her appropriate racial and marital status, while shots of her parents' substantial brick ranch house served as the middle-class "Smith home." This construction aided Susan Smith's performance of classic Good Motherhood, despite the fact that her story was sketchy and ever changing, even in the early days of the investigation.

Class status was a running subtext in this framework of motherhood. In these first days of sympathetic coverage, national reporters did not mention Susan Smith's full-time secretarial job at a local textile mill, although her occupation would take on immense significance in journalistic narratives after her confession. One nightly news segment briefly mentioned Smith's past job at a local store, where she met her future husband while she was still in high school.[23] There were no other indications of outside-the-home occupations in these televised reports until after Smith's confession. In this narrative, Smith's working life implicitly stopped when her life as a mother began. Reporters instead focused on David Smith's job as a Winn-Dixie manager, a firmly middle-class occupation in economically depressed Union. NBC's Bob Dotson described an idyllic memory of the family at the grocery store where the boys played in the aisles.[24] The omission of Smith's working status coupled with her sobbing quotes about her boys' daily needs to produce an image of Smith as a full-time housewife.

Smith's non-working status was a key component of her Good Mother image. As a cultural ideal, round-the-clock mothering ascended to dizzying heights by the 1990s. This was the era in which the media urged women to abandon their careers for the "mommy track." Launched in 1988 by *Good Housekeeping* magazine, the "New Traditionalist" movement swept the media, urging women to "cocoon" at home with their children and abandon the "superwoman" dilemma of balancing work and family. Predictably, Hollywood tapped into this trend. Films like *Fatal Attraction* and *The Hand That Rocks the Cradle* warned women not to wait too long to fulfill their maternal destiny, lest they succumb to the psychotic, baby-snatching proclivities of the childless thirty-something. Alternately, the feel-good plots of *Baby Boom* and *Steel Magnolias* revealed that, even though it might come at great cost (a lucrative career, or, in the case of Shelby in *Steel Magnolias*, functioning kidneys), the joy of motherhood was worth the sacrifice.[25]

Despite, or perhaps because of, the fact that most Americans had long since ditched the nuclear family ideal of the stay-at-home mother—by the mid-1990s, there were "more than twice as many single-mother families as married, homemaker-mom families," and most married mothers worked outside the home—the "mommy track" was a prescription, not just one among a range of options. According to the contemporary media panic, working women who sent their children to day care were courting certain danger. A discernible hysteria surrounded the issue of day care in the 1980s. Nightly news-watching Americans learned of sexual, satanic, and/or ritual child abuse at centers across the nation throughout the decade, beginning with the McMartin case in California in 1983. In the *Nation* several years later, Alexander Cockburn described the day-care hysteria as a modern-day "witch hunt" for the "body-snatchers of America's children." Physical abuse at day-care centers was only the most extreme of the perilous possibilities. Attachment issues, improper socialization, and germs topped the list of problems working mothers would have to face with their children if they relied upon outside-the-home care. A 1984 issue of *Newsweek* asked, "What price day care?" while televised news reports like Tom Brokaw's "Daycare Nightmare" asked mothers, "How safe is your child if that child is in day care?" In 1987, the journal *Family in America* compared day care to a dangerous, birth defect–causing drug by asking, "Day Care: Thalidomide of the 1980s?"[26]

These questions inspired fear, or at the very least, guilt. If churches, schools, day cares, and playgrounds—places expressly dedicated to the well-being of children—were off-limits, it seemed that nowhere was safe. A high-ranking military official in the Reagan administration argued that working mothers who "send their children to faceless centers rather than stay home to take care of them are weakening the moral fiber of the Nation." Although working mothers did not respond by pulling their children out of day care en masse—how could they with no alternatives?—they were met with nightly mother-shaming on the national news. This was not simple psychological manipulation. Media studies scholars argue that media panics are inherently, if not deliberately, political: "Although media panics rarely begin as a conscious effort to bolster the power of government authority, they often inadvertently reinforce conservative political stances and policies not shared by the majority of the population."[27] The media panics over kidnapping and day care had a singular, if unspoken, conclusion that dovetailed with New Right patriarchal ideals: the only safe place for children was at home, with their mothers.

Perhaps this anti–working-mother context explains why reporters failed to mention Susan Smith's occupation for several days. By October 1994, she had worked at Conso, one of the largest employers in Union County, for about two and a half years. The first reporter to "discover" this information was Gary Henderson of the *Spartanburg Herald-Journal*. Henderson recalled that, in her timeline of that fateful day, Susan Smith had mentioned that she picked her sons up from Judy Cathcart's house that afternoon. On Friday, October 28, three days after the Smith boys' disappearance, Henderson looked Cathcart up in the local phone book. The conversation yielded the informational "nuggets of gold" that Smith worked at Conso and her sons spent their days at Cathcart's in-home day care. Henderson used his interview with Cathcart in an article the following day, but he omitted the name of Susan Smith's employer. Although they often followed Henderson and other local journalists' leads, the national reporters stationed in Union failed to pick up on Smith's working status, information that would have increasing salience in the days to come. Deliberately or not, many reporters seemed to be following a script: a working mother was not a Good Mother, and any mention of her neighbor's much-needed services for local parents would reveal that Susan Smith selfishly put her children in harm's way by leaving them each day to go to work.[28]

The two reigning maternal cautionary tales—the shrinking ranks of white mothers and child endangerment—were not just the province of a narrow Republican program. By the late 1980s, the "new momism" permeated both sides of the political spectrum. It had become a widespread cultural ideal, not just a party platform. In 1988, none other than *Ms.* magazine, the glossy voice of feminism created by Gloria Steinem in the early 1970s, captured the tone of the "birth dearth" hysteria with their "Special Mothers' Issue." The cover photo encapsulated the public panic perfectly: in it, a glowing, blonde mother held her angelic, white child with "ENDANGERED?" stamped over them in large, alarming script.[29]

In the "Editor's Essay" of the issue, underneath a photograph of a stereotypical 1950s family (children clamoring around a father who has clearly just returned from work, mother looking on with a smile and a doll in her hand), Anne Summers asked some of the key feminist questions about 1980s motherhood. Would new reproductive technologies like egg donation and surrogacy further "liberate" women from their so-called "biological clocks," or would they end up creating new "hierarchies of women" based on class? Is motherhood a "question of controlling one's body," or is it a question of rights? In this new world of single motherhood and fathers' custodial rights and Hollywood's celebration of "romanticized and irresistible motherhood," Summers argued, our cultural definition of "what is a mother is challenged." Finally, she asked, during the twenty-fifth anniversary year of Betty Friedan's classic book, "is a new mystique looming?"[30]

For the *Ms.* readership and the mothers of America, these were prescient questions, and the first few articles in the issue set a feminist tone by attacking the family-values crowd and questioning the assumption that mothers are "natural caretakers,"[31] But almost halfway through the issue, something happens. The article topics switch to real, regular, American mothers—not reproductive technologies like surrogacy and abortion, or family-values politicians, or legal struggles over the "Baby M" surrogacy case—and the tone of the issue changes drastically. In "A Transcendent Moment," a white, middle-class professor and mother of three experiences "transcendence" at the hospital birth of her first grandchild. A glowing drawing of a grandmother, mother, and baby accompanies the piece—a doubly maternal scene that seems to tout the ideal, even implying the availability of the "new momism" to women who are beyond childbearing age. The next article brings readers back to stark reality with harsh, red-tinted photographs of Cherryl Bellefleur, the subject of that month's "Tracking the Dream" series. "Twice married, twice divorced," proclaims the subheading sadly, "Cherryl lives with her son Jesse in a trailer she may lose. She longs for a real house and a relationship with a good man."[32]

In this second half of the "special" issue, it is not just the personal narratives of women that define Good Motherhood. Advertisements hammer home the particular cultural dangers of being a poor, single, working mother. An eight-page Chevy ad, placed in the middle of "Cherryl's Story," features a series of mothers in soft focus. The first mother sits on a sofa with her young daughter in her lap, listening intently to her in front of a glowing window. The copy reads: "Sometimes the best way to talk about things is heart to heart." On the following page, a young, worried, white mother holds her baby, who is facing the camera over her shoulder. Chevy implores consumers: "Don't spend the next six years wondering if you did the right thing." The ad continues in this vein for eight pages, each bearing the Chevy logo: "The Heartbeat of America."[33]

This advertisement, longer than most of the articles in the issue and positioned in the middle of a profile of a hard-working single mother, had a clear message. If readers somehow missed this caution, they turned the page to confront stark photographs of cigarette-smoking, coffee-drinking, prematurely aging Cherryl and her son Jesse in their cramped trailer. In large, bold print in the middle of a page, Ms. details Cherryl's maternal desperation: "I am really afraid of failing, of not giving him what he needs. He's got such a quick mind, it would be a waste. But Mommy's there, Mommy does it." Another article in the magazine drove in the final nail of the "back-to-home" message to mothers. Under the headline "Careers and Kids," the author asks, "Many of today's most successful women stayed home to raise their children—Are young mothers now trying to do too much?"[34]

The obvious answer to the question was "yes." Even through the pages of this issue of Ms., a feminist publication that was very much resistant to the New Right, we can track the change in the prescriptive image of American motherhood. The careerist mommy-in-a-power-suit of the previous decade— the kind of mother who might opt for the some of the new reproductive technologies highlighted early in the issue—morphs over the course of several articles into a professional, full-time mother. These new moms, concludes Edith Fierst in her piece on careers and kids, "will surely want to take into account the experience of those who have managed to have both a family and a successful career by doing so sequentially." As in the pages of Ms., the options for American mothers had changed by the end of the century: "The supermom of the 1980s who managed to stagger into the '90s [was] told that she just can't 'have it all' and presumably she should feel guilty for continuing to try."[35] In 1990s America, mothering was a full-time job, and mothers were professionals whose children took up all of their time. The good ones had no room, or desire, for outside work or careers.

The "new momism" took hold of American culture early in the 1980s. Despite the vibrant feminist critique of the institution in the 1970s, maternal struggles were such a taboo subject that the editors of Why Children? a 1981 collection, could not find women who were willing to go on record about any of their negative experiences with motherhood. These American mothers did not necessarily internalize the "mommy myth," but they recognized the dangers of criticizing the maternal ideal. Rather, they voiced anonymous complaints. The year before the Ms. "Special Mothers' Issue" hit newsstands, a 1987 survey of over one thousand mothers revealed the truth: American mothers tended to cite "ambivalence" rather than fulfillment when they spoke of their experiences of motherhood.[36]

The employment numbers also belie this pop-cultural message. The influx of women into the workforce did, in fact, slow down in the 1990s as compared to the previous half-century. But the white-collar "supermoms" of the 1980s did not appear to be racing to the "mommy track": the National Bureau of Economic Research found that married working women of the 1990s were less likely to leave their employment or even to reduce their hours than they were in the 1980s, even when their husbands experienced significant pay increases. The media of the 1980s, however, indicates that family values won the war of rhetoric, even if it did not change the behavior of most working women. Even many feminists at least partially internalized the neotraditional "mommy myth" that made criticism of the institution nearly impossible. By 1992, "never had the baby been so delicious," according to feminist scholar Ann Snitow in a plaintive essay criticizing the "rising national babble of pronatalism," the burial of mothers' experiences within "family values," and the utter lack of a coherent feminist response.[37]

The cultural attack on working mothers continued unabated into the mid-1990s, reaching its apex the very year of the Smith murders with the advent of Dr. Laura Schlesinger's wildly popular radio talk show. Dr. Laura, as she calls herself, is best known for her tirades against working mothers (although, as her critics delight in pointing out, she is one herself). She begins and ends each radio show with the refrain, "I am my kid's mom," and she berates callers daily into similarly arranging their lives around their children. Her promotion of the "new momism" on the airwaves helped her become the second most popular radio show host in the nation by the late 1990s (Rush Limbaugh was first) and the top radio host in Canada. Dr. Laura's enormous following certainly suggests that she began dispensing advice via the airwaves at a time when Americans were particularly receptive to messages about traditional motherhood.[38]

In the early 1990s, the ranks of acceptable mothers narrowed, and Susan Smith, with her low-paying textile-mill job, estranged husband, and daily reliance on a neighbor's in-home day care, would surely fall outside of that boundary. According to the dictates of the "new momism," to be a Good Mother was to be a mother who did not work outside the home, neither by necessity nor by choice. During those first few days of her national fame, Susan Smith, the devastated mother who leaned heavily on her husband and alternated between public tears and seclusion, could not have been further from the familiar maternal stereotypes of the exhausted "superwoman" who tried unsuccessfully to "have it all," or Cherryl, the working-class single mom who led her son in the early-morning dark from their trailer to his day care.[39]

The class requirement of the "new momism" glossed over the fact that most mothers in this country could not financially afford to stay at home with their children whether they wanted to or not. Media consumers could assume, then, that if Susan Smith was a full-time mother, her husband's income was firmly middle-class. Key shots and sound bites that positioned her as the kind of mother who met even Dr. Laura's impossible standards aided this assumption. On location in Union a few days after Smith reported her sons missing, ABC's Mike von Fremd reported that the Smiths were "well-liked" in the small town, quoting a local woman who said Susan "came from a very good upbringing." Shots of Susan's parents' suburban ranch house, where the family gathered during the investigation, accompanied these reports as visual proof of the Smiths' appropriate class status. National reporters failed to mention that this large house was the home of Susan's much better-off stepfather, or that Susan and David Smith, prior to their separation, actually lived in a cramped brick home on the other side of town recently purchased with loans from their parents. Prior to that, they lived with David's grandmother in her tiny rural home outside of Union.[40]

Along with middle-class status, the bedrock of the "new momism" was a secure marriage and a stereotypical nuclear-family model. For almost three days, reporters failed to pick up on the well-known local melodrama that was Susan and David Smith's troubled marriage, legal separation, and impending divorce. Susan Smith appeared before cameras with David in tow, and often they were actually touching—holding hands or physically supporting each other in front of a bank of microphones. Broadcasts in these early days showed David Smith pleading with the carjacker via television camera, but Susan Smith rarely appeared solo. Indeed, after her confession, some reporters looking for pictures of Susan Smith alone ended up cropping David Smith out of photos taken during the investigation. Although it was common knowledge in Union that Susan and David Smith were in the midst of a nasty divorce on the grounds of his adultery, this information did not appear in print for three days. As with Smith's occupation, this failure to scrutinize the parents more closely need not have been a deliberate media cover-up. But, given their explicit personal doubts about Smith's story, as well as the fact that immediate relatives are always the most likely suspects in kidnapping cases, it is surprising that reporters did not investigate the Smiths' family situation more thoroughly from the outset.

This rendering of the Smiths as a married couple significantly aided the Good Mother script. The anti-mothers of neoconservatism were almost always single, part of a dysfunctional family structure in which the father—the normative leader of the household and the figure whose income allowed full-time, stay-at-home "new momism" to flourish—was missing. Like kidnappings, the "birth dearth," and day care, a media panic surrounded the issue of single motherhood and its corollary, the "absent father" epidemic. By the early 1990s, the failure of many American men to uphold their end of the bargain as providers and protectors reportedly resulted in a record number of single women and fatherless children. The year of the Smith case, editorial rants about "deadbeat dads" abounded as some states began posting "wanted" posters for fathers who failed to pay child support.[41]

This fatherlessness allegedly caused dysfunctional behaviors in children ranging from teenage pregnancy to homosexuality to crime sprees. Reports and politicians held single mothers responsible; they were, after all, the ones raising these deviant adolescents. By the 1990s, the "culture of single motherhood" became shorthand for the national poverty rate as well as a direct progenitor of the nation's crime problem. Because they posed such widespread threats to the fabric of society, single mothers were necessarily Bad Mothers. According to the late-twentieth-century maternal mythology, Good Mothers functioned solely as parts of patriarchal, nuclear families.[42]

For three days, Susan Smith appeared in the national media as a "new mom," the maternal linchpin of a middle-class, nuclear family. Inevitably, however, reporters and investigators had to shift the frame due to the utter lack of clues, resulting in increased scrutiny of Susan Smith, the only "witness" to the alleged crime. Twila Decker-Davis of the *State* newspaper explained that editors initially vetoed reports from anonymous sources expressing suspicion in Union, but after a few long days of intensive national coverage, they began to extend more "leeway" to their reporters. The newly suspicious stories were not based on new leads; there weren't any. In fact, there were no clues at all, only Susan's ever-changing story of the night of the carjacking. "We do not have the car. We do not have the children. We do not have the suspect," a visibly frustrated Sheriff Howard Wells told reporters in an evening press conference on October 28, three days after the boys' disappearance.[43]

Day three, it seems, was a turning point in the media coverage. Almost imperceptibly, the frame of the Good Mother started to shift. That night, national news programs collectively featured a "break" in the case—or rather, because it was not new information to investigators or even locals, the details of the Smiths' troubled relationship was a break in the mediated image of Susan

Smith. The damning information was there for the asking all along; some reporters had begun to hear the rumors about the impending divorce as soon as they arrived in Union. As a legal separation, it was public record, as Gary Henderson, who covered the story for the nearby *Spartanburg Herald-Journal*, learned when he went to the county clerk's office on the third day of the investigation. Henderson's "find" spread quickly from the local to the national media. The day after his visit to the Union County Courthouse, October 28, 1994, all of the major media outlets focused on the Smiths' rocky marriage, legal separation, and impending divorce, for which Susan Smith had filed the paperwork just weeks before her sons went missing.[44]

The information that Smith was a single mother in a tumultuous relationship with her estranged husband combined with the frustrating lack of clues to set in motion the rapid destruction of the Good Mother image. The news of the divorce unleashed a flood of suspicion accompanied by newly negative images of Susan Smith. That night, Smith's façade began slowly to unravel, but in order for the public to consider the "inconceivable," reporters had to dismantle the Good Mother they had helped to build. This journalistic deconstruction featured a trajectory of strategic attack points that simultaneously destroyed the ideal image and created a new, oppositional "Susan Smith" for public consumption. The new narrative leaned heavily on issues of class and marital status, with an undercurrent of deviant sexuality in the form of infidelity. Before Smith ever admitted to harming her children, she had transformed, in public representations, into a familiar "anti-mother": divorced, single, working-class, and, perhaps most damning of all, sexually active.

On day three, the news of the divorce appeared in two different morning newspapers, Spartanburg's *Herald-Journal* and the *Charlotte Observer*. It immediately became a major news peg, appearing on all three networks' nightly programs. Outing the Smiths' separation three days into the national coverage made it seem as if they had somehow deceived the public about their marriage, although they never lied about their relationship to investigators or to the press. Even worse, it provided an implicit motive to kidnapping: a possible custody battle between mother and father, as Rick Bragg suggested that day in his first of many stories on the case for the *New York Times*. Bragg also outed Susan Smith as a working mother in this article, saying simply that she worked for a "textile company," but other national reporters did not utilize this information until after her arrest.[45]

That night, three days into the investigation, it appears that, once the details of the divorce spread among reporters stationed in Union, editors and producers gave the go-ahead to report on leaked information from anonymous sources, information that, in some cases, reporters had been sitting on for days. CBS's Randall Pinkston paired the news of the divorce with the damning speculation that the Smiths had gotten "inconclusive" results on their lie detector tests, although Sheriff Wells refused to confirm or deny any information about the couple's polygraphs. Although NBC's Bob Dotson included no actual statistics in his nightly report, he pointed out the suspicious circumstances of the crime, stating that "kidnappings are rare, and carjackings are rarer, in rural areas." Susan Smith was "in seclusion at home," refusing to discuss this "big mystery with lots of questions." In less than two minutes, Susan Smith's story transformed from "every mother's nightmare" to an extremely unlikely and suspicious occurrence.[46]

Almost as one, print and television reporters refocused their coverage. The family, the town, and law enforcement officers were no longer key players. Susan Smith, alone, was the story. On October 28, three days into the investigation, Smith's mediated image shifted dramatically as the national media followed local reporters' lead in outing the Smiths' divorce. The very same day that the Smiths' troubled relationship made headlines, journalists also began to detail the many discrepancies in Smith's account of the carjacking—and there were many.

The newly suspicious images of Susan Smith in the media may have shocked many viewers, but law enforcement officials suspected Smith from the beginning. Parents are always the most likely suspects in kidnapping cases, and Susan Smith's carjacking tale had key problems from the outset. Many of the officers involved in the investigation knew Smith's family well. In fact, Union County Sheriff Howard Wells maintained a very close relationship with her family: he was godfather to Susan's brother Scotty's two children. The night of the Michael and Alex's disappearance, local police questioned Susan and David Smith for many hours, finally releasing them around 4:30 the following morning. In his summary of one of his interviews with Susan Smith that night, Sheriff Wells wrote that she seemed confused about the type of hat the carjacker had been wearing; she described it as a baseball cap to one officer and later as a "toboggan" (or a "sled") to Wells. Roy Paschal, the SLED (State Law Enforcement Division) sketch artist reported even more suspicion. Although Smith initially told him that she would not be much help because she had only seen the carjacker in profile, once Paschal began to draw, she provided many details. Smith did not follow the "usual pattern" of description by traumatized victims, and she approved of every facial feature he drew immediately, without offering suggestions or revisions. He remembered thinking that finishing the composite sketch in an hour must have been "some kind of record."

By Wednesday, less than twenty-four hours after the alleged carjacking, law enforcement officers knew about Smith's most recent break-up with Tom Findlay. In fact, they had seen the "Dear Jane" letter, provided to them by David Smith, and they knew that Susan's children were part of the reason Findlay ended the relationship. Susan Smith vehemently continued to deny any involvement in the disappearance of her sons, and that afternoon, still less than twenty-four hours after the alleged carjacking, she agreed to take a polygraph test. David Espie of the FBI quickly determined that Smith had lied, based on the test results as well as her nonverbal behavior. With the results in hand, he confronted Smith, who denied her deception and demanded to leave. As she hurried out of the witness room, SLED Agent David Caldwell caught up with her and confronted her with the question: "Why haven't you been completely honest with police during the course of the investigation?" He was talking about Wal-Mart, Smith's primary alibi for the evening.

In her plot of the events leading up to the carjacking, Susan Smith told investigators that she had taken the boys, who had been "fussy" all night, to Wal-Mart for a few hours to get ideas for Christmas presents. They spent much of their time in the toy section; Smith said she saw many people, but no one she knew by name. She asked Michael if he wanted to go see Mitchell Sinclair, a close family friend and the long-time boyfriend of her best friend, Donna Garner. Michael said yes, and they headed in the direction of Sinclair's home. At a stoplight on the way there, she told investigators, an African American man jumped into the passenger side of her car.

Armed with the knowledge that Mitchell Sinclair had not been home that evening and that not one single person at Wal-Mart identified Susan Smith as a shopper from the night before, Agent Caldwell confronted her. Smith, caught in her lie, admitted that they had never gone to Wal-Mart. Rather, she had been driving around all night, but she thought it "would sound dumb" that she "was just riding around." As Caldwell continued to push her on this point, Smith told him she had been driving around because she had "had a bad day," and she and Michael were singing in the car. Yet she had previously told Agent Espie and others that the boys were crying a lot that night. When Caldwell pointed out this contradiction, Smith clammed up and, because she was not under arrest and free to go, she left shortly thereafter. Within about twenty hours of the initial report of the crime, then, there were already major contradictions within Smith's story of the night before.

Two days later, on Friday, October 28, as nightly news anchors informed surprised viewers of the Smiths' tumultuous relationships, the leaks and media speculation forced Sheriff Wells to acknowledge the problems with Smith's story, although he refused to describe them in detail. Wells reluctantly voiced his frustration: "In twenty years of law enforcement, I've never worked a case that had so little to work with." He hastened to add, "But there's not anything more that can be done."

By the next day, Saturday, October 29, the leaks had become more specific. The *Union Daily Times* led the attack with a morning report that Susan Smith had failed a lie-detector test; the reporter included the facts that Mitchell Sinclair's home, Smith's alleged destination when her children went missing, was empty that night and that no one had seen Smith at the local Wal-Mart that evening. The *State,* the newspaper of Columbia, South Carolina, also reported that Susan Smith had gotten "inconclusive" results on a polygraph test, although authorities would not confirm or deny the rumor.[47]

That evening, although they were armed with a growing list of discrepancies in Smith's story, some reporters still tempered their broadcasts, pairing the increasing suspicion with kidnapping statistics that legitimated parental fears of "stranger danger." Others included damning statistics that had been at their disposal since the outset of the investigation: NBC's Bob Dotson told viewers that "it is one thousand times more likely that a child would be taken by someone in their family." Sheriff Wells protested at a press conference that Susan Smith was a "victim" in this case, although the "public was trying to make her a suspect." He added: "It would not be unusual for any mother, frantic over the abduction of her children, to give conflicting statements to the police." But NBC's final words of this first day of explicit suspicion pitted the frustrating nationwide search against the embattled image of Susan Smith, the Good Mother: "There is still no evidence in this case after four days of searching—only a mother's word." The old tag of the collective "fear of parents everywhere" became, in a few short days, the overwhelming public scrutiny of one mother in particular.[48]

By Monday, October 31, six days into the investigation, all of the nationally televised reports openly challenged Susan Smith's story. Despite the fact that Sheriff Wells confirmed that Smith's interviews were not going well, reporters generally did not focus on the ever-widening cracks in her account of the night of the carjacking. They had already destroyed the image of the Smiths as a normal nuclear family by reporting on the impending divorce, but a week into the search for the boys, the singular goal of this journalistic narrative was to focus public suspicion by attacking Smith's character.

The journalistic repositioning of Susan Smith as a duplicitous divorcee summarily precluded any possibility of maintaining her former Good Mother status. One by one, the building blocks of her maternal image came tumbling down. Curiously, national reporters—Rick Bragg of the *New York Times* was the exception—failed to mention Smith's job as a secretary at a local mill, although it is difficult to imagine that correspondents could spend a week in the small town and not learn something about Conso Products, Union's largest employer at the time.[49] Instead, Smith's plunging class status was based on her marital status and family history in these reports. A "good girl" no more, she could also no longer be a Good Mother.

One week into the national coverage, the confirmed rumors of the many inconsistencies in Smith's story were fair game for news reports. But the *NBC Evening News* chose to attack Smith's familial identity rather than her sketchy story. "There's something fishy about it," former neighbor Dot Frost told NBC's Bob Dotson. But the "fishy" details included in the segment had nothing to do with Smith's carjacking allegations. The short report revealed that there were many proverbial skeletons in this seemingly ideal family's closet. "[Frost] says their home life wasn't always happy," NBC's Bob Dotson revealed over headshots of Susan and David Smith, reminding viewers that the couple had recently filed for divorce. "On October 7, [Susan Smith] was awarded custody of the children, a repeat of her own childhood. Susan Smith's father, Harry Smith, killed himself one night after his divorce. Susan was then six."[50] Again, this was strategic narrative framing on the part of reporters; Smith's childhood trauma was public knowledge in the small town, but once Smith became a public suspect, the information acquired new salience.

Smith's family history served, in this instance and for many months to come, as evidence of her potential pathology, not as a basis for sympathy. Dotson ended his Halloween report by saying that people had begun to question everything about the case, "even the parents"—but the extreme close-up of a weeping Susan Smith left no doubt in viewers' minds which parent they should be questioning.[51] It was the first time viewers saw shots of Susan Smith alone, without a male protector, and the effect was devastating to her public image.

Reporters also went about the difficult work of sexualizing Susan Smith, which was not a small task if one remembers the televised images of the plain, sweatshirt- and glasses-clad young mother whose face was puffy from crying. On November 1, 1994, several networks reported that local police had begun to investigate the relationship between Smith and Mitchell Sinclair, the longtime boyfriend of Smith's best friend and the person she said she had been on her way to visit the night of the carjacking. The *Atlanta Journal Constitution* reported that Sheriff Wells, "intrigued" by Sinclair's interview on the tabloid show *A Current Affair* a few days earlier, planned to interview him again. Juxtaposing headshots of Smith and Sinclair, NBC reported that both had been interviewed numerous times and were questioned about "where they were"—together—on the night of the crime. The headshots remained on the screen while the 911 tapes, released to the public that day, played in the background. Smith's freefall down the social ladder, from the middle-class wife to the single woman with suspicious boyfriends and an even sketchier alibi, eliminated all vestiges of her short-lived, lofty maternal status. Reporters had only to throw a man into the mix, and the ensuing narrative revisions suddenly made sense.[52]

Amidst this media onslaught, on Wednesday, November 2, eight days into the investigation, local police privately dropped a bombshell on Susan Smith. At a Baptist Church in downtown Union, where law enforcement had recently moved in order to throw the media off the scent, SLED Agent Pete Logan administered another lie-detector test. Smith failed. Logan seized upon a particular detail of her carjacking tale. The stoplight in nearby Monarch Mills at which the criminal allegedly leaped into her car was a triggered light. The signal on Highway 49, the highway from which Smith had approached the light, remained green unless a car came to the intersection along the cross street. In other words, Smith's Mazda could not have been the only car at that intersection; there would have been a witness to the carjacking if it had occurred as Smith reported. Logan himself checked the stoplight that morning, and the trigger worked just fine.[53]

In response, Susan Smith quickly altered her story. The carjacking, she insisted, really happened in Carlisle, some sixteen miles outside of Union. She said she had told the police that she had been in Monarch, which was just a few miles from her house on Toney Road, because she did not "have any good reason" to be so far from home that night. Logan asked Smith to go home and write a new statement including all of the new information she had just revealed. Authorities knew then that Smith's lies added up to involvement in her children's disappearance, but the various discrepancies brought them no closer to finding the boys.[54]

The media did not yet know about the triggered stoplight, but they were on the attack nonetheless. The increasing refocus of media reports put the Smith family on the defensive and forced Susan to do something she reportedly did not want to do: speak for herself. In a press conference on Wednesday, November 2, 1994, the family spokesperson read a message from Susan and David Smith detailing the agony of missing their sons. Local papers printed the statement in full. The words read like a primer on Good Motherhood: "It is so difficult not knowing where they are. We can't feed them; we can't wipe away their tears; we can't hold them; we can't hug them. The things we take for granted as parents, taking them for walks, giving them a bath, playing with them. It hurts so much not to be able to do these things. . . . We remember their first smiles, first words, first steps, but we need more than memories. We need Michael and Alex home where they belong."[55]

The grieving mother then directly addressed her boys: "I want to say to my babies, your mama loves you so much. I can't express how much you're wanted back home. Be strong, and take care of each other. Mama and Daddy will be right here waiting for you." NBC paired Smith's pleas with long camera shots of authorities searching Susan and David Smith's small brick house, which reporters identified for the first time as the couple's family home. Footage of police rifling through Smith's belonging gave way to the mother's tearful words. "I just want to say to my babies that your mama loves you so much," she cried, removing her glasses, flanked by her mother and David. The segment ended with a shot of Susan and David Smith hugging as correspondent Bob Dotson explained pointedly that Susan Smith "now seems to be the center of this investigation."[56]

The following morning, Susan and David Smith appeared on all three major networks' morning shows to do more damage control. Americans awoke to the televised image of the couple live via satellite from her stepfather's living room, holding hands while they addressed the media and the alleged carjacker. Both parents wore pictures of their sons on their lapels. David Smith, shell shocked and tear stricken, barely spoke. In her longest public interview to date, Susan Smith put forth an impassioned defense of motherhood: "I would like to say to whoever has my children that I constantly am praying each day that they are taking care of them and giving them the necessities that they need to survive. It's very difficult to understand right now why anybody would want to take anybody else's children away from them, and I find it very difficult to handle not being there for my babies. I've been there for them from day one, and the hardest part is not knowing, I mean just not knowing. . . . Since day one I've known everything, everywhere they've gone, I knew where they were, and this one time there's absolutely nothing I can do and that's very painful."[57] In this monologue, Susan Smith presented herself as the ideal mother the nation had rallied around for nine days. Televised tears notwithstanding, without the aid of sympathetic media images, Smith's last-ditch effort to reclaim her former Good Mother status proved to be her curtain call.

The collective withdrawal of media support apparently destroyed Susan Smith's duplicitous resolve. That very afternoon, she met with Sheriff Howard Wells, and he told her a lie of his own. The Carlisle stoplight where the man jumped in her car, he explained, was under surveillance for drug activity, and yet officers did not see her car there that night, much less witness a carjacking. Finally, she broke. Sobbing hysterically, Smith confessed to murdering her sons by rolling her car, with the boys in the back seat, into a local lake. Although her written statement would not leak to the media for several weeks, Susan Smith repeatedly emphasized her primary motive to murder: her fears of failure as a mother. She barely mentioned her carjacking lie except to say that she knew "the truth would prevail," and once it did, she "felt like the world was lifted off of [her] shoulders."[58] The truth was out, the nationwide manhunt was over, and the American public was outraged.

Given that the building blocks were already in place by the time she confessed to murdering her sons, making Susan Smith over into a Bad Mother would not be a difficult task in the weeks to come. After her shocking admission, another issue, one that had been implicit in the coverage of the nine-day investigation, reared its ugly head. For the few weeks following Smith's arrest, the media had a new peg, one that had functioned invisibly within the tone and content of the coverage thus far: race. Immediately after her confession, the frame shifted from the implicit detail of her supposedly innocent whiteness—a subtle but crucial anchor of Smith's former Good Mother status—to the outright racism of her carjacking lie. Smith had manipulated the public with historical images of race that made her story seem more believable. By combining the roles of the Good Mother and the white woman in danger of the black male criminal, she had ensured that many viewers would reflexively believe her story. When she confessed to Sheriff Wells, Smith forced media-consuming Americans into a defining moment: would the nation's willingness to believe Smith's facile lie result in a public referendum on race relations?

"A HARD WEEK TO BE BLACK IN UNION"

WHEN SUSAN SMITH confessed to the murder of her young sons after a nine-day, nationwide kidnapping investigation, the public was outraged. NBC's Bob Dotson, who was stationed in Union during the manhunt, the confession, and the trial nine months afterward, later explained that the Susan Smith case fascinated "because evil looks so much like us."[1] The idea that an infanticidal mother could look so normal, that a lying murderer could inhabit the body of a young white mother, intrigued Americans, but that alone does not account for the overwhelming attention paid to Susan Smith. During the nine-day search, the criminal did not look, as Dotson argued, "like us" to all viewers. Evil was racialized: the violence was perpetrated by the stereotypical dark-skinned carjacker complete with the black-hooded sweatshirt and matching knit cap. Innocence was race-based, as well: the victims of this dark danger were young, defenseless, and white.

In essence, Susan Smith committed two crimes: the murders and the lie. The anger at Smith's confession was, according to one journalist, "largely a reaction to the idea of a mother murdering her own children, but even so it was another abrasion on a sore spot already rubbed raw." The wound of which he wrote was, of course, race. Smith called upon the most familiar face of criminality when she claimed that an African American man had carjacked her. The images of the black male criminal and the white female victim have a well-documented history in American culture, and Susan Smith put herself squarely within this tradition when she uttered her infamous lie.[2]

Just as Susan Smith's appalling confession provided a (missed) opportunity for cultural self-reflection about the impossible ideals of motherhood, so too did it provide an opening for the frank analysis of race relations at the end of the twentieth century. Yet few reporters delved meaningfully into the subject of race in the days immediately following Smith's arrest. These reports graced front pages and nightly news broadcasts only briefly during the days of national shock that followed Smith's confession. The news peg was short-lived—a few weeks at most—and generally replaced by the summary denial of the role of race in the case.

Despite this pervasive journalistic avoidance of the issue, race clearly played a significant role in perceptions of and responses to Susan Smith from the moment that she "cried wolf" to the time of her trial nine months later. The racialized responses to Susan Smith's confession reflected the political rhetoric known as the "new racism." After the cataclysm of the civil rights movement of the 1960s, race-based politics of the old-school, Dixiecrat, George Wallace style slowly fell out of favor, as the "solid" Democratic South of the Jim Crow era transformed into a "solid" and "forcibly reformed" Republican South. But anyone familiar with American politics at the end of the twentieth century knows that this transformation did not entail the eradication of racist policies in the South or even in the nation. Since at least the 1970s, racial violence and other forms of overt racism against African Americans have been generally condemned, although they still occurred with some frequency. In the place of aggressive, overt racism, a complicated racial code developed, one that hinged on the intertwining of race and gender. The result was a language of "clever and thinly disguised references to 'law and order,' welfare, quota, taxes for 'social programs,' food stamps, 'states' rights and local government,' urban decay, 'big government,' crime, and 'personal responsibility.'"[3]

The images of whiteness and blackness that surrounded the Susan Smith investigation were holdouts from the unconcealed racism of the pre-civil rights movement era, and they endured as New Right icons. These images relied upon the gendered code of "family values," as well. By the 1990s, historian Paul Harvey argues, "patriarchy had replaced race for overtly religious, Southern conservatives as the defining principle of God-ordained inequality."[4] The public attempts to make sense of the role of race in the Smith case—or more accurately, the attempts to write race out of the case—represented the new racism and the corresponding new sexism at a crucial moment in the evolution of this political code.

Many white media consumers would have had little trouble digesting the familiar criminal blackness of Smith's alleged carjacker, just as many of them did not initially question his white female accuser. The iconic pure white woman had long served as a "pervasive fixture of racist ideology" in the United States, and by the time of the Susan Smith case, the image of the criminal black male was one that had also enjoyed wide circulation in

American politics and popular culture for several generations. The image of the African American male as a dangerous sociopath, and as a specific danger to white women, became particularly potent post-Reconstruction. It was not until the 1880s and beyond that white people, primarily southerners, began to make frequent accusations, mostly false, of rape against black men. The alleged objects of their brutal lust were always white women, and accusations of rape served as a primary means of socioeconomic and political control.[5]

Around the turn of the twentieth century, the "rape myth" of lynching, in which white men avenged sexual assaults on white women by murdering the accused black men, seeped into the regional and national consciousness. One of the leading historians of southern lynch law has called the brutal practice a "ritualistic affirmation of white unity," but, as a joint venture in the exercise of patriarchy, this "affirmation" hinged on both race and gender. The stereotypes that justified lynching were uniquely sexualized: the white male protector, the white female virgin, and the "black beast" rapist. During the decades surrounding the turn of the twentieth century, conventional white wisdom in the South lay much of the blame for lynching on black men. That is, the imagined prevalence of uncontrollable and necessarily violent black male lust for white women led white male mobs to lynch the offenders in order to protect "their" women from rape. This was not just racial vengeance or the simple protection of women from a perceived threat. The heights of brutality reached by white mobs seemed to indicate a far deeper psychological motivation, as did the sexual imagery and rituals that surrounded the violent practice. White supremacy and patriarchy dovetailed in the "rape myth," with white women serving as the "crucial defensive perimeter," as repositories of presumed racial purity, and as pretext to extralegal punishment. The "black beast" was no ordinary criminal; he was the ultimate threat to the southern social order.[6]

Although the symbiotic images that constituted the "Southern rape complex"—the white woman in danger and the "black beast brute"—enjoyed wide currency in the nation at the turn of the century, they did not, of course, accurately reflect historical realities. Contemporary observers and historians have shown that only a small percentage of African American victims of lynch mobs were actually accused of rape. Ida B. Wells-Barnett, a black activist who famously challenged the "rape myth" in the 1890s, and Jessie Daniels Ames, the white female leader of the Association of Southern Women for the Prevention of Lynching, were particular critics of the "rape myth" and its attendant images of the "black beast" and the innocent white "lady." The numbers have varied over time, but historians estimate that, at most, only one-fourth of black male lynching victims were even accused of rape at the time of their murders.[7]

The white patriarchal paranoia became a historical force in its own right, despite the fact that, as Wilbur Cash famously pointed out, the odds of a white woman in the South being raped by a black man were less than her odds of being struck by lightning. The complicated equation of African American freedoms in society, the economy, and the political arena with black intrusions into the white man's bedroom fostered a pervasive fear of black male sexuality and a convoluted rape complex among southern whites. One Atlanta lawmaker went so far as to propose in 1906 that white "ladies" be "prohibited from riding in the front seat with black drivers because a mere 'touching of garments' was enough to incite the beast to immediate and wanton sexuality." In fact, accusing a black man of rape could be a means of power for white women in the turn-of-the-century South. By uttering just a few carefully chosen words, a white woman could set in motion the entire machinery of white patriarchy. Such accusations were never taken lightly; they could result in a lynching before trial or even before an arrest was made.[8]

The dominant racial stereotypes and resulting theories of rape in the early twentieth century made the crime a solely interracial affair in which black men violated white women, despite the fact that throughout history, sexual assault is more likely to be intraracial. This "rape myth" was "a dramatization of cultural themes, a story [white men] told themselves about the social arrangements and psychological strivings that lay beneath the surface" of daily life in the turn-of-the-century South. This was not just violent daydreaming; the "rape scare" masked its own white supremacist motivations. Black males' purported propensity to sexual assault meant that economic opportunities and political equality were treacherous experiments. African American men at the polls, for instance, would constitute a "horrendous occurrence" leading them to "presume that they could claim equality in other places—most dangerously with white women."[9]

Although the practice of lynching waned over the first few decades of the twentieth century, the accompanying sexual stereotypes remained, and white mobs still occasionally avenged alleged attacks on white women through mid-century. In 1931, a "legal lynching," or a speedy trial in an all-white legal system, placed Scottsboro, Alabama, on the national stage. The "Scottsboro Boys" were a group of nine African Americans who were accused of raping two white women on a train in Alabama. A mob surrounded the jail the night of their arrests, but the local sheriff prevented a lynching by calling in the National Guard. The "boys" went to trial shortly thereafter, and eight of the nine were found guilty. Despite the reversal of these convictions twice by the United States Supreme Court and the recanting of the charges by one of the women, the "boys" spent between six and nineteen years in prison. To white Alabama in the 1930s, they were, according to a local journalist, "beasts unfit to be called human."[10]

The "black beast" that Smith called upon in 1994 remained a criminal icon throughout the twentieth century. Although the frequency of lynching decreased, the "black beast rapist" enjoyed enough cultural currency in the middle decades of the century that Richard Wright based *Native Son* (1940) on the image. Fifteen years after Wright published his acclaimed novel, and twenty-four years after Scottsboro, two white men from Money, Mississippi, murdered fourteen-year-old Emmett Till, a young black Chicagoan who was spending the summer with his extended family, for reportedly "wolf whis-tling" at a white woman. Local authorities arrested and indicted the two men for murder, but all observers expected legal "whitewash," to use *Jet* magazine's term, and that is what they got. It took the all-white, all-male jury sixty-seven minutes to return a verdict of not guilty.[11]

Despite all efforts by activists to bury him for good, the "black beast" did not disappear with the civil rights movement. In fact, the black militancy that grew out of the movement in many ways fed into racist and sexist images of African American masculinity. Eldridge Cleaver, a member of the Black Panther Party who wrote his memoir, *Soul on Ice*, while in prison, revealed that he routinely raped white women as an "insurrectionary act." Because white women, especially in the South, were the pinnacle of the socio-racial hierarchy, the ultimate white possession, raping them was a kind of guerrilla tactic aimed at white patriarchy. White Americans were duly horrified. Ronald Reagan, outraged by Berkeley's invitation to Cleaver to speak on campus, warned Americans in the late 1960s: "If Eldridge Cleaver is allowed to teach our children, they may come home one night and slit our throats."[12]

As the political party realignment took shape in the late 1960s, Eldridge Cleaver toned down his rhetoric, and Ronald Reagan and his ilk shifted their language to reflect the post-movement racial dynamics. The coded language of the new racism dictated that overt fears of African American sexuality and aggression were transformed into vague public concerns over "law and order." But racial profiling persisted, and explicit racism was, in certain instances, still publicly acceptable to some. In 1984, when four black male teenagers asked a white man on a New York subway for five dollars, he pulled out a gun and shot at all of them, paralyzing one for life. The man, Bernhard Goetz, was dubbed the "Subway Vigilante" by the tabloids, and he became an urban hero. According to one author, Goetz was "a man who had fulfilled the secret fantasy of every New Yorker who has ever been mugged or intimidated or assaulted on the subway." At trial, the jury acquitted Goetz of all charges of assault and attempted murder.[13]

According to much of the media coverage, like a lynch mob in the rural South, Goetz had simply taken the law into his own hands and battled the black predator on his own terms. In the 1980s and 1990s, the "black beast" was once again ubiquitous. He played a recurring role in new forms of televised entertainment such as the reality show *Cops* and legal dramas like *Law & Order*. He entered Americans' living rooms daily through fearsome headlines about "inner city" violence and the "superpredators" who preyed on innocent urban residents.[14] And, like the paranoid popular images of the "black beast rapist" of the turn of the century, he served a political purpose.

A primary difference between the "black beast" at the beginning of the century and his criminal brothers at the end of it was that the latter image was often divorced from images of racialized sexuality. The carjacking panic of the 1980s and 1990s, which Susan Smith clearly tapped into with her lie, was a case in point. Victims could be of either sex, but there was a clear racial component to the perception of the crime: the particular fear of this crime in the suburbs indicated that whites felt especially vulnerable. The stereotypical carjacker was universally black, perpetrating a "mini-epidemic" that led the *Economist* to argue that stopping your car at a light in Detroit would probably mean that you would "lose it for good." One study in the 1990s found that, the more violent the crime, the more likely white Americans were to assume that the perpetrators were African American, enabling the wholesale application of racialized stereotypes to crimes like carjacking. This criminal image set in motion the entire plot of Tom Wolfe's best-selling *Bonfire of the Vanities* when "master of the universe" Sherman McCoy, a white bond trader in New York City, assumes the worst of an African American youth in the street and strikes him with his car as he tries to flee the presumed predator. Yet a Department of Justice survey of police reports revealed that African Americans were more likely to be victims of carjackings than whites, while just over half of victims of any race reported that their attackers were black.[15]

Although he was seen as a universal predator, and rape was no longer his sole *modus operandi*, white women in particular still lived in fear of the inner-city black male. This omission of sexuality in discussions of violence is part of the new racist code. Media expert John Fiske explains: "The fact that the white horror of sex between a black man and a white woman cannot be spoken aloud in post–civil rights America does not mean that it has disappeared." Scholar Wendy Kozol agrees, arguing that the long history of the image functioned as subtext: "The fiction of the black male perpetrator automatically sexualized a nonsexual crime."[16]

So when a black man, or black men, actually did attack a white woman, the event made major headlines, as seen in the so-called "Central Park Jogger" case. This was the name given to a woman who was raped, beaten, and abandoned in Central Park in 1989. The victim was a young, white investment banker; the perpetrators were young, working-class, African American and Hispanic males. Almost without exception, the young men appeared as "beasts" in the media—literally, as animals that gathered in groups to go on rape sprees known as "wilding."[17]

The image also played a controversial role in the presidential election of 1988 when Republican George H. W. Bush used it against his opponent, Michael Dukakis, then governor of Massachusetts. Bush's stance in his infamous campaign ad was "tough on crime," and the issue was Dukakis's policy of "weekend passes," or furloughs for state inmates. One such individual was Willie Horton, an African American man who had been convicted of first-degree murder and sentenced to life in prison. While on a weekend pass, Horton escaped, kidnapped and assaulted a white couple, stabbed the man, and repeatedly raped his girlfriend. An anti-Dukakis ad entitled "Bush and Dukakis on Crime" capitalized on Horton's violence, informing the public that Dukakis opposed the death penalty and allowed murderers out of prison on the weekends to wreak havoc. Over Horton's menacing mug shot, the narrator listed his crimes: murder, kidnapping, assault, and, last but not least, rape. The ad ended with the tagline, "Dukakis on crime." The implications were clear: a Republican vote was a vote against the "black beast."[18]

This new racism was a thin but clever disguise. The code was blatantly transparent to its progenitors, if not yet to the American public; former racist demagogue George Wallace, upon hearing the speeches of some of the Republicans of the 1990s, reportedly lamented, "You know, I should have copyrighted all of my speeches." Although the Bush campaign vigorously denied responsibility for the Horton ad—it was released by a partisan group that was "technically unaffiliated" with the campaign—Republican strategist Lee Atwater later apologized for it. Even so, conservatives consistently denied that the ad and the issues surrounding it were about race. This was an issue of "crime and punishment," with Willie Horton as the poster child. Despite the fact that he clearly functioned as the "black beast" du jour, his race was allegedly unimportant. The silent pairing of the generic term "crime" with the visual image of a black male face and white victimization allowed Republicans to deny charges of racism. The media largely complied with this denial. As Tali Mendelberg argues, "the closest journalists came to condemning the Horton appeal was to label it a negative partisan tactic, not a negative racial tactic."[19]

According to the logic of the new racism, the explicit deployment of racist images was not permissible in late-twentieth-century American culture. Indeed, when such a manipulation occurred, it gave white Americans an opportunity to absolve their racial guilt by condemning the offending white party. This is precisely what happened when Charles Stuart, a white Boston man, claimed that he and his pregnant wife had been shot on their way home from a Lamaze class in October of 1989. His wife died in the hospital, while Stuart survived to participate in a months-long investigation in which the Boston police rounded up African American men all over the area, interrogating many and detaining a few. The case prompted national media coverage. By January 1990, almost three months after the crime, the state had a black male suspect that they were ready to try, only to be tipped off by Stuart's guilt-ridden brother that the family was suspicious of Charles himself. Charles Stuart essentially admitted guilt and summarily ended the investigation when he committed suicide shortly thereafter.[20]

Like Susan Smith a few years later, Stuart's deliberate racial profiling to cover up his own violent crime violated the rules of the new racist code that carefully avoided explicit mention of race. The Boston police became momentary outcasts, and several members of the force were charged with the violation of the civil rights of many of the men they had questioned and detained, including the suspect who would have been the defendant in Carol Stuart's murder trial. However, as the trials of the officers dragged on over the next few years, public interest waned, and the officers were exonerated in the end. On July 8, 1995, two days before the start of Susan Smith's trial, a jury cleared the last officer in Boston of official misconduct.

By the mid-1990s, overt racism still surfaced frequently, but to a mixed reception. During the O. J. Simpson murder trial of 1995, Americans again witnessed racism in the subtle efforts to depict O. J. Simpson as the "black beast." *Time* magazine famously darkened their cover photo of Simpson to make him appear more menacing. But the case underwent a rapid transformation when charges of racism against the LAPD entered the courtroom. The entire theme shifted from the sexual politics of domestic violence to the sociolegal politics of race, resulting in Simpson's acquittal.[21] Thus, the complicated rules of the new racism allowed and even encouraged stereotypical images of black deviance and criminality, but they discouraged the aggressive, explicit racism of the pre–civil rights movement days.

National headlines implicitly cautioned Americans about these rules: the trials of the Boston police who perpetrated the racial profiling in the Charles Stuart case were ongoing at the time of the search for the Smith boys. Law enforcement officials in Union County thus proceeded more cautiously than their forefathers as they hunted for Susan Smith's missing sons and their alleged kidnapper. Reporters described Susan Smith's carjacker blandly as a "black male, 20–30 years old," wearing a "dark blue toboggan cap, plaid jacket, and blue jeans." Sheriff Howard Wells reassured the public that the carjacker had no motive to hurt the children, and he was more likely to put them out somewhere unharmed. Wells was being practical: crying children were an unnecessary burden that any carjacker would drop off immediately. But the unspoken fear remained; the "black beast" of the American imagination was fully capable of "losing his patience" with two defenseless white children.[22]

The Smith family's whiteness dictated the amount and the tone of news coverage as much as the alleged attacker's blackness. Historian Glenda Gilmore speculates that the status afforded by Susan Smith's race and gender was the one thing that could save her from her horrible deed: "When all else failed Susan Smith—parents, marriage, career, love—she used the one morsel of status left to her as a poor white Southern woman with a past. If threatened by a black man, she could become beloved again, cleansed in the blood of her lambs. She could even use the power of the black male rapist myth to get away with murder. Or so she thought."[23] And for a few days, Smith's whiteness served her well, as did the porcelain skin tone of her sons, the most obviously innocent white victims in the kidnapping investigation. The Union police and local volunteers copied a favorite family photograph of Michael and Alex Smith and distributed it nationally to media outlets and other law enforcement agencies the morning after their disappearance. In the photograph, Alex, a chubby baby, sits on Michael's lap in a white wicker chair. Both boys are wearing white shirts, denim overalls, and big smiles. The picture of the boys became something of a fetish associated with the case; locals, law enforcement officers, and reporters wore miniatures of the photo pinned to their lapels.[24]

As Ron Rosenbaum pointed out in the *New York Times* months after Smith's arrest, it was all too easy to see in this photo "the perfect idealized children" that most parents "never had." "Idealized," in this instance, implicitly meant "white." After Susan Smith confessed to double homicide, some observers made this meaning explicit, arguing that the outpourings of emotion, the overwhelming media coverage, and the unprecedented public participation in the search for Michael and Alex Smith rested subtly upon their race.[25] Although few of these critics drew specific links to other famous cases, those that did had a point: kidnappings and missing children were a prevalent contemporary news peg, but the cases that received the most attention, like Adam Walsh in 1981 or Polly Klaas in 1993, always featured white children.

This is true of the twenty-first century, as well. Most Americans will remember the more recent Elizabeth Smart case; her parents got international media attention when they reported that their young daughter had been kidnapped from their million-dollar Salt Lake City home. Of course, Smart was not the only missing child in the United States that year. An equally horrible kidnapping occurred in Milwaukee the month before Smart disappeared: seven-year-old Alexis Patterson vanished on her routine walk to school in May of 2002. Although the city's media outlets provided extensive coverage of the case, CBSNews.com's David Hancock called the Patterson kidnapping a "non-starter with the national media." A spokesperson for the Milwaukee NAACP warned that many locals suspected that the national media was "racist and one-sided." They voiced their charges when they phoned in to local radio shows to ask: "Who is this white girl getting all this coverage?" In "A Tale of Two Kidnappings," the CBS report that compared the two cases, David Hancock acknowledged that "race and class are unavoidable factors in journalistic decisions," but experts listed other factors as well, including the role of the police and the parents in disseminating information.[26]

Hancock's report did not serve as a call to action: Elizabeth Smart still made the national nightly news, while Alexis Patterson remained a name known only in Milwaukee and the surrounding areas. Hancock was unique in his critique of racism in media practices, and his network, CBS, was singular in its coverage of race in the Susan Smith case. While the other major networks dropped the racial angle just days after Smith's arrest, CBS profiled the racial overtones of the case for far longer, offering periodic in-depth reports and interviews with African American scholars, legal experts, and community representatives until the eve of the trial. Of the mainstream news outlets, CBS was alone in its prolonged focus on the racial aspects of the Smith case.

Over a decade after Smith's trial, David Bruck, her defense attorney, ruefully explained this dynamic of the investigation coverage: "Precious, adorable, little black children in those white wicker chairs would not have seized the imagination of this majority white country in anything like the same way that Michael and Alex did." Some locals in Union agreed with Bruck's assessment. When Oprah Winfrey brought her show to town the week after Smith's arrest, the audience of three hundred locals "disagreed loudly on issues such as race and the death penalty." An unidentified Unionite argued on her nationally televised talk show: "Now if it had been two black children and a black man kidnapped them, hijacked them or something, the sheriff would come out and did his little job. . . . But the news media wouldn't have been here."[27]

The subtext of this visual media coverage was that whiteness was besieged, victimized, endangered, and it was necessarily front-page news. As Smith was the mother of these idealized white babies, her race was clearly related to her reception as a mother, but it was also a key component of her performance of female victimhood. The historical plot line of the "black beast" criminal was not enough to ensure widespread belief in Smith's carjacking story. There was a catch: while all African American men ran the risk of being accused of violent crimes, not just any woman could be a believable accuser. Historians have found that a female accuser's class mattered as much as her race when it came to public opinions about her victimization. According to the evidence in early twentieth-century court records, for example, some southern jurors believed that "the magnitude of the damage an assault inflicted on a woman was directly related to her place in the social order and to her position as the repository of white civilization and racial purity." When the public weighed a woman's acceptability as a victim at the beginning of the twentieth century, they also judged her class status. In the 1990s, even in the wake of second-wave feminism, "certain women's bodies [were] more valuable than others."[28]

It is this dynamic, this race- and class-based fault line within the gendered social order, that dictated the media focus on Susan Smith's class and her marital status. If Susan Smith were a married, middle-class, housewife and mother, then she was a suitable victim. When journalists depicted her this way, she became the lead feature on local, regional, and national news throughout the

investigation. Just as they had helped to create the Good Mother image, journalists aided Smith's performance of victimized whiteness, specifically endangered white womanhood, by adding the necessary but unspoken elements of
middle-class status and proper paternal protection. When the camera showed
Smith leaning heavily on the arms of various white men—her husband, the
sheriff, or other law enforcement agents—it upheld the performance of white
patriarchy that historically accompanied the assault of a white woman by a
black man.

But as suspicion of Susan Smith grew, viewers expressed more skepticism,
and some observers zeroed in on the image of the carjacker as a particularly
weak point of her story. Several days into the investigation, local African
Americans began to share their fears with journalists. "While no one was
openly critical of the generic sketch," reported the *Boston Globe*, "some blacks
here are wincing at the fast response to every wooded sighting of a black
male." A local man laughed when he told reporters that his co-workers kept
commenting on his resemblance to the composite sketch.[29] But during the
first week of the search for the boys, reporters and even editorialists refused to
openly challenge the image of the black male criminal or even to point out his
dubious ubiquity. To do so would have been to challenge the sacrosanct word
of a white mother.

By Wednesday, November 2, 1994, when authorities released the 911
tapes in which the McClouds reported the carjacking—"And it's a black guy,
she says," can be heard clearly on the tape, which played on all of the major
television networks—journalists were still unwilling to broach the race angle
in their coverage.[30] The following day, Smith's confession irrevocably transformed the tone of all coverage, and the unspoken issue of race immediately
surfaced. Although most had been initially reluctant to challenge the tenuous
story of this white mother, reporters easily demonized Smith as a racist as
soon as she was behind bars.

The "raw wound" of race and the immediate, angry responses to Susan
Smith's confession reflected the intricate linguistic rules of the New Right
1990s. Once Susan Smith had admitted the terrible deed and was whisked off
to jail, never to return unshackled to the streets of Union, Americans had to
deal with the complicated racial fallout. They, too, had been complicit when
they rallied around the duplicitous young mother. At this point, there were
three options for reading race in the Smith case. First, Smith's carjacking story
could serve as a widely publicized example of the continuing cultural currency

of age-old racist stereotypes, an instance of overt racial profiling that gave lie to the new racism. Her lie, in essence, could serve as a public referendum on race. But the second option let viewers off the hook for their belief in her racist allegations: Smith could be ostracized as a lone racist, a throwback whose falsehood contradicted the progress made in American race relations in the second half of the twentieth century. Finally—and this third option required some major mental gymnastics—the significance of race in the case could be denied altogether.

To their credit, many members of the media at least briefly chose the first option in the days immediately following Smith's arrest. Initially, some journalists ruminated on the state of American race relations in what could have been a self-reflective, even productive, manner. The earliest editorials that addressed the issue after Smith's confession condemned the use of Jim Crow–era racist images, arguing that the carjacking lie was representative of the lack of racial progress in the United States. According to these reports, Smith was not the only person at fault in this scenario. The American public, because of their willingness to believe Smith's poor performance of distraught motherhood for over a week, was implicated in her lie, as well.

This journalistic narrative surfaced literally the moment that Smith's confession became public. Among the crowd that had gathered to hear Sheriff Wells announce that he had arrested Susan Smith for the murder of her own children was Gilliam Edwards, a local African American man. As the gathered group expressed their shock and sadness, Edwards finally voiced the racial anger he had felt for the past nine days. "Speak up, black people, don't be afraid," he told the African Americans who had amassed for Wells's press conference. "We don't murder people," he shouted, exhorting the crowd to join him in his protest of the racist image. The *Atlanta Journal Constitution* reported that about thirty African Americans joined Edwards, "some raising their fists and shouting." Maria Eftimiades, a *People* reporter who wrote one of the first books about the Smith case, printed Edwards's diatribe in full. "It's always a black man, always a black man," he yelled to the crowd: "It's time for us to stand up like men and women and stop the whites from accusing us of hideous crimes that they commit against themselves and they have committed against us for 484 years. . . . What kind of people accuse defenseless people? We black people are totally defenseless. We shouldn't accept that no more. We got to fight back. We don't stand up for ourselves."[31] The angry shouts of this unknown South Carolina man summarily exposed the new racism. Many news reports carried some of Edwards's comments the following day, letting his rage serve as racial analysis with little commentary. Predictably, the attention paid to Edwards in the media was short-lived.

The image of the black male criminal was a core part of the story for the next few days, at least until Smith's written confession leaked to the media. The night of Smith's arrest, *Nightline* opened with the words of an African American man from Union: "A black man has been falsely accused again. I mean, we've had problems before and this is just unfair." Later in the broadcast, anchor Ted Koppel returned to the theme. Locals were devastated by the murders, but they were also angry at Smith's lie. An unidentified Unionite vented: "Everything that comes up that's wrong, everything that's bad, first thing they do is pick a black man as the epitome of evil." Tyrone Mason, an African American man from Chicago, agreed, explaining wearily to the *New York Times*: "As long as its allegedly a black man involved, America will fall for anything." The day after Smith's confession, television journalists tentatively acknowledged this racial anger, highlighting interviews with local African Americans who wondered "if Union would ever again live up to its name." NBC's Jim Cummins ended his segment that evening by arguing that Susan had "played to antique fears" with her racist lie.[32]

Except for the brief report a few days later of Smith's family's apology to Union's African American community, that was the last mention of race in the coverage of the Susan Smith case on the *NBC Evening News*. ABC followed suit. The day of her confession, Mike von Fremd interviewed some local African American men at a barbershop in Union. One asked plaintively: "Why were so many people prepared to believe?" Another local man warned: "If it had gone any further, it could've torn this town apart, between blacks and whites." Others nodded in assent as von Fremd awkwardly ended on a positive note: "But at Dawkins Barber Shop, they praised police; there was no wholesale rousting of black men." The report shifted to the subject of Union's small-town quaintness, and with that, it seems, the issue of race in the Susan Smith case was resolved enough for the network.[33]

Although most television reporters easily dropped the racial angle, print media held on to it for a while longer. When Susan Smith accused a black man, "the authorities here were quick to start ransacking our community for a suspect," Vincent Dawson told a *Washington Post* reporter. "But since she confessed, no one has rushed forward to apologize. That doesn't make for a very strong community spirit." Francine Krenshaw, another local African

American, agreed: "Race relations were already bad here. Now they're going to be worse." Locals told the reporter that police questioned at least a dozen black men during the investigation, and authorities had gone door-to-door in African American neighborhoods looking for information and suspects. "I was scared at first," Harold Browning, a construction worker who was questioned for several hours by local police, said. "I knew I didn't do it, but people started to look at me kind of funny after that." It was, a local woman proclaimed, "a hard week to be black in Union."[34]

Charles Sennott of the *Boston Globe* mined local racial anger in his immediate post-confession coverage, as well. He wrote that, when Smith first reported the carjacking, "police cruisers rolled into the Monarch Mills neighborhood," drifting "slowly past the knots of black men hanging out on the front porches and side streets of the town's oldest black community, which straddles the railroad tracks on the outskirts of town." The police questioned many local black men, prompting some African American teenagers to tear down the "crude" composite sketches hanging all over downtown Union. For many African Americans, Smith's admission that she had murdered her sons was not the "worst possible outcome." According to the *Boston Globe,* "the worst-case scenario in their minds would have been for an innocent black man to be convicted of the crime and executed amid national hysteria."[35]

Five days after Susan Smith's confession, Oprah Winfrey brought her immensely popular daytime talk show to town. She set up camp in Buffalo United Methodist Church, the scene of Michael and Alex's funeral just a few days before. The entire audience was made up of locals, and the discussion grew heated at times. Dot Frost, Susan Smith's former neighbor, who was not at all camera shy during the investigation, introduced race into the conversation, arguing that in her experience, white people were more outraged by Smith's confession than African Americans.

The general theme of the show centered on exploring the community's sentiments about the proper punishment of Susan Smith, but several locals kept returning to the issue of race. Samuel Vanderpool, a local African American, described the humiliating experience of the police coming to his parents' house to question him because he resembled the composite sketch. Vanderpool told Winfrey that the police did not "pick him up," or take him to the station for further questioning, but coming to his family's home was enough: "The cops came to my mother's house—my father's house to come get me, you know what I'm saying? Before this happened right here, I been—felt pressured—racial pressures or whatever against the police department and everything. But when they came to my house looking for me for this right here, that right there was preposterous. It made me feel like they disrespected my family, they disrespected me, they disrespected me as a human being." A local woman agreed, arguing that Vanderpool's experience was a familiar example of racial profiling, or "the fact that so many times a black man is who the crime is put on." A man in the audience, inspired by her words, argued that Smith's lie was a crime aimed at an entire race: "From the standpoint that when she pointed her finger and said one black man did it, she pointed her finger at every black man in this country. And when the point—when this happens, you take the black man as a hostage." Some audience members protested at this drawing of racial lines, claiming that "not all white people believed her" and that everyone, regardless of race, "fell in love with these children."

Locals clearly needed to air their feelings, and each time Winfrey moved the discussion back to punishment, tension rose in the church. Producers played a series of clips of Susan Smith begging for the safe return of her children, and Winfrey followed up by asking, "Do you not feel some sense of severe betrayal by that?" The audience answered in unison, "Yes!" Capitalizing on this anger, Winfrey explained that, although she understood "that we should feel compassion," she was uncertain in this case. She asked: "But do we really care what frame of mind she was in? Do we really?" "No!" the audience answered in unison.

But when they got the chance to speak individually, many locals expressed more complex feelings. In response to Winfrey's question about Susan Smith's "frame of mind," Samuel Vanderpool—a direct victim of Smith's carjacking lie—asked for Christian forgiveness: "These people here are jeering for this lady to be killed. And we call ourselves human beings, you know what I'm saying? That ain't even right because we're supposed to be God's children." An African American woman also pleaded with the audience to "think from your heart" and to "ask God to forgive and let us all live." Another woman seconded these thoughts, raising her voice over the loud interruptions of another pro–death penalty audience member to argue "it's up to us as human beings to come together as one." At the end of the show, Winfrey and a local pastor had the final words. He argued for forgiveness, and Winfrey concluded vaguely that belief "in the power of God can restore us."[36]

Winfrey's attempt to reach a harmonious, Christian conclusion was in keeping with the mainstream media coverage of the case during the week after

Smith's arrest. But not all locals agreed with this assessment. Although most of Union's small African American population did not join Gilliam Edwards on the streets of Union to protest the public's willingness to believe Smith's lie, they agreed with his dismal opinion of local race relations. John McCarroll, of the nearby West Spartanburg NAACP, told Rick Bragg of the *New York Times* that the case exemplified what many people tried to ignore, that there "is still a lot of prejudice between the races" in South Carolina. "We try to turn our back on it, hoping it will go away," he explained, "but sometimes it just gets worse." Reverend McElroy Hughes was the president of the local chapter of the NAACP at the time of the Smith case, and, like Edwards, he had some strong opinions of Smith's crimes. Hughes argued that the media story about the races coming together in the search for the boys was a convenient "camouflage" for simmering racial conflict, a "band-aid instead of major surgery."[37]

According to Hughes, racial problems were endemic to Union. There was a clear power disparity; for example, black and white children attended the same schools, but most of the teachers and administrators were white. Until the 1990s, a black man "minding his own business" on a downtown street was likely to be arrested for loitering. Unemployment rates were higher and average annual salaries lower among African Americans. "This town is cursed," he told *New York Post* reporter Andrea Peyser. "It will remain cursed until we create a situation in which the black man is equal." Hughes's depiction of conflicted race relations in Union had a shelf life of about one day in media coverage. He says that very few reporters approached him, even those that produced segments that explicitly addressed race. According to Hughes, "people want to say nice things, and they want to hear nice stories" about race, so reporters gave him a wide berth; the stories he had to tell did not have happy endings.[38]

Yet even if they refused to interview him, a few journalists initially agreed with Hughes's assessment, and they openly challenged the popular teleology of racial progress that undergirded the new racism through their coverage of the Smith case. Small newspapers all along the eastern seaboard featured reports that argued that white racism, far from being a relic of the southern past, was alive and well. One reporter argued that, although Sheriff Wells and his team of investigators skillfully avoided accusing random black men in Union County, the widespread white belief in Susan's lie could have easily turned into a mob mentality if they had not handled the case properly. A Louisiana reporter argued that Americans "have a blind spot when it comes to white criminals" that enables them to believe in the enduring image of the black male attacker. Not surprisingly, journalists across the nation referenced Charles Stuart as a case in point. Kevin Ross, a Los Angeles County district attorney who wrote an op-ed for the *New York Times* one week after Smith's arrest, protested the use of the well-worn image of the black male criminal, but he also offered a broader context. Throughout the investigation and the massive media attention surrounding the case, "the country [was] cozy in bed with *The Bell Curve* by Charles Murray and Richard J. Herrnstein," a best seller that posited that racial differences in intelligence quotients were the products of genetic factors. Media outlets across the nation carried generally favorable reviews. Ross saw a connection between the "black beast" criminal and the best-selling racist tome: "For many, justification that blacks have lower intelligence quotients perpetuates the scapegoating."[39]

These articles represented a potentially seminal moment in American racial reflection. Yet this national conversation about race ended quickly. In most media outlets, the race angle lasted less than a week, and in some papers, it lasted only a day. With the singular exception of CBS, most major newspapers, magazines, and televised news programs offered a stock editorial or two on the historical image of the black male criminal, and then they focused on Susan Smith herself, never to return to the broader racial dynamics of her case.

Those few media outlets that continued to address the racial angle did so from a safe distance, one that did not involve implicating observers. These reports isolated Susan Smith as a lone racist, with Sheriff Howard Wells serving as the community's savior through his expert handling of the investigation. Wells and his team questioned suspects cautiously and professionally, and the good sheriff single-handedly solved the case when he coaxed a confession out of Susan Smith after nine long days of lies. Unlike the Boston police over five years earlier, local and state law enforcement did not indiscriminately round up African American men for questioning, and the men they did question were, without exception, released within a few hours. According to one Florida journalist, Sheriff Wells had "learned the lessons of the 1989 Boston case" of Charles Stuart. In this report and others, journalists anointed Wells the hero of a case in which there were few laudable figures. "If there is a bright spot in the entire sordid mess," argued one reporter, searching for a positive angle, "it is that the case fell under the jurisdiction of a modern Southern lawman with impeccable credentials whose actions and words were carefully crafted to do everything possible to solve the murders while doing everything he could to control what could have been a violent situation."[40]

In this heroic narrative, which was a popular one for several days after Smith's arrest, no one could blame Sheriff Wells and his team of investigators for believing Smith's facile story. Most reporters argued that Smith's alleged carjacker was simply a familiar image. As Richard Lacayo put it in *Time* magazine the week after her arrest, Susan had only to "reach for available nightmares" to cover up her crime. The physical characteristics of the alleged carjacker—the "stranger in the shadows"—would have come to Smith naturally, perhaps subconsciously. "Susan Smith knew what a kidnapper should look like," Lacayo explained. "He should be a remorseless stranger with a gun. But the essential part of the picture—the touch she must have counted on to arouse the primal sympathies of her neighbors and to cut short any doubts—was his race. The suspect had to be a black man. Better still, a black man in a knit cap, a bit of hip-hop wardrobe that can be as menacing in some minds as a buccaneer's eye patch. Wasn't that everyone's most familiar image of the murderous criminal?"[41]

Although the caption underneath the accompanying photo informed readers that the "sketch of Smith's 'attacker' says a lot about our fears," Lacayo's final argument served to absolve Americans, especially white Americans, of racial guilt. He referenced the Stuart case as a turning point. According to this message, law enforcement officials were less quick to believe a white accuser. Times had changed, and racism had an individual face. Susan Smith was an isolated artifact from the racist past, not a representative of the troubled present: "The ploy of the dark-faced stranger works only when those around you share your worst assumptions. And this time, in this case, enough people were prepared to recognize that the face of the killer could be hers."[42]

Positioning Smith as a lone racist at least acknowledged that race played a role in the case, but even this news angle changed quickly. The week after Susan Smith's confession, her brother Scotty Vaughan gave a press conference to formally apologize to Union's African American community. According to Scotty, Susan Smith saw a man on her drive that fateful night, and she later grafted him onto her desperate lie. He told the press corps that the family was sorry not so much that Smith had told a racist lie, but that anyone would see the lie as racist. "It is disturbing to us to think that anyone would ever think that this was a racial issue," Smith's brother told the waiting reporters. She saw a man on the side of the road as she drove that night, and she later incorporated him into her story. He continued: "Had there been a white man, a purple man, a blue man, on that corner that night, that would have been the description Susan used. . . . We hope that you won't believe any of the rumors that this was a racial issue."[43]

A related media tactic, one that many African American religious leaders backed, was to explicitly deny the role of race in Smith's choice of attacker. The racial dynamics that had so angered people were, according to this line of thinking, the product of another time that had been recycled for the purpose of sensationalism. When Reverend Jesse Jackson publicly condemned Smith's choice of a black male criminal, a Tennessee reporter retorted that his accusations were those of a bygone era. "I know where Jackson is coming from," he wrote. "If the sheriff had drawled, 'Well, well. Looks like we got another case of nigrahs steppin' out of line heah. You dep'ties go out and find me a boy, and we'll have this thing wrapped up 'fore suppah,' people of every race would have gone through the ceiling. Justifiably."[44] In this narrative, Howard Wells stood in grand contrast to the stereotypically lynch-hungry, small-town southern sheriff. Likewise, the tiny town of Union was no angry white mob. Racism was the problem of a few "morally warped" individuals, not a persistent social issue that had subtly changed form after the civil rights movement.

Others sought to deny the role of race in the case completely. One popular angle that erased race as a theme in the case was a victim-centered narrative, in which all Americans, regardless of race, were the unwilling prey of Susan Smith's lies. In fact, in an ironic twist given the awful new sexist stereotypes of black motherhood, some post-confession coverage of the Susan Smith case prominently featured African American women as good mothers. "It was cold and dark and [the Smith boys] had to be out there by themselves, drowning," cried one African American woman to a reporter. "This is not a black-white thing," another sorrowful black mother told a reporter. "This is babies." Chris Burritt wrote in the *Atlanta Journal Constitution* that this mother shouted these words in protest to Gilliam Edwards's outburst following the announcement of Smith's arrest. Edna Meadow, an African American grandmother from Union, told reporter Gary Henderson of Spartanburg, South Carolina, that the lie was "not a race thing." "It's about how those pitiful babies left the world," she cried the day before Michael and Alex's funeral.[45] As people grieved for the boys nationwide, the media tactic of positioning African American mothers as good, grieving mothers served as a subtle means of defusing the racial tensions surrounding Smith's confession.[46]

The primary race-denying tactic centered on the new racist idea that the predatory black male criminal was simply a fact of life, not a racist stereotype.

Many observers argued that Susan Smith unthinkingly chose an image that she thought would make the most credible cover-up for her crime. ""I do not believe that young lady would have concocted that story if she didn't think it was the most believable [scenario]," argued U.S. Representative Jim Clyburn, an African American Democrat from South Carolina. Reverend Tom Currie of Union echoed this opinion when he explained that Smith chose a black man as her imaginary attacker because, "at the time, carjackers were minorities."[47] Journalists did not challenge this circular logic in print or on television.

This argument that Smith's choice of criminal was not at all racialized was especially popular among local leaders in Union. A clear goal of this message was to forestall any lingering anger in the local African American population. Just hours after Smith confessed, local leaders had already begun working to defuse racial tension. Reverend Alan Raines of Union explained: "I believe that just as prayer brought us together in the last eight or nine days of looking for the hope that those boys would be returned, the same thing [will happen] as we exercise our faith day to day." The media readily promoted this message of healing, either by avoiding the issue of race altogether or by offering small reports on how the races of Union had pulled together to overcome tragedy. Don Wilder, the editor of the *Union Daily Times,* argued to *Editor and Publisher* that Smith simply chose "someone exactly opposite her" on which to blame her crime. He continued: "If she were living in a community where there was Chinese or Hispanics, she might well have chosen a Chinese, the exact opposite of what she is."[48]

Reverend Bob Cato agreed that local demographics helped to determine Smith's lie. Monarch, the small mill town just a few miles outside of Union where Smith said she had been carjacked, was a community of "good, quality mill people," and besides, there "were few blacks living there." Smith "did not want to hurt anyone," especially the white people of Monarch that she likely knew or could even have been related to, so she invented a black attacker. "It did not have so much to do with race as community," Cato concluded. Cato was part of the coalition of popular local ministers who set about neutralizing racial tension within the community almost as soon as Smith confessed. According to Cato, people who saw this case as one of race were "unlearned people" who were "looking for a story."[49]

Reverend A. L. Brackett, the prominent African American minister of Union's First Baptist Church, quickly emerged as the local voice of reason on the issue of race. Brackett did not believe that Susan Smith was a racist, although he clearly saw the potential for racial tension following her confession and the exposure of her lie. The evening of Smith's confession, as Gilliam Edwards attempted to rally local African Americans against Smith's racist lie, other Unionites directed reporters to Brackett to dispel the aura of racism hanging over downtown. "We're trying to encourage people not to even think that way," he told the *Union Daily Times* the night of Smith's arrest. "I want to point out the fact of the good relationship the black and white have here in this community." The reverend's initial sound bites made him the de facto voice of black Union County, a role that resulted in a slew of interviews in local, regional, and national media outlets. By November 5, two days after Smith's confession, Brackett had already planned a church forum for "citizens to voice their feelings on the case"; he explained that Susan's lie "had made some blacks angry." The meetings were meant to help locals "pull together as citizens and work for the good of Union," tending to racial wounds that Smith's lie may have reopened.[50]

Brackett's handling of the race issue proved to be very popular with the media: the Sunday after Smith's confession, the day of the boys' funeral, CNN broadcast Brackett's sermon worldwide. He received letters from as far as China commending him on his Christian response to Smith's crimes. An old friend of Jesse Jackson's, Reverend Brackett helped organize the famous minister's visit to Union. Although some local leaders expressed the fear that Jackson would stir up racial tensions, his visit was tame and his message was subdued. Jackson deemed the murders a "human, not a racial tragedy," and local ministers agree that his visits to a group of local leaders and to Union High School, where he had an audience of almost fifteen hundred students, helped to reduce any lingering racial anger in the community. The overwhelming message from religious leaders, and the primary narrative in the media, was one of healing and of the races grieving together. In fact, Reverend Brackett argued on the *Sally Jessie Raphael Show* that the investigation actually brought Union's races closer together in their search for, and later grief over, the Smith boys.[51]

Journalists excerpted interviews with Union residents that wholeheartedly endorsed the ministers' official assessments of race relations in the weeks following Smith's arrest. Union understandably wanted to get to work on healing, rather than dwelling on the horrible lie. Just after Wells's announcement, Unionites took down the yellow ribbons that had covered Main Street, replacing them with black and white ones in commemoration of the boys, and perhaps in a silent gesture of healing across racial lines.[52] And yet, underneath the surface of this message of a community valiantly pulling together in a time of tragedy, the trappings of the new racism were subtly visible.

The town fathers' handling of the racial issue does not, in fact, appear to be unique to the Smith case. Union County's historian, Dr. Allan Charles, argues that there has always been a "genuine friendliness between the races" in Union. Race plays a negligible role in Charles's *Narrative History of Union County, SC*, and when it does appear, Charles offers a harmonious narrative of black-white relations. Dr. Charles still finds Union to be historically moderate, though not liberal, on the issue of race. The only modern racism Charles could pinpoint in Union in the 1990s was the ostracization of those who "mixed," or had sexual relations with, those outside their own race. Betraying his own prejudices, he explained that the "lower elements of white women" sometimes "took up with" black men, which resulted in them getting "cast out of the white community." Union as a whole, however, was a "poster child for integration": the races were equal in education, employment, and government. Union also has a "black bourgeoisie," which was, for Charles, apparently proof of equality.[53]

While it is perhaps not a complete "whitewash," Charles offers a rather rosy view of race in the South Carolina upstate in the early twentieth century in his official history of Union County. Yet bloody facts belie this vision of the region. The "Negrophobic" governor and senator Ben Tillman, notorious for his 1892 pledge to lead a lynch mob to avenge the rape of a white woman, was from nearby Edgefield. Lynchings increased "dramatically" during Tillman's tenure as governor in the 1890s; in fact, during the 1890s, lynchings in several upcountry counties, including two that bordered Union (Laurens and Newberry), outpaced legal executions by the state. South Carolina ranks tenth in the number of lynchings nationwide, and mobs leveled the charges of rape or attempted rape against almost half of the state's black male victims between 1881 and 1895. South Carolina mobs lynched at least seventeen African Americans in one year (1898) alone, many of them in the upstate. The rampant extralegal violence led one contemporary scholar to deem South Carolina "nothing more or less than a mobocracy."[54]

Although with less frequency, lynchings continued into the postwar period, most famously when a white mob murdered twenty-four-year-old Willie Earle of Greenville, South Carolina, in 1947. Even as massive resistance transformed into the new racism over the course of the civil rights movement, South Carolina had its fair share of racial tension, including the Orangeburg Massacre of 1968, a race riot sparked by attempts to integrate the only bowling alley in Orangeburg. By the time of the Smith murders, the major source of racial anger in the state was symbolic: the Confederate battle flag flying over the South Carolina statehouse made national headlines in 1994. When the NAACP protested to have it removed, the state GOP balked, approving the continued display of the flag by a wide margin at the Republican primary in August of 1994. As journalists and observers debated Susan Smith's motive that November, some South Carolina business owners filed a lawsuit against the state legislature, arguing that the flag controversy hurt business by frightening investors and courting an NAACP economic boycott.[55]

Racism persistently plagued South Carolina throughout the twentieth century, and Smith's lie laid bare this problem. Not surprisingly, many observers disagreed with their official historian's optimistic assessment of the county's race relations, but their voices seldom appeared in media coverage. Andrea Peyser, the *New York Post* reporter who produced the first book on the Smith case just a few months after the young mother's arrest, argued that the "relations between the races" in Union were "pretty similar to the relations between the sexes—It all depends on whom you ask." She described a small but significant forest on a rural highway in Union County, explaining that "every Southern town has its infamous trees." David Smith's mother told Peyser that when her family moved to Union in 1972, "people told me that was where they hanged black men if they tried to date a white woman. . . . I got the impression it wasn't a whole long time since those trees were used."[56]

Peyser wrote of a Union that was "just a generation removed from segregation." Marty Keenan, owner of a local barber shop, recalled a 1952 incident in which a black man, who was leaving a store with his arms full of packages, "'brushed up' against a white woman," and was imprisoned for years for the contact. Even more recently, in 1993, a white woman had reported being mugged by a black man in Union, but rumors abounded within the African American community that she had concocted the story to hide her gambling problem. Union had a small-town southern culture in which "Susan faced sharp criticism when she briefly dated a black student" in high school. In the 1990s, interracial couples freely strolled the downtown streets beneath the Confederate flags that adorned the local pawnshop, some houses, and many car antennae. If overt racism had largely disappeared, statistics still supported systemic discrimination. In a county that was approximately one-third African American, the average annual income for a white Unionite in 1989 was $10,939. For black Unionites, it was $6,711. Five years later, when Smith made the national news with her carjacking lie, the county's total unemployment rate hovered at 7.3 percent. For local African Americans, it was 10 percent.[57]

Nevertheless, in the wake of the Smith case, many local whites argued that, as in the nation at large, race relations were no longer a problem in Union. Kevin Kingsmore, who attended Union High School with Susan, offered the evidence that their graduating class was "half black," they had an African American principal at the time, and he never witnessed any racial tension, much less violence. Michael Roberts, who served as a juror during the trial, agreed; the races generally had to get along for such a small community to function. According to some, the search for the Smith boys brought the races together. "We were all lied to, and we all searched together," said Phil Hobbs of Union's WBCU radio station. Locals generally argued that the racial angle was a product of the sensation-hungry media that was searching for controversy. The evidence of local racism came from, in the words of various locals, "crazies," "people we didn't know," "malcontents," "rabble-rousers," and "fringe folks."[58]

Torance Inman of the Union County Chamber of Commerce acknowledges that there were and are racists in Union, "but they pretty much keep to themselves." According to Inman, the overt racists in Union, it seems, were African American—a claim that clearly echoes the New Right mantra of "reverse racism." Inman argued that no Unionites were surprised when Gilliam Edwards tried to rally the crowd after Wells's announcement of Smith's arrest. "He's a self-professed Muslim, Nation of Islam, very radical," Inman said, a slight smile on his face. "He's going to show up for everything." McElroy Hughes, formerly of the local NAACP and curator of an eclectic Black History Museum in the basement of his church, Inman simply deemed "eccentric." He concluded that Edwards and Hughes are part of a small minority of local African Americans who are "inherently distrustful of white people."[59]

Journalists rarely, and then only briefly, challenged Union's official racial vision of itself in those first weeks of coverage, and within two weeks of Smith's arrest, with the exception of CBS, race fell out of the coverage altogether. Even as the trial approached and the preparations of both sides were daily national news, race was not a factor. But some later argued that race played a silent role in the trial: as a white woman, Susan Smith would never receive capital punishment, regardless of the brutality of her crime. Conversely, if a black male carjacker had actually murdered the Smith boys, he would most certainly get the death penalty. In response to my initial question about this ten years after the trial, Rick Bragg replied flatly, "I think if it had been a black carjacker, he would have died by now. . . . He would have made it to trial. Howard Wells would have made sure he'd made it to trial. . . . It would have been a quick trial, and he would have died by now."[60] Likewise, according to this line of thinking, if a black mother had committed the crime, a jury would just as surely have voted to execute her. Race lingered around the margins of the trial, but in accordance with the new racism, these arguments remained unspoken.

In fact, the racial issue had become so diffuse in public responses to the case that it hardly factored into coverage of the trial, even though the prosecution tried to make Smith's lie a fundamental part of their strategy in the "guilt phase" of the trial. On the last day of the trial, NBC quoted prosecutor Tommy Pope's attempt to play to racial anger one last time in his closing statement of the sentencing phase. He addressed the jury directly: "For nine days, she was telling us it was a black man." He paused for dramatic effect. "The black man was her." Pope's words called upon the historical image of the "black beast" even as he exposed Smith's lie, implying that when she killed her children, she was every bit as dangerous, threatening, and evil as the presumed worst elements of society, African American male criminals. Perhaps predictably, this sound bite stood alone; journalists provided no analysis or supporting interviews, and the racial angle did not play a major role in the television coverage of the trial at all.

Race appeared in televised coverage of the case just one more time during the year of the Smith trial. When CNN's talk show *TalkBack Live* came to Union during the first week of the trial, audience members and callers demonstrated a singular, if underreported, preoccupation with the issue. Union resident Carolyn Jeter argued that Smith was treated with far more "compassion" because of her race. Jeter recalled hearing "racial slurs" during the investigation, "including comments about taking the alleged carjacker and 'drag him up and down Main Street.'" The show, predictably, ended on a more positive note, as did the few news reports that covered it; a Spartanburg resident argued that "Susan Smith could have said any one of us could have taken those children." In other words, race was not really an issue in this case.[61]

With the exception of this locally filmed CNN call-in show, the racial angle of the Smith case was a null story by the summer of 1995. By that time, other images had acquired immense explanatory significance in the case of Susan Smith. These images easily eclipsed race, and they allowed Americans to bury the painful subject safely under the covert language of the "new racism." Journalist Cynthia Tucker pinpointed the problem just a week after Smith's confession. Tucker wrote of the "bitter legacy" and the nation's failure to make Smith's case useful. Smith's name would stand for many things in the years to come, she argued: "Deteriorating family structures, the loss of innocence in small-town America, infanticide. And, despite her family's forthright apology for her lie, she will also be a symbol of our failure as a nation—a failure that belongs to all of us, whether white or black or brown—to bring clearheadedness to the subject of crime and race."[62]

Despite this general public reluctance to discuss the role of race in the Susan Smith case, the connections between race, crime, and legal justice were on the minds of many Americans in the mid-1990s, largely because of the impending trial of O. J. Simpson for the murder of his ex-wife. The trajectory of images in the Susan Smith case inverted the imagery process of the Simpson case, which was tried that same year in California. Wendy Kozol argues that the Simpson case initially made the news as a public conversation about domestic violence, feminine vulnerability, and gendered power relations. Images of race and masculinity, specifically racist white policemen and a victimized black man, quickly subsumed this narrative.[63] The post-confession coverage of the Smith case reversed this process: the initial narrative was one of race, specifically the racism of her carjacking lie, but this narrative quickly faded from headlines as issues of gender quickly became the primary means of explaining Smith's actions.

The rapid retreat from even the most generic racial theorizing was very much in keeping with the new sexism. As in the Smith case, in public analysis and policy, gendered representations had subtly replaced race. Moral assertions about sexuality and class had become, in 1990s America, key components of the complicated linguistic code of race. Perhaps it was inevitable, then, that when Smith's confession destroyed all vestiges of her ideal maternal image and her class status went into free fall, the public latched on to the explanatory power of deviant female sexuality, long after the "black beast" carjacker exited the stage. The sexualization of Susan Smith solved many of the narrative problems in the story: it eclipsed whiteness and modern white racism as focal points; it allowed further demonization of Smith based on the previous suggestions of her sexual misbehavior and tenuous class status; and, perhaps most importantly for observers, it provided a motive for Smith's actions.[64]

3

"THE MODERN-DAY MEDEA"

MATERNAL INFANTICIDE, or more specifically "filicide" (the murder of one's own children), so thoroughly violates our cultural common sense about motherhood that it is one of the most confounding crimes in American culture. The words commonly used to describe the Susan Smith murders—"unspeakable," "unimaginably evil," "unthinkable," and "unfathomable"—bespoke a pervasive inability to understand Smith's actions. The young mother's confession, according to one stunned journalist, was "one of those universal moments that hit everyone in the gut." Veteran reporters shed tears. "If time had weight," proclaimed NBC's Bob Dotson the day after her confession, "this day would be crushing." The images of Susan Smith that circulated during the investigation, and the racialized readings of Smith's carjacking story immediately after her confession, simply could not answer the question on everyone's minds: how could she do it?[1]

Of course, speculation about Smith's motives to murder began as soon as Sheriff Wells made his shocking announcement. The media saturation of the kidnapping investigation, and the nationwide involvement of hundreds of citizens and law enforcement officers in the search for the children, ensured that outrage was the overwhelming public response to Smith's confession. "I hope she fries in the electric chair," argued one woman, speaking for many Americans who felt personally betrayed by Smith's revelation. "Hell's too good for her," added another as she flipped through *Newsweek*, which featured a cover story on Susan Smith the week after her confession. Amidst other, more profane shouts, a lone bystander cried, "We believed you!" at Smith as she went into the courthouse for her bond hearing the day after her confession, making it clear that Smith had committed two crimes: the murders and the lie.[2]

Smith's surprising confession necessitated extensive revisions in the coverage of the case that went far beyond the superficial racial analyses discussed in the last chapter. Even the damning cracks that had developed in Smith's façade as the investigation dragged on did not begin to explain why she would kill her children. As Smith settled into her jail cell, journalists vied for explanatory power, rapidly sorting through available scripts. News vans swarmed over Union "like ants" in the days following Smith's arrest, searching for new leads that would explain the fatal twist in the story.[3] As observers searched for answers, reporters and anchors searched for images that would dispel the dissonance between the murdering "monster mom" and the "Good Mother" Americans had rallied behind for so many days.

A rapid narrative revision was in order, and in the context of the early 1990s, there was a well-known cultural image that fit the bill. By the early 1990s, New Right anxiety over the destruction of family values had honed its attack to three primary targets: female sexuality, single motherhood, and the perceived assault on the traditional breadwinning father. Neoconservatives saw these three issues as the inevitable devil's spawn of feminism. Pat Robertson, the televangelist, would-be politician, and major voice of the New Christian Right in the last two decades of the twentieth century, perhaps best captured this dubious connection. In a 1992 letter campaigning against Iowa's proposed state Equal Rights Amendment, Robertson famously summed up the New Right paranoia of women's rights: "Feminism is a socialist, anti-family, political movement that encourages women to leave their husbands, kill their children, practice witchcraft, destroy capitalism and become lesbians."[4] For a few months in 1994–95, Robertson's "feminist" nightmare found its embodiment in the figure of the one woman dominating national headlines: Susan Smith. The third of the "seven Susans" was an anti-feminist caricature, a sexually wanton, habitually violent, scheming single mother. This "Susan" cuckolded her salt-of-the-earth husband and murdered her sons to bed the wealthiest bachelor in Union. This narrative—the "boyfriend motive"—transformed Smith's crime from the "incomprehensible" act of an aberrant mother to the representative crime of a familiar female deviant, placing her within a recognizable new sexist framework of maternal evil and female sexuality.

As we have seen, by the time Smith confessed, her impending divorce was public knowledge. Her single-mother status opened her up to all manner of attacks, which became more vociferous as the vague details of Smith's personal life began to trickle into the media coverage. Almost immediately after Smith's confession, a shadowy new character emerged: the boyfriend for whom she allegedly killed her children. During the investigation, as Smith's maternal façade and alibi of that fateful night began to unravel, reporters erroneously zeroed in on Mitchell Sinclair, the man Smith had allegedly been on the way to visit when the carjacker leaped into her passenger seat. Sinclair's appearance on the tabloid news show *A Current Affair* raised some suspicions when he said he believed the "truth would come out." Although Sheriff Wells and his investigative team quickly ruled Sinclair a non-suspect, many news reports speculated that Sinclair was Smith's lover and that he knew more than he had told.

In fact, he did not. Sinclair was a long-time, very close friend of Smith's family. He was the boyfriend of Smith's best friend, Donna Garner (the two later married) and he was very close with Susan, her parents, and her sons. The media spotlight cast upon him late in the investigation seemed utterly ridiculous to Smith's family and to everyone in Union who knew Mitchell Sinclair, for two reasons. First, everyone knew how serious he was about Donna. And second, many knew the identity of Smith's real boyfriend at the time.

After a brief reconciliation with David between June and August of 1994, Susan Smith formally filed for divorce in late September on the grounds of her husband's adultery. She resumed a relationship with Tom Findlay, the son of her boss at Conso. Smith had dated Findlay for a few months in the winter of 1994, but they broke up when a jealous David Smith, from whom Susan was separated at the time, threatened Findlay. But on October 17, 1994, Smith's fling with Tom Findlay abruptly ended. At the time of the break-up, Smith believed she was falling in love. For Findlay, the relationship was a casual affair; in fact, he dated other women that fall. In his "Dear Jane" letter, Findlay cited many reasons why the two could not continue to date, including their very different backgrounds and her children. He had reason to believe that the relationship was casual for Susan Smith, as well. He called her "a bit boy crazy" in the letter, citing an instance in which Smith kissed another man during a party (Findlay himself had sex with another woman during this party). Findlay left this letter on Smith's desk on Tuesday, October 18, and she cried as she read it. The two agreed to remain friends.

That Thursday, October 20, David babysat the boys while Susan Smith met some friends after work. When she came home, they readied the boys for bed together, and then Susan Smith fell asleep. David seized the opportunity to go through her purse, where he discovered the letter from Tom Findlay. Convinced that he could counter-sue Susan Smith with proof of her adultery, David did not want to awaken her by leaving. So he called his girlfriend, Tiffany Moss, who raced over to the Smith home, took the letter to her church to copy it (there were no copy shops open in Union at night, but

Moss's mother was a secretary at the church and had a key), and returned the letter to David, who stowed it back in Smith's purse. The following morning, when David came to pick up his sons while Susan Smith was at work, he revealed his find, and they had another in a long series of heated arguments. Smith was upset that David had gone through her things, but she insisted that her relationship with Findlay had begun only after the legal separation. David screamed at her that he could prove she was lying, because he had been stalking her. "He told Susan he had more evidence against her," Smith's mother wrote later, citing Susan Smith's account of the fight. "He had a tap on her phone. He had friends following her. He claimed he knew every step she had taken lately."[5]

The information that David Smith knew her every move was very upsetting to Susan Smith, because in addition to the Tom Findlay affair, there was another man in her life that she did not want anyone to know about. Although the details are very sketchy, Smith appears to have also been sleeping with her boss, Cary Findlay—Tom's father. The fear that David would reveal this information to Tom plagued her all weekend. At her request, a Southern Bell employee came to her home on Saturday, assuring her that David had been lying about tapping her phone. But Susan Smith still believed that David knew more than he had revealed during their Friday morning fight, and she resolved to talk to Tom Findlay. A few days later, on Tuesday, October 25, Smith approached Tom at work and asked to speak to him in confidence. "I've been involved with your father," she said through tears. Findlay was shocked, of course, but he graciously agreed that they could remain friends. At the trial months later, he said he tried to be compassionate because she was very upset and possibly suicidal. His reassurance was for naught; Smith continued to cry and ending up leaving work early that day. That night, she took the boys for a drive, and they disappeared forever.[6]

At the time of Smith's arrest on November 3, 1994, the Smiths' legal separation was well known, and many in Union knew of her relationship with Tom Findlay. The affair with Cary Findlay, on the other hand, was an absolute secret. In fact, because Susan Smith later recanted the information, it is still not clear whether that affair actually occurred (Cary Findlay certainly never confirmed it). At any rate, there were enough open secrets about Smith's relationship history floating around Union that national reporters easily picked up on the sordid facts almost as soon as Sheriff Wells announced her incarceration.

After Smith's arrest, sexuality and class rapidly transformed from subtle undertones to *the* explanatory factors of the case. A few years after the murders, feminist Annalee Newitz argued that Smith summarily "violated the most sanctified code of 'family values' when she chose to kill her children."[7] The "boyfriend motive" and its attendant image of Smith as a "boy crazy," divorced single mother fit seamlessly into contemporary New Right fears about changing female roles in society and the corresponding deterioration—or, in the parlance of the day, "crisis"—of traditional American manhood. The "boyfriend motive" positioned Susan Smith as a national scapegoat for various social ills, serving her up as a cautionary tale of feminism run amok.

The initial sex-based, post-confession image offered by the media was entirely predictable, a sort of "Dr. Jekyll and Mr. Hyde" split personality meant to explain the contradiction between the crying mother who pleaded with the alleged kidnapper on national television versus the affectless "baby killer" Americans saw being led through a mob to the courthouse for her bond hearing. In this reactionary analysis, there were, in effect, "two Susans": Smith wore a maternal mask, one that effectively covered her "heart of darkness."[8] It was a useful motif, because one of the primary post-confession narrative problems was the fact that no one, not even Smith's estranged husband, could furnish any proof that this "monster" had actually behaved badly as a mother prior to the murders.

Having discarded most halfhearted attempts at racial analysis of the case, reporters stationed in Union recentered their narratives on this mask worn by the duplicitous mother. In interviews, neighbors cited the loving pictures Susan had taken of her sons and the many parties she hosted for them. "She was perfect," a Union woman told *Newsweek*. "You've got your bad girls at high school and you've got your good girls. She was your good girl." Locals provided laundry lists of evidence of Smith's alleged "goodness": "She dressed well, in clothes that were considered on the preppy side (a denim miniskirt and pink polo shirt in one yearbook picture), and didn't smoke or drink." Union residents who had known Smith for all of her twenty-three years simply could not understand what would drive this mother, whom they all knew as a "sweet girl," to murder. The young woman who had made excellent grades and volunteered with the Special Olympics in high school just five years before must have had "another side" to be able to do such a thing to her children. "I've seen her with those babies," sobbed a local business owner to *New York Times* reporter Rick Bragg. "She came from a good family. I don't understand any of this."[9]

Bragg, a veteran reporter, knew from past experience that public scandals were often accompanied by "shock and a certain amount of revisionist history," making the perpetrator seem less sinister, "somehow more pure," than they really were. But in Susan's case, there was "absolutely nothing in public record or in the minds of people here that even hint[ed] at a capacity for murder." Bragg, stationed in Union for the *New York Times*, wrote at length of the town's utter confusion: "To the people of Union who grew up with Mrs. Smith, who remember tying ribbons in her hair when she was a little girl, who enjoyed her smile—everyone talks about the smile—it is as if there are two Susans. They ask over and over about what caused her to kill her own children, but nothing, to many people, will ever explain how this woman, who seemed to be a perfect mother and so hard-working and devout, could do such a thing."[10] Susan Smith's mask of decency, it seemed, had been fatally flawless.

It was, of course, a staple of popular crime analysis, but the trope of the mask was more than a cliché. Susan Smith's exploitation of idealized motherhood was a direct assault on the gender politics of the era. The mask motif was a remedy that consoled readers and viewers that Susan Smith was not painful proof that the idolized "Good Mother" was capable of cold-blooded violence. The public quest for motive quickly took the form of a search for previous evidence of her dark side. Many articles cited Smith's troubled family history, especially her father's suicide in her childhood and her impending divorce, as factors that contributed to Susan's own alleged mental instability. There was ample evidence of deviance in her past, reporters argued: "From reports that Susan Vaughan [Smith's maiden name] was pregnant with son Michael when she wed David three years ago to the recent separation from her estranged husband and the alleged extramarital affairs, Mrs. Smith lived what appeared to be a lie."[11]

According to this narrative, Smith lived a "lie" to hide her own deviant behavior, and with her confession, she became sexually suspect. After nine long days in the backwoods of South Carolina, journalists seized upon this gory plot twist with zeal. Suddenly, Smith was a tabloid staple, and even the mainstream media trafficked in sensationalism in their post-confession coverage. "Nobody admits it's exciting, of course," wrote journalist Bob Herbert the week after her arrest. "Nobody would dare say it was entertaining. But when Phil Donahue and Oprah Winfrey decide to set up shop in Strom Thurmond country, you know there's something titillating going on. Sex, lies and infanticide in Union, S.C."[12]

The two-pronged obsession with motherhood and female sexuality permeated the media coverage of the case: if Smith was not the Madonna, she must, then, be the whore. Although this sexualization generally rested upon rumors, the initial source of this angle was a known authority on Susan Smith's romantic encounters: her soon-to-be ex-husband, David Smith. The couple had been separated for several months by the time of the murders, but David knew a disturbing amount of details about Susan's personal life. He had, of course, stolen the break-up letter from Smith's purse a week before the murders, and his girlfriend, Tiffany Moss, copied it so they would have evidence. The night of the boys' disappearance, Moss "had been keeping tabs on [Susan's] movements almost every minute" at David's request, although she lost track of Smith once she left home that evening with the boys. Days later, when he turned the letter over to authorities as part of the investigation, David Smith unwittingly scripted a sexualized narrative of the case.[13]

This letter—a "Dear Jane" penned by Susan Smith's short-lived, post-separation boyfriend—would become infamous. Indeed, it quickly became the "smoking gun" that explained Smith's motive to murder. With this letter, Susan Smith's sexuality acquired sudden salience in explanations of her crimes. Journalists focused on one part of the letter, repeatedly quoting the paragraph addressing Smith's children:

> Susan, I can really fall for you. You have so many endearing qualities about you, and I think that you are a terrific person. But like I have told you before, there are some things about you that aren't suited for me, and yes, I am speaking about your children. I'm sure that your kids are good kids, but it really wouldn't matter how good they may be. The fact is, I just don't want children. These feelings may change one day, but I doubt it. With all of the crazy, mixed-up things that take place in this world today, I just don't have the desire to bring another life into it. And I don't want to be responsible for anyone else's children, either. But I am very thankful that there are people like you who are not so selfish as I am, and you don't mind bearing the responsibility of children.[14]

Suddenly, it all made sense. Those feelings expressed by the author of the break-up letter—the active desire to avoid having children, selfishness, a lack of responsibility—had, in public representations, become Susan Smith's own. They were her motives to murder. Selfishly, heartlessly, she did it for a man.

Like the previous images of Susan Smith that circulated in the first few

weeks of her national fame, this new image of Susan Smith relied upon rumors, strategic shots and sound bites, and the omission of messy details that
did not fit the script. Its explanatory power was obvious, and a few networks
got right to business, floating the romance script immediately after Smith's
confession. Within a few hours of Sheriff Wells's announcement, CNN unof-
ficially broke the story of the "boyfriend motive," reporting that authorities
searching Smith's home had allegedly found a "Dear Jane" letter from a boyfriend "saying he wanted to be with her but 'did not want any kids around.'"[15]
CNN's "scoop" ensured that almost all reporters covering the story would
feature this sinister male character in their coverage within twenty-four hours
of Smith's arrest.

The "Dear Jane" letter immediately eclipsed all other possible motives,
and media outlets from *Hard Copy* to the *New York Times* quoted the letter
extensively, days before they even knew Tom Findlay's identity. As horrifying
as this image was to viewers, it was a familiar one in American culture. The
idea that "sensual women were likely to be criminals" was a criminological
truism. In the second half of the twentieth century, this connection between
female sexuality and violence acquired enormous explanatory power in cases
of maternal filicide. According to Ann Jones, the leading authority on homicide by females in the United States, in times of social change, the "witch-
hunt" mentality reigns: social anxiety "surfaces from time to time in American
society in the same form it took in Salem: a sudden notice of the crimes of
women."[16] By all accounts, the final decades of the twentieth century were
a time of major social change and corresponding anxiety amongst those proponents of more traditional gender norms. In particular, the transformations
wrought by second-wave feminism enabled women to have sex more freely,
postpone motherhood, divorce more easily, and enter the workforce in droves,
resulting in a renewed cultural scrutiny of female sexuality and behavior. In
this context, when a woman was accused of violently discarding the maternal
mantle, her alleged crimes easily fit the anti-feminist cautionary tales spun by
New Right politicians.

The sexy (or at least sexually active) murdering mother was not a new figure in American headlines. In 1965, a banner year for second-wave feminism,
the "boyfriend motive" for filicide made national news for the first time. That
summer, as above-the-fold headlines blared "Sex Discrimination in Jobs Is Big
Problem" and "Women Complain of Bias on Jobs," Mrs. Alice Crimmins, a
working-class New York mother, reported her two children kidnapped from

her Queens apartment. Despite evidence that indicated that someone had tried to get in from the outside, Mrs. Crimmins was charged with murder.[17]

The law enforcement agents involved in the Crimmins investigation did not deliberately "set out to convict an innocent woman." Rather, "many people almost immediately assumed she was guilty because she was 'like that.'" Mrs. Crimmins's separation from her abusive husband combined with her job working long hours and her alleged sexual activity to paint a lurid picture. Although most acquaintances described her as a shy woman, the media seized upon the prosecutorial image of Crimmins as a "strident" and "rebellious housewife" whose pancake makeup, tight slacks, and "little black book" full of men's names provided the evidence necessary for conviction. Rumors of numerous boyfriends, including one with shadowy mob connections, provided the most damning evidence. *Front Page Detective* dubbed Crimmins the "Sexpot on Trial," and the name stuck. According to the tabloid media, Crimmins was representative of modern feminism: she was "an erring wife, a Circe, an amoral woman whose many affairs appear symptomatic of America's Sex Revolution." Inevitably referred to as an "ex-cocktail waitress" to underscore her working-class status, Crimmins was found guilty of manslaughter in three separate trials.[18]

Much like Susan Smith a few decades later, Crimmins's name was "synonymous with tabloid sensation" for years. After a brief respite from fame, during which she served her prison sentence, Crimmins resurfaced in the media when it was reported that she had married a wealthy suitor. Photos of her aboard her new husband's yacht accompanied headlines announcing her parole in 1977. Crimmins was a tabloid mainstay for over a decade, and her case inspired numerous true-crime books, novels, plays, and films throughout the 1970s.[19]

Five years after Alice Grace (née Crimmins) disappeared into the sunset on her new husband's yacht, yet another "Sexpot on Trial" captured national headlines. In 1983, Diane Downs, a recent divorcee, claimed that she and her three children were shot in the course of a carjacking by a "bushy-haired stranger" on a rural road in Oregon. One of her children died, and the others were severely injured, while Downs herself suffered only a superficial wound on the arm. Although Downs, like Crimmins, consistently maintained her innocence, the media and, later, popular crime writer Ann Rule (who achieved best-selling status yet again with her account of the case) followed the prosecution's line of attack, charging that Downs shot her three children in cold blood to facilitate a reunion with a former lover. As in the Crimmins case,

Downs's sexuality was a key issue in her trial. Media accounts and trial testimony focused on Downs's extramarital affairs and her volatile, post-divorce relationship with a married co-worker. This final affair served as the "smoking gun" in the investigation; law enforcement officials believed that Diane shot her children in a desperate attempt to win back her ex's affections. The media promoted this narrative of the case, as well. The *Weekly World News,* a grocery-store-aisle tabloid, featured a full-page picture of her on the cover accompanied by the screaming headline: *"Kids Cramped Her Style . . .* So the Fiendish Mom Shot Them."[20]

Unlike the Crimmins case, there was damning evidence against Diane Downs: one of her remaining children positively identified her on the witness stand as the shooter. The jury found Downs guilty on all counts of assault, attempted murder, and murder, and the judge sentenced her to life in prison plus fifty years for the illegal use of a firearm. But as with Crimmins, Downs's incarceration was not the end of her fame. She made national headlines again in 1987 when she briefly escaped from prison. Authorities discovered her at the home of a fellow inmate's husband, where she claimed to be searching for her children's murderer. That same year, Ann Rule published her book on the case to rave reviews and even better sales. Downs surfaced periodically in the media over the next few years. In 1988, she appeared live via satellite on the popular *Oprah Winfrey Show.* Winfrey focused on Downs's alleged violence and her sexuality: "In addition to being accused of shooting your three children, you were always sleeping with everyone else's husband, always preferred married men. . . . You befriend an inmate, you escape from prison and you go move in with the inmate's husband. . . . You look like the girl next door, but the girl next door looks like she's turned bad."[21]

The following year, Rule's bestselling book about Downs inspired a popular television miniseries—"Part *Fatal Attraction,* Part *Mommie Dearest"*—complete with a drunken, leather-clad Farrah Fawcett as the offending mother, prompting another wave of media coverage. Her sexual behavior, and the "boyfriend motive," is what people remember most about Oregon's most famous murderess. Even now, TruTV's (formerly CourtTV) "Online Crime Library," the most thorough account of her case besides Rule's book, is titled "Diane Downs: Her Children Got In the Way of Her Love."[22]

The "boyfriend motive" of infanticide had thus achieved national headline status periodically during the two decades before the Smith murders. In journalism, a story's mythic quality, or its basic structure in terms of plot and characters, often has a greater impact on its audience than the actual details of the event being covered.[23] The "boyfriend motive" in the Crimmins and Downs cases had become, by the time of the Smith murders, the foundational myth of maternal filicide in the United States. In the case of Susan Smith, the basic "boyfriend motive" plot structure mattered more than the actual details, most of which were unknown in those early days.

This model of motive should be even more familiar to twenty-first-century readers than it was to observers in the 1990s. As I finish this manuscript, the Casey Anthony trial just ended in an acquittal. Anthony was accused of murdering her daughter Caylee in 2008, but the jury found her not guilty because, they said, there was not enough hard evidence. Nevertheless, the media trafficked widely in the sexualized script of maternal filicide. Casey Anthony was a single mother; in fact, the identity of Caylee's father has remained shadowy throughout the wall-to-wall coverage of the trial. Cue the "boyfriend motive": Anthony, like Susan Smith, was a lying, scheming slut, more interested in sex and partying than motherhood. Proof of this motive ranged from pictures of Anthony at bars to the tattoo she got a few weeks after her daughter went missing. "Bella vita," it said—the "good life," which was precisely what reporters and prosecutors believed Susan Smith sought when she killed her children. Anthony's tattoo, like Smith's "Dear Jane" letter, served a central role in the media as an indication of motive.[24]

In their attempts to shore up the mythic quality of the "boyfriend motive," journalists turned to even older examples to explain the Smith drama. It was perhaps inevitable that reporters would deem Susan Smith a "modern-day Medea" in reference to the ancient Greek tale of betrayal and infanticide. It was, *Newsweek* pointed out, the prototype of "how much evil can lurk in even a mother's heart—something we've known for 2,300 years." Reporters solemnly quoted Euripides: "No cowardice, not tender memories. Forget that you once loved them, that of your body they were born. For one short day, forget your children; afterwards, weep: Though you kill them, they were your beloved sons."[25]

As in the sketchy narratives of the significant details of Susan Smith's life, the media took liberties with the Greek classic in their coverage of the Smith drama. Ignored were Smith's suicidal tendencies, her professed love for her sons, her fears that she could not be a good enough mother, all of which she expressed in her two-page written confession. Reporters quoted only those lines that supported the "boyfriend motive." A family lawyer tersely summarized the debate over motive for the *Washington Post:* "Medea kills following rejection." Journalists continually misused the ancient tragedy and recast Susan as the "modern-day Medea in the person of a 23-year-old mill girl" who was "not the first woman to choose a man over a child. . . . It happens all the time."[26] But the details were fuzzy. In fact, there was no new man in Susan Smith's life; given her impending divorce from David Smith and her recent break-up with Tom Findlay, there was no man in her life at all.

This inconvenient plot problem did not keep the "boyfriend motive" from making front-page news the day after Smith's confession. Although Don Melvin of the *Atlanta Journal Constitution* began his article that day cautioning that no one could be certain of Smith's motive, the headline "Mom's New Love Often Tied to Child Killings," said it all. In Melvin's report, an expert source explained that the family dynamic shifts dramatically when "you get a new fella entering the picture," especially for young, recently divorced mothers like Susan Smith. Smith was excited about her new love, who was, according to Melvin's confidential sources, none other than Mitchell Sinclair, the man she had reportedly been on the way to visit the night of the murders. Like Alice Crimmins and Diane Downs, Susan Smith faced one major obstacle to her budding romance: her children. "Smith and her husband, David, filed for divorce in September, and some experts say parents can harm their children to save a marriage. But the head of a national children's organization said the motive more often is a desire to attract a new husband. Smith was on her way to visit a boyfriend when she reported the children abducted. WXIA/Channel 11 reported that a source close to the police investigation said the motive may have been Smith's obsession with Mitchell Sinclair. Sources said Sinclair had professed his love for Smith but did not want 'a ready-made family.'"[27] Reporters had the tone of the letter right, but they were completely wrong about its author. Mitchell Sinclair, the alleged object of Smith's "obsession," was actually a close, trusted family friend who had participated daily in the search for the boys. He and Smith had never had a sexual or romantic relationship. The mythology of the "boyfriend motive" and the journalistic race for the "scoop" ensured that reporters like Melvin readily quoted their anonymous sources, even at the risk of promoting some very specific misinformation.

Despite his unclear identity, by the following night, some twenty-four hours after the announcement of Smith's confession, the "boyfriend motive" had become the primary understanding of the crime. That evening, CBS's Randall Pinkston discarded the speculative tone of previous broadcasts.

Smith's motive to murder, he soberly told viewers, was "a man who wanted her but not her children." To those who saw Smith as a plain young woman who dressed very conservatively, even frumpily, this was surprising news. As a local minister put it, she was no "Siren Sue"; she did not remotely resemble sexy Farrah Fawcett as the unhinged murderess Diane Downs, pining for her ex in black leather and big hair and singing raucously to "Hungry Like a Wolf." It took real imagination to place this tear-streaked young woman, who had thus far appeared on television in thick glasses, oversized sweatshirts, and sneakers, in the middle of a fatal love affair. To overcome the lack of visual "evidence" of her deviant sexuality, the media leaned heavily on minute titillating details to do the work for them. Magazine exposés featured aerial views of the hot tub in which a drunken Smith had allegedly cavorted alongside quotes from the infamous break-up letter instead of actual photographs, because none could be produced in which she appeared to be sexually suggestive in any way.[28]

Although Susan Smith initially gained fame with her carjacking lie, the sensational, sexy angle of the "boyfriend motive" is what kept her in the news in ensuing months. The sexualization of female violence was part and parcel of the gender politics of the late twentieth century. The one-track focus on the "boyfriend motive," with its attendant trappings of single motherhood, sexuality, and violence, amounted to an argument that Susan Smith was an evil representative, a national problem, not some lone feminine aberration. Neoconservatives in 1990s America easily donned the mantle of accuser, using "Susan Smith," now shorthand for female evil, as the representative of various perceived social problems.

In this developing narrative, Smith's sexuality was the explanatory link: sex made her a bad mother, and it made her violent. To make her crimes legible, reporters had to rewrite Smith's life to include a history of both violence and deviant sexuality. Just seconds after they cut away from the live feed of Sheriff Wells announcing Smith's arrest, CBS scooped their competitors by producing an alternative revised plot of violence in the Smith family. A spokesperson from the National Center for Missing and Abducted Children told reporter Randall Pinkston that infanticide often occurred in one of two contexts: "to cover abuse, or it's for emotional reasons—someone who has a romantic interest and the other partner is not interested in the child, or revenge, or conflict."[29] In other words, Smith killed her sons because she was either chronically violent or blindly in love. Mere moments after the public announcement of her arrest, the expert had scripted the two images of Smith that would dominate the news over the coming weeks. More importantly, his hasty analysis merged the age-old sexualization of female murderers with a contemporary social obsession: child abuse.

By the late 1980s, "media fixations" on child abuse went hand-in-hand with the national obsession with missing children and the day-care panic. Unlike the concurrent, but unsupported, hysteria over kidnappings, the numbers actually seemed to support the fixation with abuse: according to the Department of Health and Human Services, the estimated number of abused children in the United States doubled between 1986 and 1993. These dire statistics coupled with erroneous, but widely publicized, reports that children were slightly more likely to endure abuse at the hands of mothers than fathers. A new public enemy, the abusive mother, was born. According to this logic, Susan Smith was different from other violent mothers only because her consistent abuse turned fatal. In the days immediately following Smith's confession, the answer to the pressing question of motive was often followed by national child-abuse statistics. "How could she do it?" asked Elizabeth Kastor in the *Washington Post* the day after Smith's arrest. She listed general abuse statistics, arguing that, while Smith's actions clearly were not "understandable on the level of logic," the murders were "the extreme version of something we do understand, which is child abuse."[30]

There was a crucial flaw in this model of motive: no one who knew Susan Smith could furnish any evidence of prior abuse towards her boys. In fact, her family, friends, neighbors, and acquaintances consistently supplied sound bites extolling Smith as a good mother. But the template of abuse made cultural sense; it "solved" the case by slotting Smith into a familiar subset of bad mothers. In lieu of actual evidence of abuse in Smith's past, reporters simply referenced other unrelated cases, using national statistics for validity. They seemed unable to differentiate between the two distinct crimes of child abuse and infanticide. One NBC reporter argued that abusive and homicidal parents share the general problem of "having no control," concluding feebly that Smith's crime had "raised lots of questions about young mothers and stress."[31]

There was, however, a gendered subtext to the national obsession with child abuse in the late-twentieth-century United States. In media reports, infanticide was the endpoint of the dangerously slippery slope of child abuse, the result of single mothers' inability to manage outside stressors, namely their finances and/or their boyfriends. According to this analysis, maternal violence against children increased in direct correlation with the rise in divorce and single motherhood. Child abuse and child homicide were not problems that should concern all parents; they were the individual problems of young, broke, unfit mothers like Susan Smith.

By the early 1990s, the American legal system had responded to this image in the form of "failure to protect" laws. Because fathers are generally seen as the "'invisible' parent," when charges of violence against children surface in a family, these laws hold the mother responsible even if she did not perpetrate the abuse. In other words, under "failure to protect" statutes, mothers are blamed for fathers' behaviors—a twisted version of the logic of the "boyfriend motive" in which a woman chooses a man over her child. In fact, one such maternal failure made the news just days before Susan Smith's national debut. Although her name is one most Americans do not remember, twenty-four-year-old Pauline Zile made headlines when she told authorities that her seven-year-old daughter Christina had been kidnapped from a restroom at a shopping center in Florida just three days before Susan Smith alleged that she had been carjacked. For five days, Zile appeared on the nightly news hysterically clutching one of her daughter's dolls, pleading with the kidnapper through the television cameras. Zile addressed her daughter directly, telling her not to be scared and to try to find a way to call if she could.[32]

A drastically different narrative emerged after police discovered blood in Zile's apartment during a routine search. Pauline's husband confessed to beating the child to death in Pauline's presence some six weeks earlier. Together the couple had dumped the body behind a local Kmart. Only seventeen hours before Susan Smith confessed to murder, Pauline Zile and her husband were charged with murder and aggravated child abuse in Florida.[33] Even though Christina died by her stepfather's hands, Pauline Zile was "crucified in the media as the epitome of a bad mother."[34]

The abuse narrative thus had its sexual undertones, featuring women who selfishly chose their lovers over their children. For about a week after her confession, the national media convincingly recast Susan Smith as an abusive, single mother through carefully placed expert sound bites and comparisons to other abuse cases. The emphasis on "young moms and their money worries" allowed Smith to fit easily into sex- and class-based ideas about motherhood. Susan Smith was even more of an open target than other abusive mothers because she could not transfer blame to a violent husband or "absent fatherhood."[35]

In fact, fatherhood played an important role in this narrative of abuse. As

Susan Smith's status plummeted in the eyes of the American public, David Smith's rose. When reporters trotted out abuse statistics in lieu of actual evidence, it became clear that the demonic, abusive image of Susan Smith had a sympathetic male counterpart: David Smith, the grieving father and ultimate victim of the offending woman. The sexualization that surrounded the new, post-confession image of her made David a repeat victim of her crimes—adultery, separation, the murders, the nine days of lies. The story line of David as a victim reached its height with the extensive coverage of Michael and Alex's funeral on Sunday, November 6, three days after Susan's confession. The funeral received unprecedented airtime; all South Carolina television stations suspended regular programming to simulcast the service, as did the twenty-four-hour, international cable news channel, CNN. Media outlets across the nation recorded David Smith's anguished cries and moans as he buried his sons. It would prove difficult to forget the photograph of a distraught David Smith being physically supported as he was led from the church to the cemetery. This picture, like the one of his sons seated together in a wicker chair that was used in the initial search and the close-up of his tearstained wife that graced the cover of *Time* magazine the week after her confession, is one of the enduring images of the case.[36]

During the week after the funeral, the American public reached out to the grieving father. Sympathy cards flooded the tiny Union post office, many simply addressed to "David Smith, Union, SC." Letters to editors across the nation praised David as much as they condemned Susan. Some observers suggested that the tragedy might have been avoided if the court had just awarded this poor father custody of his sons in the weeks before the murders. The judge in the Smiths' mid-October custody hearing, according to one letter writer, based his decision on the apparently insignificant detail that David had had an extramarital affair, "overlooking the fact that Mr. Smith was visiting his children nearly every day because he missed them and he loved them." The letter writer went on to defend absent fathers who failed to support their children: "Men are not money machines, and I sometimes cannot blame them for not paying their child support, due to the fact that their visitation is so limited by the courts." In other words, the epidemic of "deadbeat dads" was reactionary, or something of a revolt by fathers against an oppressive custody system that favored mothers. The letter concluded: "When are the courts going to stop assuming that the mother is always the best choice. When are fathers going to get more rights?"[37]

In cases of maternal filicide, it is a common response to question why the offending mother did not just give the children to their father if she felt she could no longer care for them. But this letter writer, concerned as she was with the "rights" of fathers, asked something different altogether. She suggests that the fathers in question do not have custody rights because the legal system that determines custody discriminates against them, a claim that ignores the fact that there are many reasons why courts might not award fathers primary custody of children. This sense of paternal victimization, of persecution even, dovetailed in the early 1990s with the perceived "crisis in masculinity": the pervasive white, middle-class, middle-aged angst over changes in traditional male roles. This new emphasis on fatherhood, integral to the growing "men's rights" movements, was part and parcel of the neotraditional family-values mentality.

By the 1990s, these victimized white men figured out how to politically voice their frustration. The year that Susan Smith killed her children was dubbed the year of the "angry white male" as that constituency flocked to the polls to vote Republican five days after Smith's confession. Scholars have generally read this "anger" that led to the Republican sweep of Congress as a reactionary attempt to preserve jobs for white men in response to affirmative action and increased immigration. In short, this anger appears to have stemmed from a sense of white entitlement. In 1990, Senator Jesse Helms of North Carolina captured the sense of white victimization perfectly in his famous "White Hands" campaign ad. Twenty-eight seconds of this thirty-second spot show a pair of white male hands, wearing a wedding ring and a respectable, but not fancy, collared shirt, reading a rejection letter from a potential employer. The hands angrily crumple the paper as Harvey Gantt and Ted Kennedy are shown together as the brains behind the affirmative-action "quota systems" that were forcing white men in North Carolina into unemployment.[38]

The ad was part of the broad attack on affirmative action in the 1980s, as the Reagan administration appointed Clarence Thomas, a longtime foe of "preferential treatment," chairman of the EEOC, and the Justice Department began to file suits against those employers who followed affirmative-action guidelines on "the basis that they instituted a new form of racism." In the wake of the 1994 "Republican Revolution," affirmative action achieved its New Right comeuppance. "All of a sudden, resentment of state-order 'preferences' became politically smart," as working-class white voters, particularly in the South, began to flock to the GOP.[39]

Thus, the New Right rallying cry of "reverse discrimination" worked to bring new voters into the Republican fold in record numbers just days after Susan Smith confessed to murdering her sons. This message bespoke a sense of white *male* victimization; in other words, this anxiety, or "anger," was over gender as well as race. Neoconservatives denounced all who might benefit from affirmative action (women and minorities) as self-proclaimed victims, "special interest groups" looking for state-mandated "preferences," insults to the American meritocracy that were taking jobs from hard-working Americans (read: white men).

In the developing political rhetoric, "reverse racism/sexism" was a key code phrase. Victimization was crucial to family-values rhetoric—with the family allegedly under attack, who better to take up the mantle of avenging hero than the traditional white father? In fact, some scholars argue that the core fear of this "crisis in masculinity" was a changing definition of what it meant to be a breadwinner, or, as our letter writer concerned for David Smith's well-being might put it, "father's rights." David Smith was, of course, a victim of Susan Smith's crimes, but the idealization of fatherhood in this case had a larger context. It served as much political purpose in the wake of Smith's confession as did the idealization of motherhood during the initial investigation.

Exalted fatherhood coupled with deviant motherhood to become the story du jour, appearing in above-the-fold headlines alongside election results the week after the Smith boys' funeral. But although he later endorsed the "boy-friend motive" wholeheartedly, David Smith refused to follow the fabricated abuse script provided by the media. Ten days after Susan Smith's arrest, in a heavily promoted news special—"How could she do it? How could Susan Smith kill her own children?" the voiceover asked as close-ups of the grieving father graced the screen—Katie Couric interviewed David Smith on a *Dateline NBC* exclusive entitled "First Words." Between tears, David Smith flatly denied any allegations of maternal abuse. "Susan, she was great, she really was," he told Couric before a watchful nation. "She was a very dedicated, devoted mother to the children."[40] This interview forced the media to abandon the "abusive mother" narrative, and it summarily disappeared from coverage as if it had never happened.

The ideal father script died a quick death, as well. For a few weeks, David Smith was a media star, but after Couric's prime-time interview, he all but vanished from coverage for several months. The media latched onto a new image of Susan Smith that fit another prevailing cultural narrative of motherhood, but only if there was no doting father in the picture. The Smiths' legal separation provided the final explosive element of the dysfunctional family dynamic. This single plot element, perhaps more so than any other, summarily placed Smith among the ranks of familiar maternal deviants in American culture: single mothers.

By the end of the century, mother-blaming took many forms, but single mothers bore the brunt of the ire. This is one instance in which the new sexism apparently trumped the new racism: for neoconservatives, the most prominent characteristic of these demons was clearly their sex. Regardless of race or class, all single mothers courted condemnation. In 1992, the most famous example of this came from the highest levels of political power in the United States. In his oft-quoted speech about the urban riots of the early 1990s, Quayle transcended both race and class in his attack on single mothers. Quayle's new target, in what was possibly an attempt to avoid sounding racist by being an equal-opportunity sexist, was the popular television show *Murphy Brown*, on which the title character, an unmarried, wealthy, white woman, had recently given birth: "It doesn't help matters when prime time TV has Murphy Brown—a character who supposedly epitomizes today's intelligent, highly paid, professional woman—mocking the importance of fathers, by bearing a child alone, and calling it just another 'lifestyle choice.'"[41] Predictably, Quayle enjoyed support from the far right. In his defense of the vice-president, pundit Rush Limbaugh explicitly connected the *Murphy Brown* debate with the violent subtext of single motherhood when he argued that Murphy Brown—again, a fictional television character—was an abusive, unfit mother whose son would turn out just like the gangsters perpetrating the Los Angeles riots.

On his television show, Limbaugh informed viewers that Brown did not even know how to hold her baby, much less care for it. "Look at her, where's the nearest trash can, what can I do with this thing?" he railed in voiceover as he showed a clip from *Murphy Brown*. "Look at the poor baby's arms, that baby can't possibly be loved and be happy. . . . Murphy, if you don't, if you don't start handling that kid right you're going to end up with a serial murderer on your hands."[42] Like her poor sisters in riot-torn Los Angeles, without a husband, Murphy Brown was destined to raise a fatherless criminal. Gender, sexuality, and marital status placed her among the ranks of maternal deviants in conservative eyes, regardless of class or race.

By the time Susan Smith made headlines, single motherhood and child abuse had come to be seen as twin "national emergencies," key points of attack in the politics of the new sexism. In early 1995, as Susan Smith prepared for her upcoming murder trial, Katha Pollitt of the *Nation* lamented that single mothers were the "demons of the moment, blamed for everything from crime to the deficit." These demons were built upon a discernible subtext of sex and violence: the perceived problem with single and/or divorced mothers was that they both raised "the same specter of women out of men's control."[43] Without men in the household to serve as providers and protectors, it seems, there was always the possibility of maternal sexual misbehavior and intrafamilial violence.

Whatever protection Susan Smith had once had from condemnation—endangered white woman, loving wife, middle-class mother—was gone within two weeks of her confession. Predictably, she became the anti-heroine in the most controversial New Right narrative that linked motherhood, sexuality, and violence against children, one that perhaps surpassed all others in mother-blaming and slut-shaming. Anti-abortion, or "pro-life," groups latched on to the Smith case as further evidence for their argument that infanticide and abortion were interchangeable. According to this analysis, American women who sought abortions were no better than the child-killer Susan Smith. Media outlets added fuel to this "pro-life" fire when they erroneously reported that Susan Smith had an abortion in her teens and later married David when she discovered she was pregnant so as to avoid having another one. Under the subheading "Abortion, Lost Lover Seen Spurring Mother's Actions," the *Boston Globe* listed several contributing factors to Smith's disturbed mental state, including her "wealthy" lover's "sudden departure" to London (which did not happen until after Smith's confession) and "an abortion she had as a teen-ager which deeply depressed her."[44]

Although the reporter quoted a law enforcement official who cautioned that "no single factor" caused Smith to commit murder, the report leaned heavily on Smith's own sexual behaviors as explanation. Her recent break-up represented the "culmination" of a tragic life, although some tragedies apparently affected Smith more than others: "If the suicide of her father, Harry Vaughan, had traumatized her, she never showed it. She did become profoundly depressed in her senior year after undergoing an abortion. . . . A law enforcement official said that Smith brought up the abortion during her confession to the murders."[45] The message was clear: any depression that Smith suffered was based on her own sexual misconduct, not on external traumas or psychological problems beyond her control. Yet there is no evidence of any kind that Susan Smith ever had an abortion. In fact, when she and David unexpectedly conceived a few months into their relationship, the two never even considered the option of abortion. Despite the fact that Susan was only nineteen and had plans to begin attending college full-time in just a few months, David wrote that "one of the things we settled right off was the abortion route." The young couple discussed it, but they quickly "realized that there wasn't much to talk about. Each of us was totally against the idea from the start."[46]

This was not just a case of journalists baiting readers with sexual innuendo and dubious facts from anonymous sources. Intentional or not, there was a political agenda behind the sensational headlines, and some media consumers were explicit in their defense of this agenda. The "abortion wars" waged in the 1990s featured physical attacks on women who sought the surgery as well as on their medical providers. This outright violence, including murder, combined with policies that offered little support to new mothers and their babies, exposing the hypocrisy of the "sanctity of life" rhetoric. The levels of vitriol and violence in the 1990s indicated that anti-abortion activists were more interested in their own nostalgic conceptions of motherhood than about the "rights of the unborn." At the end of the twentieth century, reproductive rights were tantamount to a frontal assault on the ideal of the "new momism." A woman who chooses to terminate a pregnancy summarily "strips the veil from the sanctity of motherhood," "demoting" maternity from "a sacred calling to a job."[47] Although abortion opponents would say that their interest was in preserving life, it seems that their primary concern was controlling the sexual behavior of women in a way that protected the "mommy myth."

Thus, some people reacted angrily to Susan Smith by equating abortion and infanticide. One letter writer argued that no one could blame Susan Smith for being confused by such an "ambiguous society" that "supports mothers as they decide whether to allow their children to live." Readers across the nation compared reproductive rights and child murder in their letters to editors, asking why the American public was not similarly outraged by every abortion. One even went so far as to ask anti-abortion protesters to "redirect their energies"; rather than picketing at abortion clinics, they should march on Union's Main Street during the Smith trial.[48]

In a sarcastic missive entitled "Feminists Must Unite Behind Susan Smith," a North Carolina man wrote: "Even if her children were inconvenient to her and her new boyfriend, she has the right to choose when she has children. . . . Her estranged husband has no right to imply that he should have been asked to consent to the murder of his children—that would have been an invasion of her sacred right to privacy." He concluded: "It was a long, hard fight obtaining the inalienable right to tell a woman that it's OK to kill your children; we must not go back on 20 years of progress."[49]

Despite the general feminist silence on the case, for "pro-life" observers, feminism was to blame for Susan Smith. Abortion was a key wedge issue in 1990s politics, and the "antis"—Republicans—were winning the war of rhetoric as well as the legal battles that chipped away slowly at women's access to reproductive rights. This grouping of the nation's most famous filicidal mother, the mass of women who terminated their unwanted pregnancies, and feminists was yet another weapon in the rhetorical campaign to define unborn fetuses as people. If a woman who sought an abortion was equal to Susan Smith, then her hypothetical fetus was equal to her murdered sons. This analogy foreshadowed the New Right campaign over "fetal personhood" by several years.[50]

Undergirding much of the "pro-life" rhetoric is a fundamentally misogynistic view of sexually active women. The violence against abortion providers and seekers in the early 1990s and the popular New Right line of favoring abortion only in cases of rape and incest gives lie to the "pro-life" cause. In these cases, the issue is clearly not the sanctity of "life." Bipartisan support for abortion in cases of rape or incest rests upon the idea that only women who *are forced* to have sex should not have to suffer the consequences. Women who do it willingly and get pregnant are, according to this line of thinking, already deviant before they decide whether to abort. In a 1983 essay, feminist journalist Ellen Willis ("EW") imagined the following conversation with a "Right-to-Lifer" ("RTL").

> RTL: If a woman chooses to have sex, she should be willing to take the consequences. We must all be responsible for our actions.
> EW: Men have sex, without having to "take the consequences."
> RTL: You can't help that—it's biology.
> EW: You don't think a woman has as much right as a man to enjoy sex? Without living in fear that one slip will transform her life?
> RTL: She has no right to selfish pleasure at the expense of the unborn.

Although public debate generally rests on ideas about "life" and murder, Willis concluded that "the nitty-gritty issue in the abortion debate is not life, but sex."[51]

Over a decade later, sex was still the key issue. Susan Smith became a target of anti-abortion activists not because she had ever actually had an abortion—there is absolutely no evidence of any pregnancies in her past beyond the two that resulted in her sons. Rather, the connection between Smith and the political debate over reproductive rights was the "boyfriend motive": according to this logic, Smith had murdered her children for a sexual relationship, which, in the "pro-life" discourse, was essentially the same thing as an abortion.

The summary sexualization of Susan Smith post-confession did not, in fact, adequately explain her motives to murder. It did, however, enable observers to understand her according to the age-old image of the sexy murderess, a figure made all the more compelling within the new sexist context of the mother-blaming, slut-shaming 1990s. Although the sexy "Susan" made for good headlines, an element was still missing, one that would ensure that the "boyfriend motive" would endure as the reigning understanding of the case. Once observers, journalists, pundits, and politicians added class status to the mix, an entirely new "Susan" was born, one that firmly secured Smith's place in the new sexist politics of gender.

4

PERSONAL RESPONSIBILITY

THE TITILLATING ANGLE of the "boyfriend motive" helped Americans make sense of Susan Smith as the kind of mother who could commit a heinous crime. This plot twist kept her in the headlines, but as more details leaked to the press during the weeks following Smith's confession, it became clear to the American public that sex, or even romance, was not her only motive. Susan Smith, it seemed, was a specific kind of slut: she was a social climber.

The emphasis on socioeconomic status in public representations of Susan Smith was not random, nor was it simple sensationalism. As with sex, there was an underlying political agenda. The link between class and sex was not conjured from thin air. There was, in fact, evidence: Smith herself paired the two in her written confession. "Because of my romantic and financial situation," the *Boston Globe* quoted a few days after her arrest, "I've never been so low."[1] There were also cultural precedents for the association between class and sex. Once Susan Smith's estranged husband, erstwhile boyfriend, and rumored sexual behaviors achieved headline status, it was inevitable that representations of her socioeconomic status would free fall.

We have seen the pop-cultural connection between female violence and sexuality in American culture. There is a corresponding connection between class status and morality; in the American imagination, lower socioeconomic status generally entails low morals, and vice-versa. For American women especially, a set of specific class associations accompanies sexual activity. In her genealogy of the term "slut," feminist Leora Tanenbaum explains: "Regardless of her family's actual economic status, the 'slut' is thought to be 'low-class' and 'trampy,' the kind of girl who wears gobs of makeup and whose voluptuous curves threaten to explode the fabric of her tight clothes. She lacks the polish of the 'good girl,' who keeps her sexuality reigned in and discreet (beneath a blazer, a belt, some nude pantyhose), and who will no doubt marry a nice middle-class man and raise a nice middle-class family."[2]

Author Dorothy Allison grew up in a working-class family about an hour away from Union, and she recognized this class/sex divide among the girls and young women in her small South Carolina town, as well. The "good" girls wore fashionable clothes and "virgin pins" and "went on to marry" the star football players after high school. The blue-collar girls, Allison wrote in a memoir published the year of the Smith trial, "were never virgins, even when we were." Their socioeconomic status dictated rumors of their sexual activity: "Like the stories told about Janis Joplin in Port Arthur, Texas, there were stories about us in Greenville, SC."[3]

Likewise, girls' sexual activity reflected their class status: "Sex was dangerous, a trap, trashy as drinking whiskey in a paper cup or telling dirty stories in a loud whisper. Sex was a sure sign of having nothing better to hope for."[4] As in Allison's best-selling memoirs and fiction, the rumors of sexual impropriety that formed the crux of the "boyfriend motive" determined a sea change in Susan Smith's perceived class status.

So, as journalists and observers revised their understanding of Susan Smith in the days following her arrest, class effortlessly joined sex as a key component of their analyses. Susan Smith, the "most hated woman in America," quickly found herself pictured on front pages as a working-class single mother. Through the rumors, speculation, and the seemingly less important actual details of Smith's motive to murder, we can track the essential building blocks of this most famous and lasting version of Susan Smith.

The image had both historical and literary precedents. In their coverage of the Smith case, journalists perhaps unwittingly referenced a modern literary archetype that combined sexuality, class climbing, and murder. As Susan Smith arrived for her bond hearing the day after her confession, one reporter described the screaming mob that awaited her outside the Union County Courthouse as a "scene worthy of a Theodore Dreiser novel." The description was apt; in fact, Theodore Dreiser would have easily recognized Susan Smith. With the exception of the criminal's gender, the "boyfriend motive" perfectly fit the script of what the great American novelist described as the classic American homicide. These kinds of crimes, explained Dreiser in a 1935 interview, were the result of the national obsession with upward social mobility: "It seemed to spring from the fact that almost every young person was possessed of an ingrown ambition to be somebody financially and socially. . . . In short, the general mental mood of America was directed toward escape from any form of poverty. . . . We bred the fortune hunter de luxe." For several decades, Dreiser studied real-life examples of the attempts by young Americans to "obtain wealth quickly by marriage," often at great cost and through violent means.[5]

Dreiser deemed this kind of violence the "American Tragedy" murder, and he fictionalized one such famous case in his 1925 novel of the same name. After much consideration, Dreiser chose as his subject the 1906 Gillette/Brown murder trial in which "an ambitious young man killed 'Miss Poor' to marry 'Miss Rich.'" Although there were some problems with this narrative—there was no evidence that the accused, Chester Gillette, was even really dating two women at once, for example—this class-climbing motive served the purposes of the press and the prosecution well. In Dreiser's novel, young Clyde murders his working-class, pregnant girlfriend Roberta in order to marry into the wealthy Finchley family. The crime, his lawyers argued, was one of passion—for wealth, not women. According to his defense team, Clyde suffered from "a 'brain storm'—a temporary aberration due to love and an illusion of grandeur aroused in Clyde by Sondra Finchley and the threatened disruption by Roberta of all his dreams and plans."[6]

Although the original "American Tragedy" case featured an offending man, the "now-familiar narrative" based on the novel has featured social-climbing criminals of both sexes as it has replayed over and over in American culture throughout the twentieth century. The phrase has come to refer to any murder in which a "'tie that binds' is severed for the sake of upward mobility." Dreiser's model featured the "woman in danger" plotline familiar to any television viewer or moviegoer, but public representations of "American Tragedies" have just as often featured violent women who kill a loved one to bed a wealthy man. Significantly, when a woman is cast as the violent criminal, sexual obsessions seem to play as much a role as class desires.[7]

Journalists assigned to the Susan Smith case perhaps unwittingly paid homage to Dreiser's criminological model, referring to the murders as an "American Tragedy."[8] Front-page articles and cover stories trafficked widely in lurid (and often inaccurate) details, providing an overarching narrative framework recognizable to media consumers. With the advent of Dreiser's quintessentially American "boyfriend motive," Susan Smith became a representative criminal rather than an incomprehensible monster, a combination of the classic femme fatale and Dreiser's "fortune hunter de luxe."

There was a seamless connection between sex, violence, and class in public representations of Susan Smith, but as always, the lingering question in this case centered on motherhood. In An American Tragedy, the young mother-to-be is the murder victim, not the murderer; Dreiser's drama thus provided no script that explained how maternity might factor into an archetypal "American Tragedy" perpetrator. But Susan Smith committed her crimes in the very specific context of the "new momism," that pervasive "siren song blending seduction and accusation," or idealization and condemnation.[9] Mothers who violently violated the boundaries of the "new momism" were one of the most suspect groups in the 1990s. Adding class status to the list of Susan Smith's damning characteristics placed her effortlessly within the most derided group in 1990s America: poor single mothers.

As with the other characteristics of the new, post-confession "Susans" in the media, positioning Susan Smith as blue collar involved dismantling the previous image of her as a middle-class, stay-at-home mom. To keep the developing plot of Smith as a familiar deviant on track, this revised narrative needed a rich man to complement Smith's lowered socioeconomic status. Journalists hit pay dirt when they discovered the true identity of Smith's most recent ex-boyfriend, the author of the infamous "Dear Jane" letter. Although they may have had to stretch the truth quite a bit to portray Susan Smith as poor or even blue-collar, the class status of her boyfriend fit the wealthy requirements of the "boyfriend motive" perfectly. As the son of the biggest operating mill in a small town in the "Textile Belt" of upstate South Carolina, he was, essentially, royalty.

At the time of the murders, Susan Smith worked as a secretary at Conso Products, the largest textile mill in Union County. The owner, J. Cary Findlay, bought the mill on the edge of Union in the mid-1980s to supplement his $25-million-a-year business ("The World's Largest Manufacturer of Decorative Trim," at least according to the sign in front of the Union mill). When he purchased this mill, Union was in a severe economic recession—unemployment was as high as 30 percent in the 1980s—and some in the county saw Findlay as a "savior." David Smith argued that Conso "practically kept the whole county afloat." When the Conso mill opened, the Findlays moved into Fair Forest Plantation, an eighteenth-century plantation home just southwest of Union in a heavily wooded area on the banks of Fair Forest Creek. Although it was no longer a working farm, the gargantuan house, lengthy stone fence, and wrought-iron gates presented an imposing fortress, the likes of which most Unionites, or Americans for that matter, had never seen. David Smith called it a "huge estate outside of town—not just an upper-crust ranch home like Bev and Linda's [Susan's parents], but a real mansion." In 1994, Conso

International's sales from their various plants worldwide totaled over $41 million. Cary Findlay and his wife, Koni, by far the wealthiest couple in Union, made names for themselves as philanthropists throughout the 1990s.[10]

Their son and heir, Tom Findlay, was a balding bachelor in his late twenties who was immensely popular with the single women of Union, including Susan Smith, whom he dated briefly in the fall of 1994. Locally, the Findlay estate was known as "the Castle." Tom Findlay, who lived in a guesthouse on the Fair Forest property, was "the handsome scion of what [was] considered the county's richest family," "the Catch" of Union County. The entire town of Union separated Smith's neighborhood, where she and David shared a cramped brick home paid for by her parents, from the Findlay estate, a sprawling eighteenth-century stone mansion on a hill overlooking a small river and the thick forests that made up much of the county. According to the *Boston Globe,* as Smith drove from "her small ranch-style house through the stone and wrought-iron gates of the Findlay estate, where Thomas lived in a guest house and was famous for 'hot tub parties,'" she allegedly dreamed of a life with Findlay in London, where his father was building another Conso plant.[11]

With the appearance of Tom Findlay in media reports, class joined sexuality as the fundamental motive to murder. In the cases of Alice Crimmins and Diane Downs, their sexual histories and extramarital affairs served as the damning evidence that irreparably destroyed their "good mother" status. In Smith's case, her alleged affair combined with her rapidly deteriorating class status to explain the enigma of maternal filicide. The media juxtaposed Smith's near-poverty—clearly an exaggeration, and an image that thoroughly contradicted the middle-class narrative of motherhood that had circulated just a few days before—with her ex-boyfriend's vast riches. In this narrative, Smith, a working-class, soon-to-be divorced single mother, used sex to get Findlay's attention, and she used violence to remove the obstacles—her children—to his wealth.

It took less than a week after her confession for class, violence, and sex to paint a vivid portrait of Susan Smith, the scheming mill girl, in almost every media outlet, from tabloids to the nation's newspapers of record. A newly single mother who brought home a little over one thousand dollars, plus $115 from David in child support, each month, Smith reportedly "sacrificed" her sons for a "deluded dream of wealth, love, and status." Under the telling headline "Bid to Climb Social Ladder Seen in Smith's Fall to Despair," the *Boston Globe* reported that the murders were the result of Smith's "desperation to jump from the listing boat of the working class." According to the report,

Susan Smith lived "somewhere between the two worlds" of the "working-class and the white collar," and her relationship with Findlay was her ticket out of this socioeconomic limbo. As sexy photographic evidence of the couple's class divide, a popular news magazine later featured in its centerfold an extreme close-up of Susan's tearful face opposite a map of Tom Findlay's father's estate, with the hot tub (the alleged scene of drunken parties) circled in lurid red. In just a few days, Susan Smith had become a single mother "on the fringe" of the working class, with only "two hundred dollars in her bank account" who saw Tom Findlay as her ticket to "life beyond Union County." She murdered her children to replicate her mother's successful social climbing and "marry up."[12]

Smith's rapidly deteriorating class status in news reports belied the fact that, over the years, young Susan had actually experienced a taste of life at each level of the social hierarchy in her small hometown. Union, South Carolina, was a representative mill town at the end of the twentieth century: stagnant growth combined with long, slow deindustrialization to create a thoroughly depressed economy. Susan Smith was born into a decidedly blue-collar family, and she came of age during a prolonged and severe local recession. Her mother, Linda Russell, left home at the age of sixteen to have a baby with Harry Vaughan. They married young, and Linda bore two sons in quick succession. Just before her second son, Scotty, was born, the Vaughans moved out of Harry's parents house and into an apartment in Union's small row of public housing downtown. For the broke, teenaged couple, the apartment represented progress. "I was proud of that apartment," Linda later wrote. "We had two cribs, an old bedroom set, a hand-me-down sofa, a kitchen table, and TV." Her parents helped them buy a washer and dryer. Linda worked at a local textile mill while Harry bounced around jobs, including night watchman, mill hand, and the fire department. His drinking was a source of conflict, as was his jealousy, and Linda experienced single motherhood off and on when the two separated periodically during the 1960s.[13]

In 1971, during a period of reconciliation in which the family again lived in public housing, Linda gave birth to Susan. When Susan was almost four years old, Linda left Harry, whose alcohol addiction and depression had reached intolerable levels. Harry terrorized his ex-wife, coming in and out of her apartment at will, following her to and from work, and phoning her to threaten suicide. After one such incident, Harry shot himself. His death devastated six-year-old Susan. Less than a year later, Linda began dating Beverly Russell, the owner of a local appliance store and nephew of a former governor. After their marriage, Linda and her children moved into Russell's house in Mount Vernon Estates, a neighborhood David Smith called an "uppity subdivision" on the edge of Union. Linda worked for "Bev," as he was known about town, at his appliance store and cared for the family while he pursued his local political ambitions.[14]

Young Susan's life changed dramatically when her mother "married up," as the papers put it in the coverage of her case decades later. An avid churchgoer and staunch family-values Republican, Bev Russell could not have been more different from the hard-drinking, often unemployed Harry, and the rolling green lawns of Mt. Vernon Estates were a far cry from Union's cramped public housing. During high school, Susan worked part-time at the local grocery store, but the family viewed it as a temporary, after-school job, not as a career move. They were solidly middle-class, and Susan Smith set her sights on higher education. She and her brother Scotty were the first of their family to have the luxury of considering college.

It was at this point that Smith's experience diverged again from a typical middle-class story. During her senior year of high school, Smith expressed a strong interest in attending Winthrop University in neighboring York County. Her mother, however, did not feel that she was "ready to leave home," and she convinced Smith to attend the Union branch of the University of South Carolina for one year. She complied with her mother's wishes, but at the end of that school year, she quit to work full-time so she could buy a car, the burgundy Mazda that would, a few years later, become quite famous. Her reasons for this decision are unclear; she had performed well in high school, graduating with a B average, and she was doing well in her college courses at USC-Union, so it was not because she could not handle the pressures of college. Her plan was to work for a year, pay off the car, and save money for college. Her parents paid for her coursework at USC-Union, but it is probable that they refused to pay for college elsewhere, and they were not supportive of her decision to work instead of taking classes for a year. One can only speculate that Smith saw her new car and her new savings as a possible way out of Union.[15]

Of course, things did not work out that way. The year that Smith quit school, she worked the third shift at a textile mill and part-time at the Winn-Dixie, where she met and began to date David Smith. Her parents did not approve of her choice. David explained that he was not "exactly Linda's dream for her daughter"; the Russells would have preferred "somebody with a college education, making $40,000 or $60,000 a year."[16]

Susan Smith's plans to return to any college dissolved in the winter of 1991 when she discovered she was pregnant. She and David married, and their relationship was tumultuous from the start. They lived with David's grandmother until Beverly Russell loaned them the money to buy the small brick house on Toney Road, a modest neighborhood of tract housing just outside Union. Most of their neighbors worked in the local mills at Conso, just a few miles down the highway, or in Buffalo, an even smaller mill town that bordered Union. David Smith later wrote that the little house was never really "home" for Susan, who spent a lot of time at her stepfather's expansive ranch house across town. In retrospect, as he tried to make sense of the murders, David Smith saw socioeconomics as one of the biggest conflicts in their marriage. "No matter how much work and love I put into our home, it would still be a tin-roofed country shack," he wrote. "Susan thought she saw the life she'd lead there: she would be out in the yard barefoot, a kid on her hip, picking collards for dinner. *Uh-uh*, Susan thought. *Not me*."[17]

After the birth of their second child, Susan went to work at the Conso plant as a secretary, a major step up from the knitting-room floor of another local mill where she had worked just after quitting college. There, she met Tom Findlay, Conso's heir apparent who lived in the sprawling mansion outside of town.[18] To get to the Findlay estate from her home on Toney Road (a row of small houses outside of town that was anything buy tony), Susan Smith had to drive through the poor neighborhoods that dotted the highway outside of Union, past the Conso plant that was the source of Findlay's wealth, through a few miles of thick woods, and into the massive stone and iron gates that separated the "castle" from the rest of Union. The distance was only a few miles, but the drive was a veritable tour of the various levels of the social hierarchy of Union.

These, then, were Susan Smith's various experiences of class by the fateful night at the lake. A middling-class mother who killed her children did not fit the "poor girl/rich man" narrative; for the "boyfriend motive" to work, Smith's precarious financial status had to stand in stark relief against her boyfriend's enviable wealth. Middle-class mothers made headlines as either ideals or victims only. But poor, single mothers, particularly those who depended on public assistance, were sensational front-page material. In the context of the new sexist 1990s, this was the stuff of political cautionary tales.

This class-based narrative revision of Susan Smith's motive to murder would have made less sense in previous historical eras. American society and politicians had not always viewed poor women as public enemies or as leaches on the system. During the first few decades of the twentieth century, lawmakers conceived of welfare and social services as aid to women and mothers whose poverty resulted from widowhood or abandonment (i.e., the loss of the traditional masculine breadwinner in a normative nuclear family). These aid recipients were seen as necessary caregivers, and the state stepped in as paternal authority when a husband/father could not. In the conversations about the inclusion of Aid to Dependent Children (ADC, the precursor to AFDC, Aid to Families with Dependent Children) in the Social Security Act of 1935, poverty-stricken mothers were conceptualized as helpless victims. Historian Linda Gordon explains that the debates over public assistance rested upon the gendered assumption "that women did not normally face the economy as individuals, as workers." Thus, legislators "saw no problem in grounding women's social rights in their dependent position."[19] Widowed and abandoned mothers, perhaps more than any other group, constituted the "deserving poor."

For over two decades, ADC was an uncontroversial public assistance program, and it functioned relatively unhindered by public opinion or political opposition. By the late 1950s, however, the program began to be seen as problematic. The origin of the rhetorical attacks on poor mothers appears to be in 1962, when policy reform ushered in the newly conceptualized AFDC. The accompanying new language of welfare—a precursor to both the new racism and the new sexism—was born in the midst of two cataclysmic social changes. First, unprecedented numbers of women flooded the paid workforce. Women working outside the home changed the roles of recipients and the state in the welfare system. Gone were the "worthy widows" of decades past; in their place were women who had apparently willingly discarded their proper domestic roles. These new poor mothers were encouraged, though not coerced, by the state to "earn" their aid.[20]

The second major change had to do with race. The growing welfare controversy coincided with the emerging civil rights movement, and race increasingly played a role in policy debates over and public opinions of social programs. The breakdown of segregation meant that African Americans gained new access to rights, opportunities, and assistance. Prior to the 1960s, state and federal public aid had openly discriminated against African American mothers. The movement exposed America's dirty secrets about poverty and racism, and it also inspired many African Americans to demand their due assistance from the state. In the 1960s, the racial make-up of the welfare rolls began to change.[21] These changes combined with the new gender composition of the workforce to create a completely transformed image of welfare recipients.

The social upheaval caused by the destruction of the old racist system engendered a reactionary association of race and class with disorder, crime, urban riots, and general civil disobedience. The rhetorical association between race, class, and crime would become increasingly clear in the new racist calls for "law and order" in decades to come, and it was already evident in the early 1960s in the welfare debates. Poverty was a function of more than just economic problems, argued President John F. Kennedy in his congressional address introducing the reforms. "Relief checks," he explained, were "not likely to provide a lasting solution" to "complicated social or personal problems." Instead of "relief," lawmakers began to speak of "rehabilitation."[22] Poverty was increasingly associated with dysfunction, and the political language surrounding the debates over public assistance and welfare programs became increasingly gendered.

By the Nixon era, a new term had entered the policy lexicon: "workfare." While "welfare" positively connoted "well-being," "workfare" was more ominous. Instead of victims of circumstantial poverty, mothers on welfare had come to be seen as lethargic dependents who needed the strong hand of the government to push them to work to support their families. As poverty-stricken African Americans sought their due from the system, this negative image became increasingly racialized. In the 1970s, the primary promulgator was Ronald Reagan, then governor of California, who carefully constructed an image of mothers on public assistance loaded with language meant to ignite righteous anger in the hearts of taxpayers. "Lazy parasites," he called them, and "pigs at the trough." By the time of his failed 1976 presidential bid, Reagan had developed a full narrative of the so-called "welfare queen" whose aliases and numerous children allowed her to bilk the state of Illinois to the tune of $150,000 (this was later debunked by journalists; the woman in question had four aliases and had collected about $8,000). Reagan carefully spoke in the coded language of the new racism and the new sexism. In fact, he was the primary midwife of the code; it was Reagan who definitively feminized the image by "changing the pronouns." The "welfare queen" hinged on a subtext of sexual deviance. She eschewed monogamy, and she bred children for the sole purpose of receiving state money. As feminist scholar Patricia Hill Collins pointed out, the image was inherently one of a woman with "low morals and uncontrolled sexuality."[23]

In political debates and public opinion, lines were being drawn between the "deserving poor" and Reagan's freeloading deviants who worked the system to support their indolent, criminal lifestyles. By the mid-1990s, research showed that this rhetorical division was not just the province of political parties. "Welfare" as a dirty word had gone mainstream. The public clearly understood the differences: 41 percent of respondents to a 1995 poll expressed negative views of "people on welfare," and 85 percent thought these people were "too dependent on government assistance." By contrast, a negligible 4 percent expressed negative views of "poor people" when references to state aid, assistance, or welfare were removed from the questions.[24]

This imagined divergence was clearly gendered. Robert Asen argues that the image of welfare mothers as slackers working the system featured a "de-privileging of mothers' roles as nurturers."[25] More specifically, the image "deprivileged" *some* mothers' domestic and family roles, namely poor mothers, while it simultaneously elevated middle-class mothers' roles to iconic status. Clearly a New Right reaction to second-wave feminism and the civil rights movement, the image of the "undeserving poor"—that is, single mothers and their ill-behaved children—had the effect of legislating a socioeconomic divide between the acceptable kind of mother/family and the unacceptable, parasitic, dysfunctional kind. By the time the image achieved headline status in the 1980s, it was coupled with its opposite: the telegenic, stay-at-home wife who had chosen the "new momism." There were mothers who should work, and mothers who should not—this divide depended on their marital and class status.

This brand of classist, sexist, and racist mother-blaming did not just represent the general anti-feminism of the GOP. No longer singularly affiliated with the reactionary neoconservatism of Ronald Reagan, this rhetoric had achieved the status of cultural common sense by the 1990s. Politicians of all persuasions preached it unapologetically. Bill Clinton—a Democrat with some feminist credentials—relied upon the available images of welfare in his 1991 campaign for president. Clinton famously remarked that welfare reform was like "God, motherhood, and apple pie; everybody's for it."[26]

It is not difficult to trace a rapid rightward shift in Clinton's welfare rhetoric during his bid for president. His original plan, laid out in his 1992 campaign book, *Putting People First,* promised pro-family—and pro–working mother—provisions such as increased child care options, child support, and health care for the working poor. But on the campaign trail, Clinton took a cue from the New Right playbook when he promised to "end welfare as know it." His later support for feminist goals like expanded healthcare for women and affirmative action notwithstanding, Clinton in essence agreed with his

Republican opponent Dan Quayle on the issue of welfare reform. During his administration, the twin evils of "single motherhood" and "absent fatherhood"—effectively, a sanitized expansion of the hated category of "welfare queens"—became daily talking points in political circles and the media.[27]

Psychologist Diane Eyer argues "behind all the venom currently directed at 'welfare mothers' is an agenda that posits all renegade mothers as the cause of our social problems."[28] Indeed, politicians found ways to blame poor and working mothers for all sorts of crimes. In the early 1990s, it seems, the fatherless, neglected children produced by poverty-stricken women were allegedly destroying the nation's major cities. In the summer of 1992, as Susan Smith tried to reconcile with her husband in preparation for her second child, Vice-President Dan Quayle blamed single mothers for the urban violence that followed the Rodney King verdict. The "lawless social anarchy" that characterized the riots was, according to Quayle, "directly related to the breakdown of family structure, personal responsibility and social order in too many areas of our society." The absence of fathers and the "illegitimacy rate" in many poor families underscored how "quickly civilization [could fall] apart." Bluntly, Quayle proclaimed that single mothers produced criminals: "Nature abhors a vacuum. Where there are no mature, responsible men around to teach boys how to be good men, gangs serve in their place. In fact, gangs have become a surrogate family for much of a generation of inner-city boys. . . . marriage is a moral issue that requires cultural consensus, and the use of social sanctions. Bearing babies irresponsibly is, simply, wrong."[29] The message was clear: poor, sexually active women bred like rabbits and neglected their children, who then grew up to become the violent men who were destroying the nation's urban centers.

Although many journalists criticized Quayle for over-reaching in his comments, the images of single motherhood that he promoted in his speech would come to characterize the domestic economic policies of the next few years. No longer the province of neoconservatives, Republicans and Democrats alike espoused this kind of gender conservatism. The roots of economic insolvency, crime, or any kind of general disorder, could be traced back to the epidemic of single motherhood. In *The Bell Curve,* published the year of the Smith murders, Charles Murray focused on "illegitimacy," or childbearing by single mothers, as the primary cause of the "selective deterioration of the traditional family" and a secondary cause of crime, poverty, and other social problems. A direct reflection of the neoconservative politics of race and gender, this racist, classist, eight-hundred-page tome was a best seller.[30]

Even as Smith's class status fell precipitously in public representations, few reporters actually deemed her a "welfare queen." Indeed, they did not have to. As seen in Quayle's oft-quoted diatribe and in the demonization of single motherhood, negative images of poor women had expanded beyond images of welfare by the 1990s. There was plenty of neoconservative rage directed at those poor mothers who used the aid provided by the social services system, to be sure. But the list of "bad mothers" had grown to include all single mothers, even the wealthy "Murphy Brown"; motherhood within marriage was seen as more acceptable than single motherhood, regardless of class status. Over the course of the 1990s, even in the policy debates over welfare, single mothers, rather than poor mothers, became the maternal demons of the decade.

Some public figures flipped the lens and spoke of "absent fathers," rather than "single mothers," as the root of the problem. President Clinton increasingly focused on these shadowy figures during his second term. "The single biggest social problem in our society may be the growing absence of fathers from their children's homes because it contributes to so many other social problems," he proclaimed at the Million Man March in the mid-1990s.[31] Positing that a strong father figure would solve everything from poverty to teen pregnancy to crime rates was another way of saying that single mothers, alone, produced criminals—without a husband, they could never be good enough mothers, much less Good Mothers. And when it came to welfare policy reform, which Clinton signed into law in the middle of his first term, mothers—not "deadbeat dads," not the wage gap that kept women poorer than men, and certainly not the cultural prescription that mothers should be the primary caretakers of children—were the clear target. Clinton was not an opportunist, as some have suggested, nor was he a liberal when it came to welfare reform. Rather, he was a direct reflection of the new sexist ideology. Although it began as a reactionary, New Right response to the identity movements of the 1960s, by the 1990s, the new sexism permeated the sociopolitical landscape to such a degree that liberals and neoconservatives often sounded interchangeable.[32]

Given the ascendance of "welfare queens'" to superstardom in the 1980s and the corresponding hand-wringing over single motherhood in the 1990s, it should not be surprising that Susan Smith, the "monster mom," caught the attention of proponents of mother-blamers on the 1994 campaign trail. Newt Gingrich, the U.S. representative of a conservative suburban Atlanta district, explicitly incorporated Susan Smith into the official New Right politics of sex, motherhood, and economics the week after her confession. Gingrich became the Speaker of the House the week after Smith's confession during the "revo-lutionary" Republican takeover of Congress, and at least one of his campaign speeches featured an explicit attack on Susan Smith.

The GOP needed to win forty seats to rule Congress, and the South was a "major battleground" in the election. The weekend after Susan Smith's Thursday confession, politicians stumped furiously across the region. At a party in Buckhead, a wealthy section of Atlanta, on the day before the elec-tions (three days after Smith's arrest), Gingrich made what he characterized as some "offhand" comments. Susan Smith, he argued, was an example of "what's wrong with America." He explained: "How a mother could kill her two children, 14 months and 3 years, in hopes that her boyfriend would like her, is just a sign of how sick the system is." He continued: "I can capture everything [Republicans] are trying to do in a sense by referring to this weekend's unbe-lievable tragedy in South Carolina, to getting at the root causes of the decay in our society." In other words, according to Gingrich, Democrats were respon-sible for creating the environment that allowed social "decay" in the form of Susan Smith. In case that message was unclear, Gingrich concluded: "I think people want change, and the only way to get change is to vote Republican."[33]

In a rather hostile interview with Tom Brokaw the following evening, Gingrich stood his ground. He dodged Brokaw's observation that the Smith family of South Carolina were people who "embraced his philosophy" of so-cial conservatism and "family values." Union County in general, and Susan Smith's family in particular, embodied the Republican family ideal in the 1990s. Ignoring these inconvenient details, Gingrich extended Susan Smith's symbolic significance even further: "I do believe there is a direct connection between the general acceptance of violence, the general acceptance of bru-tality, the general decline of civility in this society, and the patterns of the counterculture when Lyndon Johnson's Great Society began in the late '60s."[34]

Leaving aside the fact that the conservative, small-town, church-going Smith family could probably not be any *less* "countercultural," the connec-tions Gingrich made between the Great Society of the 1960s, the Republican political philosophy of the 1990s, and the popular negative images of Susan Smith are significant. In late September, just a few weeks before Susan Smith's sons "went missing," over three hundred Republican candidates for the U.S. House of Representations stood on the steps of the Capitol in front of dozens of television cameras, waving flags to the marching tunes played by a retired military band. The fanfare was the backdrop to a major political announcement that echoed the Reagan-era past and predicted the Gingrich-era future of the GOP. This announcement, deemed the "Contract with America," was both campaign promise and party platform. Reaganesque, broad in scope, and skimpy on the strategic details, the "Contract" listed ten points of new policy featuring tax cuts, a stronger military, and a balanced federal budget.[35]

Although the *New York Times* reported that Republicans focused solely on fiscal policy in their media-saturated announcement, the "Contract" also contained plans for social policy. The platform indicated that the primary social problems of the day could be fixed through changes in economic policies. The end result would be a legislated return to traditional "family values." As Newt Gingrich and Dick Armey promised in the published version of the "Contract," the election would usher in a "Congress that respects the values and shares the faith of the American family."[36] The "Contract," with Newt Gingrich at the helm, promised to legislate the mother-blaming logic of the Reagan era, and it did so through the language of the "new sexism."

Republican politicians focused a large part of the "Contract" on rehabilitating poor, single mothers, the reputed root of the systemic corruption. One of the ten points of the "Contract with America" was the "Personal Responsibility Act," a sweeping welfare reform measure designed to combat the "skyrocketing out-of-wedlock births that are ripping apart the nation's social fabric." In addition to an overall decrease in spending on welfare programs, this act "discouraged illegitimacy" by denying the extension of aid to teen mothers and to women who had additional children while on welfare. The Republican authors of the act targeted female culprits when they cited the history of welfare: "Established in 1935 under the Social Security Act, AFDC was created to help widows care for their children. It now serves divorced, deserted, and never-married individuals and their children."[37] In other words, "widows" needed help because they lacked a male breadwinner through no fault of their own; all of those other mothers did not deserve aid because they voluntarily violated the bounds of the traditional family structure.

The "Contract with America" made clear the fact that single mothers, rather than poor mothers in general, were the root of the perceived problem. According to the logic of the reforms, welfare mothers were "renegade" not necessarily because they sought public assistance, but because they were *single* on welfare. The 1996 Personal Responsibility and Work Opportunity Reconciliation Act (PRWORA)—the legislation promised in the "Contract"—rewarded married mothers on welfare while punishing women without husbands. A majority of the provisions of the reforms specifically targeted poor women's sexuality, and especially their reproductive rights. The new welfare system, Temporary Assistance to Needy Families (TANF), required paternity establishment, child support enforcement, and at least thirty hours of work outside the home per week of unmarried mothers on welfare. Married mothers, on the other hand, did not have to meet any of these requirements to qualify for assistance. Some states provided cash incentives to TANF mothers who married; others established "family caps" that prohibited unmarried women who had more children while on welfare from receiving more state assistance. The federal TANF program offered "illegitimacy bonuses" to some states that reduced the number of births out of wedlock, denied assistance to unmarried teen mothers, and, apparently in compensation, funded abstinence-only sexual education programs.[38] Controlling poor women's sexuality and reproductive capabilities was thus the solution to the socioeconomic problems described by Dan Quayle in his famous diatribe against mothers in South Central Los Angeles (and Murphy Brown) just a few years earlier. The concept of the "deserving poor" remained, only now, to be "deserving" as a mother, one had to be married.

Thus, the welfare queen had morphed into the single mother as the neoconservative bogeywoman by the mid-1990s. Susan Smith was a perfect target, regardless of the real motive for her crime, because of her working-class, single status and alleged sexual misbehaviors. Linking her to socioeconomic policy only served the New Right campaign to legislate mother-blaming. Gingrich did not need to spell out these connections in his incendiary campaign speeches. "Personal responsibility" was the remedy for immorality. According to historian Glenn Feldman, Gingrich "perfected the art of the 'new racism,'" and, in his comments about Susan Smith, he raised the coded vocabulary of the new sexism to headline status.[39] By referencing a boyfriend, "counterculture," and the welfare state (in the form of Johnson's Great Society) in an interview about the Smith case, Gingrich compared Susan Smith to the infamous "welfare queens," implying that she was an oversexed, lower-class single mother whose abuse of the welfare system was outweighed only by her violent crimes, which were, according to Newt's historical model, products of the same corrupt democratic system. And if she was one of them, why would Americans support this flawed system by voting Democratic in the upcoming elections?

Never mind, apparently, that Susan Smith had never been on welfare, or that she had been raised in a socially and politically conservative, middle-class household; neoconservatives used the working-class image of Susan Smith to their advantage. Although journalists initially ridiculed Gingrich's linking of Smith with politics, he did win the election two days after his comments, and newspaper editors published thousands of letters from supportive constituents. One reader argued: "How different is killing innocent babies through abortion than what Susan Smith did? . . . Gingrich was right about the Union case." It was a classic neoconservative conclusion: the root cause—of Smith's crime, of abortion, and of the corruption of the welfare system—was, according to neoconservative rhetoric, unrestrained, pathological maternal desires. Another reader defended Gingrich, explaining the direct link between welfare and crime: "It is this Great Society that has produced teenagers who throw Molotov cocktails through windows in Atlanta and 11-year-old children who drop a 5-year-old child from a 14th-story window in Chicago."[40]

Gingrich's message thus became a running mantra in conservative editorials over the next few weeks. One writer targeted the welfare system, comparing Susan Smith to parents who "brought children into the world, were intrigued with them for a few weeks or months, then ignored or abused them and wished them away," and so turned to the all-too-generous social services system to absolve themselves of responsibility. The few people who voiced alternative opinions—opinions that targeted the lack of government programs that might help mothers under emotional and/or financial stress—were generally met with ridicule. In an editorial sarcastically entitled "Susan Smith: For Want of a Government Program," columnist Richard Grenier explicitly attacked experts that had tried to put Smith's crimes in perspective. His primary target was the spokeswoman for the National Center to Prevent Child Abuse who suggested that, as a stressed-out, broke, young, single mother of two, Susan Smith could have benefited from some socioeconomic and cultural support, which may have even prevented the murders. Grenier's derision is almost audible in his thinly veiled swipe at feminism. His solution is a federal program to counsel mothers and a "National Fund for Counseling the Lovelorn." He suggested that First Lady Hillary Clinton could head a "new task force" for the "National Fund for Enraged Mothers," although "with Republicans now controlling both houses of Congress, funding might be a problem."[41] Grenier, like many journalists, followed Gingrich's lead in explicitly using the popular negative image of Susan Smith based on class and sexuality to identify mothers as a fundamental social problem.

Underlying all of this scapegoating is the fundamental cultural assumption, evident since at least the advent of "republican motherhood" following the American Revolution, that there is a direct connection between proper maternal behavior and the future of the nation.[42] In the 1990s, this assumption translated into the popular images and policies that blamed poor mothers for continued poverty, crime, and the oft-bemoaned disintegration of "family values." This demonization characterized the "new momism" and the mother-blaming that was fundamental to the popular culture and politics of the twentieth century, from tabloid infanticide trials to fictional characters to federal policies. Deviant mothers—loosely defined as poor, minority, single, or otherwise outside of the narrow ideal—were just as necessary a part of the "mommy myth" as their allegedly perfect white, middle-class, married sisters.

By positioning Susan Smith as one of these anti-mothers, the media, politicians, and much of the American public made her a representative of nationwide social conflicts, specifically gendered problems that legislators promised to fix after the 1994 election. This sex- and class-based image of Smith that defined the "boyfriend motive" had a long history, and she was the perfect scapegoat in the 1990s as neoconservatism went mainstream, shifting the entire spectrum of American politics perceptibly to the right. In the days and weeks following Susan Smith's confession, her story was about sex and class, because this image rendered her understandable according to the new sexist ideology of neoconservatism. In a way, the "boyfriend motive" brought Smith back into the fold; it transformed her overnight from an "incomprehensible monster" to a recognizable representative of feminine evil, a familiar she-devil among the ranks of the various mothers targeted by the gender politics of the day.

This is the image of Susan Smith that most Americans seem to remember best, perhaps because it quickly achieved complete media saturation in the weeks following her confession. This "Susan," however, faded over the months following her confession. Perhaps audiences just tired of the story, or perhaps it was because this "Susan" was based more on speculation and familiar femme fatale images than on actual details. At any rate, another "Susan" replaced her, one that would script Smith's defense at her trial. This new "Susan" deviated from the dominant narrative of evil motherhood, indicating an alternative family-values reading of the case.

5

UNION'S FAMILY VALUES

AS SUSAN SMITH'S image transformed rapidly in the media, the one trait that loosely tied each new "Susan" together was dishonesty: she lied about the carjacking, her maternal instincts, her marriage, her affairs, her class status. As murky details about her troubled past surfaced, another alleged untruth began to make headlines. Journalists delighted in accusing Union, Smith's hometown, of faking a hypocritically wholesome, small-town image. "Union was supposed to resemble Newt Gingrich's America, a place of family values and Christian fellowship," wrote Charles Sennott in the 1995 New Year's Day edition of the *Boston Globe*. The media trafficked heavily in this *Peyton Place*–like, gilded narrative of a close-knit village riddled with dark and dirty secrets.[1] Union was a made-for-television Sunday night thriller, more "America's Most Wanted" than classic small-town America.

But there was a problem with this image of Union. Like Smith herself, Union was more complicated than the easy "Madonna/whore" dichotomy. Union was both a Norman Rockwell–esque small town and a community that had had its share of personal troubles. As such, it was "Newt Gingrich's America," and it did represent the family values touted by neoconservatives. Unionites had their own corresponding analysis of their most famous resident. The town's patriarchal, regionally flavored image of Susan Smith rested upon a traditional vision of proper paternal authority, and local reactions to the case represented a community attempt at recapturing that authority—a goal that replicated the traditionalist gender politics of neoconservatism. Over the course of the winter and spring of 1995, as the small town prepared for the media onslaught of the upcoming trial, Unionites constructed and publicized their redemptive version of Smith as a helpless daughter, the fifth of the "seven Susans."

This local image of Susan Smith directly contradicted the lurid, sex- and class-based "Susan" making national headlines. Accordingly, a bifurcated "Union" joined Susan Smith in the headlines as part of the mask motif. In the weeks and months following Smith's confession, as reporters combed the small town for clues to Smith's past, a new narrative emerged: there were two Unions to match the two Susans. One "Union" was the idyllic small town duped by the evil woman—Eden to Smith's seductive Eve. Journalists seized on the southern kitsch of Union, one of "those communities that is as much family as it is town," where "people are tied together by marriage, church and Friday night football games." One reporter argued: "People live in Union County to get away from stories like this. On Sunday evenings, the streets are nearly deserted because almost everyone is in church. Crime usually means a missing stereo, and deputies know the handful of people in the county jail by their first names and the first names of their mamas and daddies." Crimes like the Smith murders just "don't happen in Union," the "200-year-old mill town with a huge sign on Main Street welcoming visitors to THE CITY OF HOSPITALITY." *Time* magazine reported that crime was rare in the tiny town where people welcomed strangers and never locked their doors. "It's a boringly God-fearing, law-abiding place," one local told the reporters. "The worst thing that happens here is like the song: Bubba shot the jukebox 'cause he didn't like the song."[2]

The other "Union" was a *Peyton Place*–like small town that teemed with poorly disguised dysfunction. Like a "pentimento on a Norman Rockwell canvas," Union's veneer hardly disguised its dirty secrets: "The Winn Dixie hides guilty lovers; the fine Christian home harbors a child molester."[3] In these depictions, Susan Smith and Union were parallels: like the offending woman, Union wore a mask of decency that hid a community rife with racial, sexual, and class conflict.

But it was *Peyton Place* with a distinctly southern twist. Reporters argued that southern politesse shielded Susan Smith from immediate detection: "The conventions of small-town life in the South place a premium on niceness, which turns out to be not very useful in predicting whether a person is capable of murder." On the contrary, small-town southern gentility, hospitality, and religiosity were facades behind which lurked Gothic violence, depravity, and lust. On the eve of the trial, *Newsweek* featured the glaring headline "Southern Gothic on Trial." The article listed the tawdry, tabloid details of the case. "Party to enough infidelities and suicides to make Faulkner—and Geraldo—proud, she's a Southern Gothic come to life," wrote the reporters.[4]

Regional stereotypes thus came to play a major role in the coverage of the Susan Smith case. Of all of the available cultural scripts, the easiest to apply to the Smith drama was the Southern Gothic trope. This quality can be tricky to define, but, as veteran southern observer Hal Crowther wrote in the *Oxford American* nearly two years after Susan Smith killed her children, Americans "know Gothic when we see it." Crowther's piece was just one in an entire issue of the magazine devoted to the question, "Is the South Still Gothic?" Historical examples include such proof of southern "benightedness" as slavery, lynchings, the Scopes "monkey" trial of 1925, and the more recent murder of basketball star Michael Jordan's father as he napped in his car just seventy-odd miles from the New South metropolis of Charlotte, North Carolina.[5]

But Southern Gothic is not characterized wholly by a preoccupation with race. Class and gender have been major themes in Gothic literature since at least the early works of William Faulkner, the so-called father of the genre. Hal Crowther points out that Faulkner and Flannery O'Connor "took the show out of town and away from the big house," focusing on working-class whites rather than the stereotypical southern gentry of the *Gone With the Wind* variety. Writers like Rick Bragg, Dorothy Allison, and Larry Brown continued this tradition, derided as "Redneck" or "Welfare Gothic" by some critics, into the late twentieth and early twenty-first centuries. Class is a running subtext in their works, and according to historian James Cobb, they "do not flinch in their portrayals of the homicidal violence, physical, sexual, and emotional abuse, and other wounds that their characters inflict on each other." Crowther quotes Larry Brown's "A Roadside Resurrection": "The world is a strange place and in it lie things of another nature, a bent order, and beyond a certain point there are no rules to make men mind." This, Crowther declares, must surely be the "Gothic Declaration of Independence."[6]

Some journalists assigned to the Smith case presented her "mask" as a specifically southern phenomenon—a facade that hid her dark, Gothic tendencies. Smith's reported "niceness" apparently fooled everyone, and the conventions of the small-town South kept neighbors from acknowledging, much less intervening in, the family's troubles. The idea that violent criminals wear masks that prevent "normal" citizens from predicting their deviant behavior is a popular one, as is the image of small towns (or, in the second half of the twentieth century, the suburbs) that seem quaint but are actually riven with scandal. News reports, films, novels, true-crime books, and even entire television series have been organized around this compelling image of the mask (see, for instance, the popular television series *Desperate Housewives* or virtually all of writer Ann Rule's library). But the image of the mask also applies to the South specifically. The idea that the deceptive pastoral setting is, in reality, peopled with monsters has been a staple of mainstream media coverage of the region. According to literary scholar Patricia Yaeger, its role is that of a scapegoat as well as an entertainer: "The South enacts horror; the North consumes it."[7]

Although many authors have tried to combat the Gothic stereotyping of the South, the identity remains, especially in national depictions of the region. On the one hand, there are the enduring film images featuring "big houses, brunswick stew, and banjo pickers" (or, in the case of *Steel Magnolias*, big hair, armadillo cakes, and zydeco). On the other, there is the barbaric South of *Cape Fear* and *Mississippi Burning* in which class and racial tensions result in violence and social chaos. The Gothic South generally eclipses the "moonlight and magnolias" South in the media and the popular imagination. And this does not just apply to cultural texts or regional history. As James Cobb points out in his recent study of southern identity, racial violence across the nation consistently conjures images of the South. In 1986, for example, New York mayor Ed Koch argued that the fatal beating of a man in Howard Beach was the kind of thing that happened only in the "Deep South." Scholars agree that, although the South may not be a distinctive region, images of its distinctiveness often serve a scapegoating function, more often than not based on ideas about race, class, and gender. In the mid-1990s, Florence King wrote in the *Oxford American:* "I can only conclude that the question of whether the South is still Gothic is beside the point. There are enough people who want it to be to turn self-fulfilling prophecies into a land-office business."[8]

When journalists depicted the Smith case as a stereotypically southern story, they were subtly, if not deliberately, arguing for southern distinctiveness—and not the down-home, good-time, *Hee Haw* kind.[9] And they were using stock characters. In fact, women, particularly working-class women, have always played integral roles in these kinds of Southern Gothic narratives. The central Gothic character in southern tales is never a middle-class white woman; hence, the need to reconfigure Susan Smith as working class. Because of her class and race, and the gruesome facts of her lie and her violent crime, Susan Smith could actually have served as a challenge to regional stereotypes; her very identity could have exploded the myth of the southern lady. Recall that the mythical southern lady was the imagined base of the entire southern socio-racial order. If her purity is only a mask, the foundations crumble.

Southern authors of the twentieth century—William Faulkner, Flannery O'Connor, Carson McCullers, Dorothy Allison, Larry Brown, Mary Karr, and others—have worked very hard to challenge this myth. In Mississippi author Ellen Douglas's *Can't Quit You, Baby*, the anonymous narrator tells the "apocryphal tale" of the white, aristocratic female body in the form of a beautiful young water-skier who is literally destroyed when she loses her balance and lands in a "writhing, tangled mass of water moccasins." The privileged lady ideal is devoured by snakes, rendering her both a relic and a Medusa-like, perhaps even predatory figure—the exact opposite of what well-to-do white women are "supposed to be" in the modern South. According to Patricia Yaeger, these authors' modern fictional female characters attack the socially constructed regional identity at its gendered core: "[They] work toward a massive category confusion in which the common classifications of Southern life no longer make sense, in which the condensation and displacement of political contradictions onto the white female body no longer take place in secret but, instead, get held up for scrutiny."[10]

Susan Smith posed the same threat to the southern order. But the trope of the mask defused this threat. Smith was not proof that the "ladies" of the South were not so ladylike after all; rather, she had never been a lady, and the misdeeds of her past proved it. The media coverage of the Susan Smith case as a classic Southern Gothic tale thus relied heavily upon the "mask" trope to describe the disconnect between the mother and the murderer. Journalist Andrea Peyser organized *Mother Love, Deadly Love,* one of the first books published about Susan Smith (it hit stands months before Smith even went to trial), entirely around the Southern Gothic stereotype. The book begins with the mask motif: readers meet Smith as she pulled out of the driveway that fateful night with her sons strapped safely in the backseat of her Mazda. The "mother's capable hands" and "smiling face" disappears on the second page as Smith contemplates the task at hand. According to Peyser, evil lived undetected in Union for twenty-three years, disguised as "a well-adjusted neighbor, loving wife and daughter, and nurturing mother."[11]

In Peyser's account, Union wore its own version of Smith's "glued-on expression." On the surface, it seemed like a classic small southern town, its streets lined with "brick cottages that have housed generations of textile workers," its "front porches filled to capacity, awash with iced tea and talk." Neighbors chatted in the parking lot of the "shiny, new supermarket," the "one concession to progress" in this "modern-day Mayberry." Union, in this account, was voluntarily backwards; residents embraced their existence outside the inexorable march of progress. They "liked it that way," wrote Peyser, because the town's "secrets are safe." For, in this town that "could be used to illustrate an encyclopedia listing for 'family values' . . . even the tidiest shutters and friendliest smiles can disguise trouble." Susan's "double life" mirrored the elaborate mask worn by her entire hometown. One local allegedly joked that Union should change its nickname from "City of Hospitality" to "City of Adultery."[12]

Passages like these offered readers two Souths: the pastoral and the grotesque. The sweet and simple exterior brought to mind the fairy tales of *Steel Magnolias* and *Forrest Gump*. But in the mainstream media, the grotesque, Gothic South, with its seedy underbelly of poverty, sex, and violence, seethed within the crumbling Union mansions and the mill houses encircling them— images that recalled the violent "rednecks" of films like *Deliverance* and *Cape Fear*. In a chapter called "Placid Surfaces," Peyser described John D. Long Lake, where Susan Smith drowned her sons. By day, she wrote, its "tranquil," smooth surface reflected pine trees and sunshine, but its deceptive calmness hid cold water and voracious catfish: "John D. Long Lake is the perfect mirror. Like Union, it takes care to conceal what lurks within." Peyser tapped into the narrative tradition of a Gothic South that featured jarring dichotomies: Union's grove of alleged "lynching trees" bloomed brightly every spring, trailers and tract housing lined the road leading to the Findlay "castle," a white mother from a good family murdered her two young sons in cold blood.[13]

This regional twist belied the fact that this story could have happened anywhere; after all, *Peyton Place* was set in New England, and novelist Richard Price later rewrote a convincing fictionalized version of the Susan Smith case in an urban, northeastern setting. The South has never had a monopoly on the grotesque in American culture, even though popular regional literary output at the end of the twentieth century still tended toward the poor, the dysfunctional, and the downright violent. Although the Susan Smith drama was not distinctly regional, journalists made sure that it had all the necessary "Welfare Gothic" ingredients: sex, violence, poverty, wealth, family dysfunction, community secrets. Unionites vociferously disagreed with this characterization; one sent a letter to Andrea Peyser's publisher expressing his disapproval. Accusing her of doing "little research" and "not even staying in Union," the unhappy local concluded that she was "critical," "judgmental," and had "little knowledge of the small town."[14]

In fact, Union accurately represented the region, although not in the dark, Gothic manner of the headlines. Union's official historian argues that the county is "so average as to constitute a virtual 'microcosm of the macrocosm'—embodying in its history the complex currents which make up the great stream of Southern history." Although the tiny town preexisted its textile industry by over a century, the mills, which began construction in the early 1890s, brought unprecedented prosperity to Union and changed its demographic and social make-up entirely. Between 1893 and 1900, five mills were constructed in Union County. The rapid industrialization had a snowball effect, resulting in the construction of railroads, especially between the mills, and attracting other industries such as knitting factories.[15]

By 1907, the mills in Union County consumed more than three times the cotton that local farmers could produce, and this productivity and growth reflected the population boom in Union at the turn of the twentieth century. The burgeoning textile industry was not a boon to the entire community, however; African Americans were not employed in the mills until the second half of the century. Union County's historian explains that "experiments with black labor always failed in South Carolina" (as they did in much of the Textile Belt). Thus, white privilege characterized the textile boom in Union County during the early twentieth century. White capitalists profited from the mills, and white laborers from the rural areas of the South toiled in them.[16]

Because they came from similar rural backgrounds and they lived and worked in very close proximity, textile mill workers made up something of a southern subculture, and Union County's workers were no exception. Generally speaking, until the groundbreaking *Like a Family* (1987), which was based on over two hundred interviews, mill workers were viewed as something of a "pitiable social type," to quote W. J. Cash. Their isolation in mill villages reportedly bred distinctiveness. One anthropologist argued in the 1950s that the culture of mill workers was even more "encapsulated" than those of African Americans in the Jim Crow South because the latter had more interaction with the regional white elites. According to this characterization, mill workers were the "rough element"—less educated, dirtier, more criminally inclined, promiscuous, and just generally cruder than the townspeople surrounding them—an image that comprised the epithet "linthead," which referred to the cotton lint that often stuck to workers long after their shifts were over. Mill workers, as well, knew they were different. In the words of historian Bryant Simon, "most mill people saw themselves not as farmers who temporarily lost their way, but as millhands, members of the largest occupational group of the Southern working class."[17]

As in other southern towns with a newly industrial economic base, Union "townies" reportedly snubbed the "lintheads" of the emerging "factory class." The official historian of Union County recalls that his father's family, who were "artisans and farmers, looked down on his mother's people on the 'mill hill,' the village of Union Mill, even though the mill workers had indoor plumbing and electricity while his father's people had to use outdoor wells and kerosene lamps." In Union as in much of the upstate, the townspeople saw the millhands as dirty, uneducated, and possibly dangerous.[18] Their disdain belied the fact that the local economy relied heavily on the labor of the "lintheads" within just a few years of the mills' construction.

Union's mills experienced their share of conflict during the labor upheavals of the 1930s, and by the 1940s, changes were afoot in the Textile Belt. Although many mill towns suffered the closing and relocation of their primary employers, Union continued to experience spurts of industrial growth. In the mid-1950s, Cone Mills built a textile printing and finishing plant on the Broad River in Union County near Carlisle, and in 1959, Conso Fastener—later the employer of Susan Smith—built a sixty-thousand-square-foot plant on the Union bypass. In the 1960s, Milliken also built a plant a few miles outside of Union on the pine-tree-lined highway on which Susan Smith was allegedly carjacked, and Ace Sweater constructed a knitting mill just outside of town. For several decades postwar, Union was atypical: while other areas of the former Textile Belt had wisely diversified by the 1970s, Union County's economy was still 94 percent "textile-related."[19]

This dependence on one industry was to have dire consequences for the county, and the resulting textile depression and late-century international relocation of textile-related production hit Union hard. Despite the "almost continuous industrial development" during the two decades following World War II, the older local mills employed fewer and fewer people as companies moved their productions overseas. Although the county welcomed new industries in the 1970s and 1980s, particularly pulpwood, Union was "having to run to stand still, as the ground was being cut from beneath its feet" with the long, slow deaths of the old mills. The recession of the 1970s combined with the depression in American textiles to hurt Union worse than the rest of the nation and even the rest of the state.[20]

Union had to reorient itself, and it necessarily looked outward, away from the hulking carcass of the empty downtown mill. The "Wal-Martization" of small-town America came to Union in the 1980s and proceeded unabated through the 1990s. The relocation of the majority of Union's commercial activity from downtown added to the small town's "sleepy" feel, and by the mid-1990s, the empty spaces and boarded-up windows downtown had the same aura of quiet decay as Faulkner's fictional mansions. The international corporations and huge interstates that graced other upstate counties gener- ally bypassed Union altogether. Several mills closed within a decade of each other, resulting in a loss of over two thousand jobs. In a county in which over 50 percent of the population was employable, these closings meant an un- employment rate well into the double digits. Despite the migration of the textile industry and the resulting lack of jobs, Unionites express a sense of community based on shared labor experiences even now. In interviews, some locals still referred to neighbors and co-workers as "Monarch men."[21] Even so, by century's end, only around two thousand residents, less than 7 percent of the county population, worked in the mills.[22]

A high unemployment rate in a deindustrializing small town in the early 1990s was not especially newsworthy. According to Torance Inman of the Union Chamber of Commerce, "for years, people thought a cloud was hanging over Union, but it's no different from any other manufacturing community. If you put all your marbles in one sock, and that sock gets a hole in it, you're going to suffer."[23] But in the context of the late twentieth century, this hefty unemployment rate combined with the developing New Right politics of race, gender, and the rhetoric of "fairness" to create the context for a massive re- gional political realignment.

According to scholars, the historic shift from a "solid" Democratic South to a "solid" Republican South during the second half of the twentieth century hinged on the issue of race, and politicians subsequently developed the code of the new racism. An "updated defense of gendered hierarchies" replaced the old strata of race, although subtle racist appeals undergirded the family-values politics of the new sexism.[24]

Conservative Protestantism was very much a part of this political shift "from Silent Majority to Moral Majority." Indeed, the transformation was due in no small measure to the influence of religious-political organizations like the Southern Baptist Convention, Jerry Falwell's Moral Majority, and Pat Robertson's Christian Coalition. In 1982, a group of historians described the platform of the youthful New Religious Political Right: at its base were tradi- tional ideas about gender, including "happy nuclear families" and "clear sex roles." These politics enjoyed great popularity in the South. Historian Glen Feldman explains that the region "has long been a bastion of patriarchy—

white male control over households and society resources, and white male loci of power. Sex, gender, and family relations have been principally defined in the region in the most narrow and male-dominated terms."[25]

As we have seen, the traditional social order of the South rested upon firm ideas about female weakness, male authority, and racial threats. This protection racket reared its ugly head during the violent phases of the opposition to the civil rights movement. It ensuing decades, it would be repackaged according to the language of the new racism/sexism, and it was readily evident in the New Right attack on affirmative action. In 1961, President Kennedy's Executive Order 10925 created the Equal Employment Opportunity Commission. He defined the governmental strategy of insuring equality in employment through "affirmative action," or "affirmative steps" taken by governmental agencies "to realize more fully the national policy of nondiscrimination" and to ensure that "employees are treated during employment without regard to their race, creed, color, or national origin." Lyndon Johnson extended this protection when he added "sex" to the list of identifying characteristics of employees in an executive order in 1965.[26] These measures, meant to redress past forms of discrimination, were clear offspring of the civil rights and second-wave feminist movements, and as such, they generated immediate opposition from conservatives in both parties in the 1960s.

This opposition characterized neoconservatism nationally, but it had a decidedly southern flavor. Although George Wallace may have been the original progenitor of populist white resistance in the 1960s, it was the GOP of the 1980s who truly honed the ideological opposition to affirmative action. Political strategist Lee Atwater—the right-hand man of South Carolina governor Carroll Campbell and Senator Strom Thurmond who allegedly "ran the South" for Reagan in 1980, deputy-managed the Reagan-Bush campaign in 1984, and ran the Bush-Quayle campaign in 1988—was a master architect when it came to redefining affirmative action. The key for the GOP was capturing the anger of certain voting blocs, and they did so by reconceptualizing economic issues as social ones. In his analysis of the 1984 presidential campaign, Atwater explained: "The class struggle in the South continues, with the populists serving as the trump card. . . . Populists have always been liberal on economics. . . . But populists are conservative on most social issues. . . . As for race, it was hardly an issue—it went without saying that the populists' chosen leaders were hard-core segregationists. . . . In 1982, we discovered we could not hold the populist vote on economic issues alone. When social and cultural issues died down, the populists were left with no compelling reason to vote Republican. . . . When Republicans are successful in getting certain social issues to the forefront, the populist vote is ours."[27] In a 1988 interview, Atwater expanded his explanation, offering a longer historical view that featured a crassly political exploitation of racism:

> You start out in 1954 by saying "Nigger, nigger, nigger." By 1968 you can't say "nigger"—that hurts you. Backfires. So you say stuff like forced busing, states' rights, and all that stuff. You're getting so abstract now [that] you're talking about cutting taxes, and all these things you're talking about are totally economic things and a by-product of them is [that] blacks get hurt worse than whites. And subconsciously maybe that is part of it. I'm not saying that. But I'm saying that if it is getting that abstract, and that coded, that we are doing away with the racial problem one way or the other. You follow me—because obviously sitting around saying, "we want to cut this," is much more abstract than even the busing thing *and* a hell of a lot more abstract than "Nigger, nigger."[28]

Atwater knew the South, and South Carolina, well; raised in Aiken, South Carolina, he attended college at Newberry, just a county away from Union. He and the rest of the GOP redefined affirmative action as not just an economic issue, but as a social one—a social force that, paradoxically, insured inequality for white men. By the late 1980s, Atwater's proposed message of new racism as social populism had become New Right gospel. Instead of "hard-core segregationists" railing against racial equality, Republicans gave themselves a makeover. They targeted "special interests" and "groups"—African Americans and women—and their unfair "privileges" and "preferences" that mandated racial "quotas" that put hard-working white men out of work.[29]

This rhetoric had particular resonance in places like the Textile Belt South, where industry had traditionally been the province of white males. By the 1990s, neoconservative attacks on affirmative action had become key issues in local and statewide political campaigns. Gone was the overt, "black beast" scare tactic of 1988; in his place there was a hard-working, frustrated white man with whom certain voters—the groups courted by the GOP—could identify. Jesse Helms's "White Hands" spot and others have been analyzed in terms of their subtle racism, but it is clear that the issue here is not just white entitlement to employment; it is white *male* entitlement. The growing attack on affirmative action rested upon a bedrock of what Njeri Jackson calls "racialized patriarchy." The discriminatory nature of this system is masked, says Jackson, in the "rhetoric of fiscal accountability, fairness, and romanticized retrievalism that nostalgically invokes earlier ages when women and African Americans 'knew their place.'" In short, the language of the new racism/sexism hides the fact that the attack on affirmative action is little more than a "marriage of patriarchy and racism."[30] Indeed, the rhetoric is more complex than a simple laundry list of new code words. "Is that *fair?*" asks the disembodied male voice in the "White Hands" ad, implying that affirmative action, in reality, perpetrates inequality. New Right charges of "reverse" discrimination, racism, or sexism are deliberate appropriations of the key terms of the very rights movements that they repudiate to defend their traditionalist position.

This belief that the ability of the hard-working white men of America to support their families was being undermined by "special interest groups" found its voice in the 1994 elections, just five days after Susan Smith's confession and arrest. Voter resentment, according to exit polls, hinged on Democratic initiatives like affirmative action and welfare. "When does fairness become 'reverse discrimination'? When is it fair to discriminate on the basis of race or gender?" asked reporters for *Newsweek.* In the mid-1990s, they argued, "Louder than before, Americans seem to be saying, 'Never.'" The "angry white male" was attempting to take back his country.[31]

These racialized politics ensured a GOP sweep of the South in 1994. The week after Susan Smith confessed to murder, unprecedented numbers of Republicans won offices across the region. The trend was mirrored in Union County when voters elected their first Republican state representative in 124 years. Republican senator Bob Inglis, three GOP incumbents at the state level, and the Republican candidates for governor and attorney general all carried the county. Although a Democratic representative and some Democrats at the county level maintained their seats, the results meant that, "for the first time since Reconstruction, Union County [was] a two-party county." Union was in the process of making the slow transition that characterized the political landscape of the late twentieth-century South: "solid" Democratic Union County was joining the GOP. Charles Warner of the *Union Daily Times* believed his county was poised on the precipice of a monumental political shift:

it can be said that Union County, now open to the GOP but still anchored by deep Democratic roots, is, perhaps even more importantly, a symbol of what is going on in many of the small rural counties of South Carolina. They, like Union County, remained loyal to the Democratic Party even as that party moved away from them on political, economic, and cultural issues. Even as the Republicans adopted positions on these issues more in tune with the beliefs of the people of these counties they continued to support the Democratic Party out of tradition. The loyalties of these counties, including Union's, are now in limbo, poised between a Democratic past and a possible Republican future.[32]

Warner essentially predicted the future of local, state, and regional politics, and his hometown was representative of a realignment that was decades in the making.

Indeed, the GOP rise in South Carolina rested largely upon the defection from the Democratic Party of white voters in rural areas and small towns like Union. The new racism was alive and well in the Palmetto State, and sometimes the old racism was, too: state Republicans sponsored a 1994 referendum on the Confederate battle flag, which had flown over the State House since 1962. This "flagrant lapse into the demagoguery of the past" resulted in a three-to-one vote approving the flying of the "secessionist standard."[33] More generally, however, South Carolina Republicans spoke in the code that highlighted white male taxpayers' perceived exploitation by big government.

Unionites might have quibbled with the post-election "angry white male" hypothesis had anyone asked their opinion. They generally had little to say about affirmative action in the wake of the 1994 elections. Jobs were not being taken from white men and given to minorities in Union County; local jobs were not going to *anyone*—the mills were shutting down with nothing to replace them. But the narrative of paternal authority that undergirded the New Right rhetoric of affirmative action and family values more broadly had local resonance. When Unionites speak of the Susan Smith case, they tell a story about the failures of paternal authority and the system of community supervision in their close-knit, God-fearing small town. "Community," in this case, meant not just the social dynamics of the tiny town of Union. It also rested heavily upon Union's vision of itself as an American ideal, an image directly opposed to the *Peyton Place* exposés and the "Gothic" dying mill town. This self-image involved explicit notions of racial and class harmony as well as a subtle, but entrenched, gender hierarchy. Union, according to its outspoken citizens, followed the lead of its town fathers—namely, the sheriff and local ministers.

When a twenty-three-year-old woman, referred to by many locals as a "girl," committed a heinous crime in their very midst, the leaders of the community presented themselves as fathers who had utterly failed one of their daughters. In essence, they were men "in crisis," seeking to reclaim their masculinity.

The community system rested upon paternal authority within households, at the pulpit, and in the local government. The various traumas that Smith suffered in the past added up, in the local imagination, to a failure of this system. The story locals told in the media, at the trial, and in interviews over a decade later amounted to an alternative narrative, one that did not call upon the preexisting images of woman- or motherhood gracing front pages and the nightly news. Indeed, theirs was an oppositional script that thoroughly contradicted the tabloid-worthy headlines about class-climbing and adultery. Instead of a nightmarish narrative about a mother and her sons, Unionites saw a tragedy about a daughter and her fathers.

Union's defense of Susan Smith began as a defense of the community. According to many locals, their lovely little town was not rife with racial tension or representative of any broader social problems. Unionites loudly voiced their disagreements with the media coverage of their beloved hometown. Many locals argued that the "malcontents" who portrayed Union negatively in the media were on the "fringes" of their insular society. "The national media always came back in and talked to people we didn't know," said Phil Hobbs, the former program director for WBCU, Union's AM radio station. "They made Union look bad in a lot of ways."[34] To them, the mask motif, and the idea that Union's sweet facade had been ripped off by Susan to reveal the carefully hidden demons within, was pure sensationalism meant to sell more papers and gain more viewers.

In direct contrast to the gritty, poverty-stricken image of the South (think Erskine Caldwell or Larry Brown), Union did not see itself as a dying mill village. According to city officials, Union is uniquely geographically situated to attract new industry and people. Three major interstates divide upstate South Carolina: I-26, which connects the South Carolina coast to the Tennessee mountains; I-85, which links Atlanta to the District of Columbia; and I-77, which runs from the Great Lakes to Columbia, South Carolina's state capital. Although Union is a good half-hour away from any of these major arteries, it "is not the middle of nowhere," said Torance Inman, holding his fingers up to illustrate the three interstates. "It's the middle of a triangle. It's in the middle of everything."[35]

Some locals supported the sweet-tea and front-porches image of the sweet, innocent small town. In many ways, they argued, Union was a friendly hamlet straight out of a Norman Rockwell painting. Phil Hobbs echoed the sentiments of many when he told me, "You won't find a better, church-going, giving community." It is the kind of town that prints wedding invitations, not just announcements, in the local paper. It is the kind of town in which the citizens might have resented the intense media scrutiny, but they still brought the journalists snacks, including homemade cookies, to make their stay more comfortable.[36]

Although some later claimed they had suspected Smith from the start, many locals seem to have truly believed her until she confessed. The resulting shock was palpable, and reporters eagerly covered the local anger in the wake of Smith's confession. The calls for Old Testament justice that rang throughout the Union of the national media belied the fact that the rage on Main Street faded quickly. The racial tensions still lingered beneath the surface, but words of hurt and rage turned to Christian messages of healing and forgiveness fairly quickly at the local level. According to popular local radio personality Carlisle Henderson, the Smith drama was a kind of test case. "This town needed revival," he argued. "We've taken each other for granted, we're not visiting our neighbors, everyone's in such a hurry. God may be saying, 'Wake up, Union.' God could be trying to tell us something."[37]

God was not the only one; local leaders took to the airwaves immediately. The day that Smith confessed, Reverend Allen Raines, the pastor of the First Baptist Church in Union, stopped by the local AM radio station, where Henderson, his locally famous parishioner, worked as a disc jockey and host of the daily gospel hour. Raines closed his message with a prayer, and the Reverend A. L. Brackett followed him on the show. The three men decided that Union would need a frequent public forum to discuss the case in coming weeks. Local churches began to hold open meetings for citizens to "voice their feelings on the case," and they continued to hold public services for the community until the end of the trial in late July.[38]

In direct contrast to the angry crowds cursing Smith on the national news, local journalists emphasized the pleas for mercy from prominent locals. William Holcombe, the Union County coroner who knew better than anyone the extent of Smith's crimes as he examined the waterlogged bodies of her sons, asked his neighbors to seek "God's help, guidance, and love." He argued that "Michael and Alex have drawn us closer together not only as a community but as a state and a nation." The local paper printed many of the thousands of letters to the editor about the case in a special section called "Many Share Their Feelings." Observers from as far away as British Columbia wrote the *Union Daily Times* editor to commend the town on the way its citizens pulled together in a time of crisis. Many sought comfort from the belief that Michael and Alex Smith were in heaven, a belief that Susan Smith herself expressed in her written confession.[39]

Sympathetic readers couched their condolences in religious language, some in poems addressed to God written from the perspectives of the "angels," or Smith's slain sons. Many letter writers pleaded for the unity displayed during the investigation to continue: "We as a community and nation need to come together in unity and not to be divided. We need to pray for the families as well as Susan. . . . May God have mercy on Susan's soul." One reader compared Smith to the biblical Moses, arguing that God forgave him for murder and he "went on to do mighty works for the Lord." He asked others not to try to guess "God's plan" for Susan, concluding: "Don't let the devil use you to hinder your life or hers, forgive and love and support her growth. Don't love the sin, but for God's sake love the sinner."[40]

Within days of Smith's confession, then, certain Unionites were already asking for understanding even as the national media coverage reached a crescendo of condemnation. Self-protection factored into Union's response to the Smith case in two ways. Initially, locals naturally sought to protect themselves from negative press and the realities of existing social tensions. Over the course of the winter of 1995, however, as past secrets became public knowledge, they began to express a kind of collective guilt, a guilt that could be resolved by protecting Susan Smith from capital punishment.

Local sympathy for Smith was couched in terms of Christian forgiveness, which should not be surprising in a town named for a "pioneer church" in which several different congregations who could not afford their own structures worshipped. Torance Inman of the Union Chamber of Commerce affirms the continuing importance of Christianity in the small town: "We are a religious community in and of itself; it is the backbone of our society."[41] In fact, it is Union's religiosity, more so than its race or class relations, that identifies the community as distinctly southern. Union, like so many other areas in the South, underwent major changes in the second half of the twentieth century. But a major continuity was the heavy sociocultural influence of Protestantism, particularly the Baptist and Methodist faiths.

This is characteristic of the region; according to historian Beth Barton Schweiger, religion has long served as "a shorthand for Southern exceptionalism." Of all of the popular images of the South as distinctive, it is religion—characterized by "its evangelical piety, its emotional fervor, its highly personal moral orientation"—that truly seems to set it apart from other regions. Samuel S. Hill, one of the foremost scholars of southern religion, identified a "Christ-and-culture" regional blend; one cannot understand the one without the other. The unique combination of a culture characterized by Christianity and a troubled regional history has led to a "Christ-haunted" South (to use Flannery O'Connor's phrase) in which one is hard pressed to find a "Southerner who doesn't believe in original sin." William H. Willimon, a scholar who struggles with the dueling identities of "Southerner" and "Christian," argues that "a Southerner can be many things, but he or she ought not to be innocent—too many bodies, too much blood for that." He recalls being told, "You know your hands are dirty. You know you were conceived in sin. You're a Southerner."[42]

This emphasis on "original sin" in southern culture combined with a unique regional relationship to the concept of "redemption." Students of southern history will recognize the term as one that describes the end of Reconstruction in the mid-1870s. This "powerful" term, argues Paul Harvey, "signifies individual salvation as well as deliverance from 'cursed rulers.'" In the concerted move to destroy the "Yankee faith" of Reconstruction, white southerners "viewed their Redemptionist activity as essentially religious, an extension of the cosmic struggle between order and disorder, civilization and barbarism, white and black." Redemption in the 1970s was a conservative counter-revolution meant to save the region from "theological liberalism and racial egalitarianism."[43] Minus the code of the new racism (Redeemers were generally proud of their overt racism), these tenets undergirding Redemption sound for all the world like those of the GOP's "Contract with America" in 1994. In other words, it should perhaps not be surprising that Susan Smith's neighbors had a ready playbook for understanding her actions, one that included an updated defense of traditional gender relations.

Although Union might not have had such an acute sense of history, locals clearly prayed according to the same theology. Unionites, like other southerners, prefer "sin and crucifixion" to "worship and incarnation." According to Samuel Hill, regional religious teachings "are centered in the themes of man's depravity, Christ's atoning death, and the assurance of salvation." The firm belief in original sin and in the salvation of forgiveness determined how locals responded to the Smith case. The Monday after Smith's Thursday confession, local ministers held an interdenominational "Community Service To Help Us Experience God's Healing," where Reverend Tom Currie preached a sermon tellingly titled, "We Are All In the Same Leaky Boat." He concluded: "Since you are dependent upon mercy, then you had better practice mercy," and it was clear to everyone in the room, although her name had not yet been uttered, that he was talking about Susan Smith.[44] Just days after Susan's confession, town leaders reminded the community that they were all sinners deserving of Christian forgiveness.

This immediate positioning of Susan Smith as a lamb lost to her flock, rather than a wayward woman or an insensate monster, was compellingly in accordance with the gendered logic of regional religion. Certain sects of Protestants, especially the fundamental varieties found in the South, are known for preaching about proper gender roles, namely female subservience and domesticity. Billy Graham, a major southern religious icon of the twentieth century, declared in 1970 in the *Ladies' Home Journal*: "The biological assignment was basic and simple: Eve was to be the child-bearer, and Adam was to be the bread winner. . . . wife, mother, homemaker—this is the appointed destiny of real womanhood."[45] The gender dynamic had changed in many denominations by the 1990s, but the southern Protestantism of Union's churches was a stronghold of traditional patriarchy. Smith's gender thus worked in her favor at the local level. It was not difficult to view her as a pathetic girl in need of protection within a theology in which women were often seen as weak and easily tempted.

Even before any of the sordid details of Smith's pre-criminal past emerged, some local religious leaders combined the traditional gender logic of southern Protestantism with a kind of popular psychology. On Sunday, November 6, just three days after Susan Smith confessed, Reverend Tom Currie of Union's First Presbyterian Church opened the morning service with a prayer for the Smith boys, for the local people that had scoured the community in vain for them, and for Susan Smith, "the mother who has done this horrible thing." He concluded: "What she has to live with is more than any of us imagine bearing through life." Reverend Currie pleaded with his parishioners to live "by faith, and not emotions." No one in the hushed church could guess Smith's motives, but Currie asked them to pray for her "especially." He explained: "What she did was unconscionable, unimaginable, unjustifiable—but I know Susan Smith as others do. None of those who know her would describe her as a mean cruel person. I truly believe that what she did was not a sick act done by an evil person, but an evil act done by a sick person."[46]

Another local minister couched Smith's crimes in terms of the very real difficulties facing young mothers. Reverend Robert Cato, who had counseled Susan and her family during the investigation and had harbored doubts about her innocence the entire time, appeared on the *Phil Donahue Show* the week after Smith's confession. With the blessing of Susan's family, Cato spoke to the nation (or at least to daytime television watchers) about Christian forgiveness. The results were mixed; some audience members spoke out angrily, but Cato reported being contacted by "hundreds" of other sympathetic mothers in the weeks following his appearance. He told me, "Mothers would just call me and confess because I was the only Cato in the phone book."[47]

Cato recalled one such woman who called him late at night from Utah and told him the story of her depression following the birth of her first son. She tried unsuccessfully to overcome the disorder; instead, she found herself standing over her son one night holding a pillow she had embroidered for his crib. As he cried, she placed the pillow over his face, and held it there long enough that he began to resist. She was startled by the ringing of the doorbell and went downstairs to find that it was a man at the wrong house. She directed him to his intended destination and reflected silently on what she had almost done to her child. She later believed that he had been sent to her by God to protect her son from her uncontrollable depressive urges. An angry *Donahue* audience member calling for the death penalty had prompted her to call Reverend Cato. She told him, "I'm more angry at that person than I am at Susan, because I am Susan." This mother was not alone. Cato received phone calls from all over the country and several different continents from parents expressing sympathy and understanding based on their troubled experiences of motherhood. He begged them to seek help and, like the woman whose son's life was saved by a mistaken visitor, to reach out to their local pastor or a Christian therapist.[48] Cato, for one, saw a very real connection between issues of motherhood, religion, and violence in Susan Smith's actions.

Reverend Cato's unique understanding of Smith's crimes, informed as it was by both Christianity and the nascent psychology of postpartum mental illness, was not the dominant Christian perspective on the case. Like the few letters and columns of other sympathetic mothers published after Susan confessed, Cato's analysis—essentially, a description of postpartum depression, a diagnosis that was not yet part of the popular lexicon—was drowned out by a more general understanding based on generic Christian forgiveness. In this narrative, Smith's motive mattered less than the process of cleansing Susan and her community of her sins. One *Union Daily Times* reader wrote: "You know God forgave us of our sins and he will forgive her or anyone else of their sins if they asked and repent and believe." Reverend A. L. Brackett received letters from all over the country from people who said they were "so angry at Susan they couldn't pray" until they saw one of his prayers broadcast on CNN.[49]

These community fathers, many of whom knew Susan Smith personally and had counseled her during the alleged "kidnapping investigation," spearheaded the effort to defuse the community's anger and begin the healing. Their approach worked. Throughout the winter of 1994–95, Union churches held interracial, open services to "promote continued cooperation between the races." By the end of the trial, over thirty local churches were involved in the open meetings. Radio host Carlisle Henderson characterized the softening of local reactions from violence to compassion for a national news magazine: "The very same people who were calling into the show a few weeks ago yelling 'Kill her!' or suggesting that she be dragged down the street are now calling in to say, 'Well, hang on, let's pray for her.'"[50]

Locals united in their opposition to the death penalty after prosecuting attorney Tommy Pope made his announcement in mid-January. This was not a simple matter of small-town residents trying to protect one of their neighbors in the face of outside scrutiny, although Smith's defense attorney David Bruck acknowledged that localism played a role: "It's just that if you're told that Beelzebub had assumed human flesh 3000 miles away, you might think, well who knows? Maybe he did. But if you're told that Beelzebub has lived among you for the past 23 years and nobody noticed, you're more likely to be skeptical and to apply common sense to that."[51] But that was not all that was going on in this case. The sin-and-forgiveness "Christ-haunted" theology of Union combined with the breaking news of the traumas in her past to produce an image of Smith as not just a lost lamb, but also as a childlike victim. At the age of twenty-three, Smith could be seen by Unionites as their own young daughter, and an abused one at that. Religion and the community's vision of itself fused to produce a pathetic "Susan" in need of paternal protection.

Although some of the traumas in Susan Smith's past were well known—everyone knew her father had killed himself when she was young, for example—others were not, and as information surfaced in the winter of 1995, locals began to see the young criminal in a new light. The emerging details of Smith's past ensured that the media soon turned its harsh attention to a new figure: her stepfather, Beverly Russell. On November 28, 1994, just over three weeks after Smith's confession, the local paper broke the story that would help script the way that much of Union responded to her case. A published report alleged that Smith had a history of suicide attempts dating back a decade, and, even more shocking, that Smith's stepfather molested Susan when she was in her teens.[52]

This was no idle gossip; local law enforcement as well as the high-school guidance counselor confirmed the reports. In 1987, when Susan Smith was fifteen years old, she shared the shocking secret with a trusted teacher, Debbie Green, while on a high-school club trip. Green had been concerned about Susan in the past because she seemed depressed. In fact, she was, and she had been for some time. Two years before, in the winter of 1985, she had confessed to her eighth-grade physical education teacher that she wanted to kill herself, and she had been taking aspirin every day believing that it would build up in her body and she would eventually overdose. According to mental health experts, Susan Smith "began to think obsessively about suicide at the age of thirteen." She was thus a troubled young teenager on whom teachers kept a close eye.[53]

On the high-school trip in 1987, Susan asked Green whether it was "appropriate" to sit on her stepfather's lap when they watched television, and then she revealed that when she did, her stepfather, Beverly Russell, often put his arms around her and fondled her breasts. Green notified the school counselor, who pressured Smith to tell her mother, Linda Russell. "Bev has done some things to me," Smith told her mother one night in May of 1987, explaining carefully how he had touched her. Russell responded with "stunned disbelief." In her account of the conversation, Russell states that she knew Susan feared that she would be angry, and she assured her daughter that she was not. But her first response was accusation: "I don't understand why you let it go that far. Why didn't you stop it?" In her book, Russell explains this response: "This wasn't a four-year-old. She was fifteen, and I felt she could have done something to make him stop. I was angry that she didn't get up and leave." She was also concerned that Susan had confided in a teacher first.[54]

Russell confronted Bev that night, and they sought family counseling with Dr. David Heatherly in nearby Spartanburg. Heatherly worked with the whole family together, with Susan individually, and with Bev and Linda as a pair. Heatherly explained that the loss of Susan's biological father rendered her "empty," "needy," and "childlike" in her emotions. Like many victims of repeated molestation, she had come to conceptualize the abuse as a consensual relationship although it clearly made her uncomfortable. Her primary concern in counseling was keeping the family together. The counseling lasted for several months. Linda and Bev stopped seeing Dr. Heatherly in November of 1987, and Susan discontinued her therapy the following month. By early 1988, the family had resumed their normal routine. Bev did not move out, and they made a family pact not to tell anyone about the abuse. Russell explains: "We felt it was an unfortunate incident that had happened in our household and needed to be dealt with there." It is not clear that, at the time, she understood the extent of the trauma of sexual abuse or the fact that it was against the law.[55]

A few months later, in early 1988, Bev Russell came home late one night after putting up "Pat Robertson for President" posters all over Union. He found Susan asleep on the couch, and at that moment, he initiated a new pattern of abuse. In early March, Susan went to one of her teachers, told her that the sexual abuse had resumed, and asked her how to stop it. The teacher went to the school counselor, who called the Department of Social Services. DSS agent Jenny Ward was at Union High School interviewing Susan within two hours. Susan revealed that Bev had repeatedly watched her in the bathtub, entered her bedroom at night, fondled her, "French kissed" her, and made her fondle him. Ward confronted Bev Russell at his appliance store, and then she called the sheriff (Sheriff William Jolly at the time). Bev called his lawyer, and Ward discussed options with Susan and Linda. They could press charges, but removal of the offender was mandatory—either Bev would have to move out, or Susan would have to be moved to a safer location. Bev quickly agreed to pack his things and move in with his mother.

Overnight, Linda decided she did not want to press charges; she worried about "what the public exposure would do to the family." She discussed this with Susan the next morning, and Susan agreed. Again, her primary concern seemed to be keeping the family together, a very common reaction to intrafamilial molestation. When they refused to press charges, Ward obtained a family court order that deemed the abuse "physical abuse or neglect," instead of the more severe "sexual abuse," because there had been no physical penetration. The order was sealed, a very unusual move; Ward said later at Smith's trial that it was the only order she had sealed in over two decades of working for DSS. The family resumed counseling with Dr. Heatherly. After several months of this, Jenny Ward came to the family home to discuss Bev moving back in, pending a home inspection to judge the proximity of the bedrooms and to make sure there was a lock on Susan's bedroom door. Linda Russell decided, for better or worse, that having everyone back under the same roof would at least allow her to monitor the situation and better protect Susan. Bev moved back in.[56]

Despite Linda's vigilance, the molestation continued. Bev Russell and Susan Smith maintained a sexual relationship, off and on, up until the spring of 1994. Throughout their relationship, Smith exhibited classic signs of trauma resulting from molestation. She engaged in promiscuous behavior, including a relationship with a much older married co-worker at the Winn Dixie when she was eighteen. She was overly dependent on men. In 1989, after her married lover dumped her and moved away, Susan attempted suicide again. She tried to overdose on pills, but her mother got her to the emergency room in time to have her stomach pumped. She received short-term, in-patient treatment in the psychiatric ward at Spartanburg Regional Hospital. When she returned to Union, the molestation and Susan's pattern of troubled relationships with other men continued. She began to date David Smith shortly thereafter. True to form, Linda never told anyone about the abuse. Bev, of course, also remained mum. Susan told only David Smith. Only her teachers knew, as well as the guidance counselor, a local pastor whom she consulted for a recommendation (he suggested Dr. Heatherly), and DSS.[57]

Unlike the vague innuendoes of the *Peyton Place* media coverage, this was the actual skeleton in the closet that almost no one knew about. When this information made local headlines, the news rocked Union. One would be hard-pressed to find a Unionite more representative of New Right family values than Susan Smith's stepfather. Beverly Russell was a prominent local business owner, tax consultant, former chairman of the Union County Republican Party, state Republican executive committeeman, and a member of the advisory board of the Christian Coalition. The nephew of former governor Donald Russell, "Bev" Russell was a conservative activist and aspiring politician. He ran unsuccessfully for state representative in 1986, and he campaigned for Pat Robertson's presidential bid in 1988 and David Beasley's gubernatorial campaign in 1994. His religiosity was also well known. David Smith, Susan's estranged husband, joked that his family used to call Bev "Thank you, Jesus," behind his back.[58]

Russell's faith informed his political activism, and this close connection mirrored the dynamics of religion and politics across the South in the late twentieth century. Unionites were appalled by the news of sexual misconduct on the part of one of their most pious and prominent citizens. When the Union County Family Court released the documents to the local media in February 1995, local reporters began to detail the physical abuse that had begun almost eight years earlier. According to the *Union Daily Times,* when the abuse began in 1988, Susan was a "popular junior" at the local high school and Russell was a "respected self-employed Union appliance store owner who just two years before had made a run for the House of Representatives while serving as chairman of the Union County Republican Party."[59]

A new vision of the Russell family unfolded slowly as locals discovered that the Social Services file on the molestation was sealed. Then it was discovered that the Department of Social Services file was missing, as was all evidence of the charges, including the Rolodex card with the family's name on it. Throughout the winter of 1995, speculation abounded that Russell had used his influence to destroy the documents so as not to damage his future political career. Despite the GOP sweep of the local elections the previous fall, at least one powerful Republican head would roll that year. After the allegations were made public in late April, Russell issued a statement saying that he was ashamed of his behavior and that he would seek professional help. Eventually, Russell resigned all political posts, agreed to a divorce, and, after the trial, left town for a while.[60]

Although the national media, like the prosecution at the trial several months later, generally included the molestation in the list of Smith's various sexual dalliances, Union residents understood this sensational detail very differently. Local journalists positioned Susan Smith in relation to different men in her life, but their story was not the "boyfriend motive" and its attendant sexual deviance. In the local narrative, the community failed Susan Smith when they allowed a powerful man to abuse her, and he was not the only culprit. Although a select few knew about Russell's sexual abuse of Susan, her troubled relationship with her estranged husband was an open secret. Bluntly put, David was "known for his shenanigans," and his extramarital affair was public knowledge around town. Everyone felt sorry for his loss, but, according to a local lawyer, "a lot of the 'poor David' was not just the fact that he had lost his children, but that he had lost opportunities with his children while they were alive—I mean, I think most people *knew that.*" To many Unionites, he was "not the epitome of the fine father," regardless of what the media said.[61]

The public sympathy for David Smith, the grieving father, slowly dissolved, especially after the *Union Daily Times* reported that he was working on a book about his life with Susan before the case even went to trial. As documents became available that spring, the local media also printed parts of Tom Findlay's deposition, which revealed that, during their separation, David had repeatedly harassed and stalked Susan Smith, hidden in her house to spy on her, and threatened Findlay with physical harm when he caught the two in a telephone conversation. Locals began to speculate that the defense might argue that Smith was "sexually abused by her husband." In June 1995, his attorney announced that David would make the rounds of television interviews—Barbara Walters, Katie Couric, Phil Donahue, and Larry King—in August plugging his new book, tentatively titled *Ultimate Betrayal: The Untold Story of Susan and David Smith.* According to his editor, Smith's support for the death penalty had "nothing to do with a six-figure advance Smith shared with co-writers or the prospect of a trial that could spur sales."[62] The book's publication was planned to coincide with the trial. David's book offended Union's vision of itself on several levels by inviting national scrutiny yet again and by admitting, for all the world to read, that the community had allowed Smith to be abused repeatedly for years.

In keeping with the Protestant visions of paternal authority, Unionites had come to understand Susan according to her relationships to a series of father figures. Russell, the abusive stepfather, and David, the straying husband, held down the negative end of that spectrum, while the respected town fathers— Sheriff Howard Wells and almost all of the local ministers—served as the avengers of their embattled community. These paternal authorities offered their protection to Susan Smith, who had begun to look less like an offending woman and more like a damaged girl.

The primary positive father figure in the case was, predictably, Union County Sheriff Howard W. Wells. Locals knew Wells as a "by-the-book," efficient policeman. Before he was elected sheriff, he was a game warden. According to local attorney Thom White, "He's the only game warden I've ever known who could stay in the woods all day long, you know, tramping around in the woods or whatever, come out of the woods his hair would still be perfectly in place and his uniform perfectly creased." Wells was "the antithesis of a redneck Southern sheriff." He had animal trophies mounted on his walls, but he also "finished at the top of his class in the F.B.I. Academy's training course," according to *New York Times* reporter Rick Bragg. The sheriff had a gun collection, but he also quoted "Supreme Court decisions off the top of his head." Thom White joked that Wells would "give his mother a ticket," and that quality made him the perfect lawman to handle an investigation that could have easily inflamed local emotions and especially racial tensions. Wells won the election for county sheriff by a slim margin of twenty-three votes; a local radio host threw many votes in Wells's direction when he argued that Union needed a sheriff that communicated well in case something big ever happened.[63] The editorial, it seems, was prophetic.

At the FBI National Academy, where Wells had gone for extra training in September of 1994, he learned from an instructor that "one student would probably be thrown into the national spotlight within the coming year." Within a month, Wells became that student; luckily, he was up to the challenge. People wrote from all over the country to praise Wells for his expert handling of the case. He personally reported receiving over one thousand letters congratulating him, and the *Union Daily Times* printed dozens more. Citizens expressed their gratitude that local police did not indiscriminately round up African American men for interrogation, as Boston police did in the infamous Charles Stuart case just a few years earlier. They also thanked him for his careful manipulation of and professionalism in dealings with the media. Wells received a personal phone call from President Clinton commending him on his work, and he won the Palmetto Award, South Carolina's highest honor for a law enforcement officer. He was later approached by film producers to tell his "heroic" story, although the film was never made.[64]

But the real focus of praise was Wells's careful manipulation of Susan Smith herself. Wells, in these depictions, was not simply a sheriff doing his job. He was a protector, shielding her from the waiting cameras while urging her to tell the truth. Once she confessed, he provided discipline like a good father, but her arrest and incarceration occurred under his cautious watch. Wells stepped into the roles played poorly by Beverly Russell and David Smith, and he restored order to the paternal authority they had corrupted. In fact, Wells already served a fatherly role in Susan's extended family as the godfather to her older brother's two children.[65]

Wells was the first prominent Unionite to speak out against the death penalty. Many locals followed Wells's lead in using the media to urge prosecutor Tommy Pope to accept a plea bargain and avoid a trial. An editorial in the *State*, the major newspaper of the state capital, Columbia, argued that it might be impossible to find "12 unbiased jurors [who] will agree to put such a pathetic defendant to death, despite the horror she has wrought." The Union paper, as well, featured op-eds about the impending trial. On behalf of his neighbors, the author argued, "the case should be pleaded out with Ms. Smith receiving a life sentence and Union County spared the media circus of a long trial." Union County residents wrote letters to prosecutor Tommy Pope asking him to reconsider his decision to seek the death penalty throughout the winter and spring of 1995.[66]

These letters were public expressions of local sentiment, and by the summer of 1995 Unionites had grown more sophisticated. Although the prosecutor ignored their pleas and proceeded with the trial, Union residents did not go blindly into the imminent "media circus." The Smith case prompted self-examination among her friends and neighbors, but it also provided an opportunity for some deliberate self-presentation, and on a national stage at that. By the summer of 1995, just weeks before the courtroom drama expected to rival that of O. J. Simpson for national attention, Union residents were extremely aware of how they were being portrayed in the media. Local leaders offered "media training" to everyone, not just Union's regular spokespeople, to help them deal with the unprecedented, international scrutiny. Union had its scars from the media onslaught during the investigation, and locals were meticulous in their preparation for their encore on the national stage.[67]

Although the national media coverage died down for a while during the winter of 1995, locals knew it was only a brief lull; in preparation for the July trial, out-of-town reporters began reserving rooms at local inns and motels in February. That spring, Union called in a PR consulting firm to advise locals on how to respond to the media. The town would soon be undergoing another crisis, and the concern was "how to keep the community from being further victimized by this situation." "This situation" meant, of course, the media presence. Media experts warned Unionites that they, as the subjects, had to remember that they were "portraying the community." The key to dealing with journalists was "anticipation." A media expert told the crowd that gathered in the auditorium at USC-Union in early June that their experiences with the media during the upcoming trial might be very different from their experiences during the investigation: "Last time the media was here for a long period of time, a vast majority were working with you [to find the children]. . . . Now they will be looking for a different story and may drive wedges between you to get that story." Because the media thrives on competition, representatives from a Greenville public relations firm told locals, "you don't want to pick an argument with CBS, because that will only make Union look bad. . . . They live by competition, and they will stay on the story."[68] Locals united defensively against the impending media onslaught. This training fostered unity and gave

Unionites the opportunity to uniformly present their own vision of their town, and of Susan Smith, to the media.

Experts from the hired public relations firm filmed interviews with city council members, ministers, and city administrators, and then they critiqued each interviewee on his or her performance. They urged everyone to be as prepared for the cameras as Sheriff Wells had been during the investigation, and they circulated tip and fact sheets around the community to help individuals deal with reporters. Ann Currie, the wife of Reverend Tom Currie and an employee at Conso with Susan Smith at the time of the murders, said the primary message of the training was "know what you want to say before the interview begins, and then don't pay attention to the questions. Say what you want to say." Those who chose not to attend the scheduled training could watch a video circulating around town for advice on how to deal with the media. Even the priest at the local Catholic church found himself hastily watching it one night after a *National Inquirer* reporter left her card on his car.[69] Everyone in Union County was duly prepared for the coming reporters.

By July of 1995, Unionites were media savvy, but they still pleaded, through letters to the solicitor, letters to the editor, and weekly editorials, for a plea deal, right up to the beginning of the trial. In the end, solicitor Tommy Pope would not make a deal. Two days before the circus began, an editorial in the *Union Daily Times* described the local mindset in this "community known for its friendliness": "It has been our hope that some deal could have been struck that would have at least somewhat served the cause of justice while sparing us the expense and pain of this trial. This, however, was not to be and now we must prepare for weeks of news cameras, microphones and reporters in our streets, our lovely courthouse transformed into an armed camp where everyone who enters is considered suspect, and the retelling of a tragic tale twisted to conform to the needs of contending legal strategies." "War, Reconstruction, Depression," and "social change" had "tested" Union before, but as always, the town would meet the challenge with "friendliness, compassion, charity, and faith." The editorial ended with a Bible quote: "This too shall pass."[70]

Jury selection began, as Judge William Howard had said it would at the second hearing in January, on July 10, 1995, in a courtroom so packed that the air conditioning stopped working; the county supervisor explained, "With the crowd Monday, it just couldn't hold up." The front page of the *Union Daily Times* that day carried these headlines: "Jury selection begins in Smith case"; "Ms. Smith ready to die, pastor says"; "Union churches plan Monday night services"; and "Media takes over Main Street." That morning, Reverend Mark Long, who had counseled Smith extensively in prison, told the media: "She made a profession of faith and turned her life over to the Lord. She had hardened her heart to the Lord, but she sought forgiveness from the church and the Lord and she knows it has been granted."[71]

Although the national media mostly ignored Long, local and regional papers quoted him extensively. Smith's hometown was in a forgiving mood on the eve of the so-called "Trial of the Century in the Carolinas."[72] The tears in the fabric of the community could be mended through forgiveness. Union would be absolved of the guilt of not saving Smith's sons if they could, instead, finally save Susan Smith. To them, Smith was a sad little girl, a "Susan" that made sense within a framework of family-values politics that featured an emphasis on traditional patriarchy. If she was not a mother because she had violently discarded her maternity, and if she was not a wife because of her impending divorce, she must, then, be a daughter. This "Susan" provided the outlines of a new, alternative script for Susan Smith—one that would, in the end, save her life.

6

"IN A LAKE OF FIRE"

THE NIGHT BEFORE jury selection was set to begin in the Susan Smith trial, reporter Bob Dotson for NBC's *Evening News* asked, in a voiceover backed by church bells: "In a town with 130 churches, people tend to be forgiving—but who can forget?" The video montage moved slowly from church steeples to Smith's tearful plea to the "kidnapper" in late October, eventually pausing on the setting sun over the now-serene John D. Long Lake in which her children drowned. The screen showed Smith's waterlogged Mazda being towed in slow motion from the water as the reporter posed the key question of the upcoming trial: "Was she crazy or merely calculating?" Was this trial, he asked, about Smith's "desperate bid to win the love of [ex-boyfriend] Tom Findlay" or was it evidence that she was a young woman "so troubled by a long history of sexual abuse that she didn't know right from wrong?"[1]

Media studies expert Elayne Rapping argues that through arenas such as the media and the courtroom—a space that is increasingly public in the era of televised trials, twenty-four-hour news coverage, and Court TV (now TruTV)—Americans "learn and relearn the gender lessons that regulate our common lives."[2] Although the judge in the Smith case refused to allow cameras in the courtroom, gender performance constituted the battleground of the final phase of the Susan Smith trial, just as it did in the televised cases studied by Rapping. The jury's perceptions of Smith's behaviors as a daughter, wife, and mother would dictate her sentence and reinscribe the gendered rules of the New Right 1990s.

In the end, the many new sexist images of Susan Smith over the nine months between the alleged "carjacking" and her judgment in court had two logical, but very different, possible outcomes. The most logical, according to family-values politics, would have been to mete out the ultimate punishment: Smith's jury could thoroughly cast out the offending woman by sentencing her to death. But there was another possible endpoint to the gendered logic of the new sexism.

The protection racket inherent in the "crisis of masculinity"—the nation's need for nuclear families, for male breadwinners, for involved fathers to right the various wrongs (divorce, "illegitimacy," abortion, single motherhood, poverty, welfare) wrought by uncontrolled women—meant that Susan Smith could be viewed in another way. Rather than a willful slut, she could be seen as a weak woman, a girl even, used and abused by various men who did not adhere to family-values prescriptions for proper paternal masculinity. This "Susan" surfaced in Union months before Smith set foot in the Union County Courthouse, but it took a media-saturated trial to legitimate it. This legitimacy came from the expert psychological diagnoses of Susan Smith, and it resulted in the image that saved Smith's life. With the advent of this "sixth Susan," a new icon worked its way into the pantheon of new sexist images: the child-like, mentally ill girl.

By the summer of 1995, the media presented a new version of the "two Susans." The victimized image of Susan Smith created by locals slowly worked its way into the national media as both sides prepared for the July trial. By early spring, *People* magazine reporters detailed a virtual reversal in "the court of public opinion," arguing that Smith's family was no longer alone "in seeing Susan as tragically, suddenly, caught in the grip of some terrible impulse." By the summer of 1995, although polls showed that some still clamored for the death penalty, the evil, Medea image of Susan was primarily the province of the tabloid media. The emerging details of Smith's past, and especially her resulting psychological problems, had become routine national headlines. By the beginning of jury selection in early July, NBC reported that "Smith looked more like a parson's wife than a confessed killer who drowned her kids." In the *New York Times,* Rick Bragg questioned whether a defendant "so self-destructive," "pale, listless, and dependent" on anti-depressants was "mentally ready to be tried."[3]

The Smith trial hinged not on disputed evidence, but on the strength of the opposing stories. "Each trial is a drama in its own right," writes law professor Charles Nesson, "a morality play watched by a public audience." The two sides in a legal case offer plots that can be told in drastically different ways depending on the "values and interests of the narrator." The cautionary tales set forth in court cases feature crucial elements of narrative with which we are all familiar: stock characters, a plot that features a disruption and eventual resto-ration of order, and a moral. At Smith's trial, the defense team did not directly challenge the facts of the prosecution's case. Rather, they emphasized different events in Smith's life, so that the jury confronted two very different "Susans." One was Medea, the "scheming slut" of the prosecutorial "boyfriend motive." The other was an entirely new, pitiable image of a girlish, fragile, mentally ill "Susan." On the first day of the trial, NBC's Tom Brokaw underscored this distinction. He opened the broadcast with the question, "Is she criminally responsible or mentally ill?" Live in Union, Bob Dotson continued. "Why did she do it?" he asked as the screen showed footage of Susan Smith crying and rocking in the backseat of an unmarked police car. "Was it a failed love affair, as the prosecution contends, or a failed suicide, as the defense will try to prove?"[4]

The opposing legal teams had to master a delicate balance: each needed to present the most compelling version of Susan Smith to the world outside the courtroom, but inside the Union County Courthouse, each team of attorneys also had to function as the most relevant voice of the community. The jury, after all, was made up of citizens of the small town that had raised Susan Smith. The case pitted Smith's defense attorney, "a polished, soft-spoken, Ivy League lawyer" against the local prosecutor (called "solicitors" in South Carolina), who was "plain-spoken" and, at thirty-two, the youngest county solicitor in the state. Although David Bruck went to law school and had practiced for years in South Carolina, Rick Bragg described the defense attorney in the *New York Times* as a "Canadian-born liberal and a Harvard man who protested against the war in Vietnam, just the kind of person many people here love to hate."[5] Bruck had lived in South Carolina for some time, and was starting to make a name for himself as an anti–death penalty attorney. On the other hand, solicitor Tommy Pope, the son of a former York County sheriff, had "blue lights in his blood." Pope was only from one county away, but he was not considered a local in Union either. His only familiarity with the small town was through playing Union High School in football (Pope played for Rock Hill High), through a few law enforcement contacts, and through his campaign efforts in the county a few years earlier.[6] Despite Bragg's depiction, Pope was no insider. The role of legal representative of the community in the Smith case was up for grabs.

The defense eventually won this unofficial custody battle. David Bruck consistently presented himself as a father figure, a protector of the various victims in the case, much like Sheriff Wells and the local ministers who had served as the voice of the community for months. Bruck's frequent references to Smith as a defenseless little girl underscored this position. He also played the role of the community protector, shielding jurors and observers from graphic forensic testimony in the courtroom, objecting repeatedly on the grounds that it was unnecessarily gruesome because the cause of death was not in question.[7] Bruck and his co-counsel, Judy Clarke, carefully led the court through the complicated connections between the sympathetic local vision of Susan Smith and the medical, psychiatric version of her that would dominate the trial.

Despite his pronounced upstate South Carolina accent, Solicitor Tommy Pope proved to be an ineffective community spokesperson. Although the state's case centered on the Smith boys at key moments, their point of attack was on Smith's character, primarily through the strategy of the "boyfriend motive." In fact, the state's duty was not to prove motive, but only to prove that Susan Smith committed her actions with "malice aforethought," a type of criminal premeditation that, in South Carolina, requires only a few seconds to be formulated (such as the moments it took for Susan Smith to position her car properly on the boat ramp, open her own door, get out, reach back in, and drop the emergency brake). Pope's focus on long-term motive, rather than on malice aforethought, was a reactionary tactic, forced by the defense's constant focus on Smith's mental state from the very first day of the trial. The content of Smith's character certainly stirred some negative public emotions, but it also urged jurors and observers to focus more on Smith's psychology than her behaviors. By the time of her trial, most Americans knew of the allegations of abuse in Smith's past, and this information helped to determine the outcome of her trial.

The defense's expert testimony legitimated the local view of Smith as an abused girl for a wider national audience. Because Smith lied on national television for nine days and then confessed to murder in no uncertain terms, David Bruck decided not to risk an insanity plea. Instead, he and his legal team chose the much murkier plea of "guilty but mentally ill." This is an ill-defined concept in the law, but it is easier to prove than insanity, in which the defendant is unable to differentiate between right and wrong at the time of the crime. Mentally ill defendants need only to prove that they had some form of undiagnosed psychological disorder at the time of the crimes. Bruck explained that most capital cases involve a focus on the defendant's mental state, and "every capital case requires the defense team to do a very thorough investigation of the person's life story." Although capital cases do not necessarily entail insanity or mentally ill pleas, Bruck knew from the moment he saw Susan Smith that this would be his approach.[8]

In his very first meeting with her, Bruck found Smith to be "out of it," "dissociated," and "inappropriately" calm, a demeanor that would not have seemed "at all inappropriate but for the fact that she had just confessed to killing and drowning her two children." Bruck also had inside knowledge of a possible mitigating factor even before he met Susan Smith the day after her confession. The Union attorney who had previously advised Beverly Russell about the legal ramifications of his molestation of Susan Smith had worked with David Bruck before. This local lawyer attempted to call Bruck after Smith's confession, but the phone lines were so jammed by the media that no calls could make it in or out of Union that night. He finally got through to Bruck's office in Columbia, South Carolina, the following morning; he explained his potential conflict of interest. Bruck, wearing blue jeans, jumped in the car, rushed to the courthouse, confronted the mob of media on Main Street, and met with Susan Smith for the first time.[9]

The jury would be made up of Union residents who, NBC speculated, could "relate to [Smith's] problems and may be less likely to execute her." The prosecution hoped exactly the opposite: that the jurors' familiarity with Smith, and especially with her two young sons, would fuel their outrage and build the case for capital punishment. Despite media speculation to the contrary, the defense had not considered requesting a change of venue. Each side hoped that the dynamics of the tightly knit community would serve their case. The collective rage of the previous fall that prompted "grandmothers" to call for "Mrs. Smith's public execution" had faded as locals "remembered that Susan Smith is one of them."[10]

Choosing the jury was thus a tricky endeavor. Legal expert Dick Harpootlian speculated that gender, rather than race, would be the key characteristic in juror selection. Indeed, he argued that the two opposing sides would be more inclined to choose mothers. The prosecution, Harpootlian guessed, would choose "young mothers, women who will think of Ms. Smith as a monster," while the defense would look for "older mothers" who were "more likely to be compassionate toward Ms. Smith because of their experiences." Harpootlian was right about this caretaker-child strategy in at least one instance: Bruck succeeded in seating the wife of a former police chief who babysat Susan as a child. It was not just this small-town dynamic, but also the various traumas in Smith's past, that would ultimately work in her favor. One juror had experienced the suicide of his father. Another had a daughter who had been sexually abused. At least three others knew someone who had attempted suicide in the past, and over half had family members in therapy.

Five jurors were African Americans. "This was not," Bruck argued later, "just white folks taking care of their own." From the outset, Bruck and his defense team strongly believed that they could convince these empathetic locals that Smith's traumas had resulted in a kind of mental illness.[11]

On July 18, after almost a week of jury selection, the day of Susan Smith's judgment had arrived—or as Rick Bragg put it in the *New York Times,* "it was all over but the shoutin'," a phrase he would famously reuse as the title of his best-selling memoir a year later. Locals and reporters turned out in droves for the long-awaited reckoning in the Union courthouse. The media had completely overtaken downtown. Twenty-five broadcasting platforms lined Main Street, and the satellite vans stretched down the hill in either direction. News affiliates from as far away as Japan filled all of the formerly empty storefronts. Almost overnight, the mass of satellite trucks, scaffolding, and wires made it look like "Hollywood" or "the fair had come to town." The circus was expected to last for about a month. Capital trials in South Carolina are divided into two phases: the guilt phase, in which the jury determines guilt or innocence based on the evidence presented by the opposing sides, and the sentencing phase, in which the jury decides which punishment will accompany their verdict. A guilty verdict in the first phase was more or less a foregone conclusion in the Smith case. The real battle for the defense team was against capital punishment in the sentencing phase.[12]

Tuesday, July 18, 1995, dawned hot and humid like so many other southern summer days, yet crowds thronged the streets of downtown Union for the much-anticipated public judgment of Susan Smith.[13] The prosecution's opening statement promised a titillating soap opera. That first morning, Pope and his legal team depicted Smith as a manipulative, sex-crazed single mother who saw her children as obstacles in her social-climbing bid to bed the richest bachelor in town—an image the media had been bombarding Americans with since Smith's confession eight months earlier. The prosecution team focused on the perceived promiscuity in Smith's past as well as the nine long days of lies in which she begged the nation to find her missing babies.[14] This approach put Smith on trial as much for her sexual history and her dishonesty as for the crime of double homicide.

"For nine days, Susan Smith looked this country in the eye and lied," began Assistant District Attorney Keith Giese in his opening statement, angrily pointing at Smith, who was crying quietly at the defense table. The "stumbling block" to Smith's relationship with her boss's son was "her children—the

children are the obstacle." This pairing of the two tropes of uncontrolled female sexuality and manipulation of the sacred maternal role depicted Susan
Smith as a broad social threat. Once Pope and Giese, with ample help from
the previous months of media attention, established this well-worn "boyfriend
motive," it was not difficult for them to portray Smith as promiscuous in all
of her relationships with men, including, most distastefully, her molestation
by her stepfather beginning at the age of fifteen. This image of "femininity
perverted," of Susan as a kind of sexual criminal, served the prosecutors by
painting her as a deceitful, sexual danger to the entire community, thus establishing the initial case for capital punishment.[15]

   "It is sadness that brings us together," countered assistant defense attorney
Judy Clarke in her opening statement for the defense. Clarke began by stating
that Susan Smith unequivocally shouldered all of the blame for the murders.
The defense asked the jury to consider the question of what kind of traumas
could place this former "good girl" in such an awful position. Instead of focusing on the crime itself and the nine days of lies that followed it, Clarke
argued that Smith's mental weakness began in decades past. The "turmoil,
distress, and confusion" of Susan's life originated with her biological parents'
tumultuous relationship and her father's suicide when she was six years old.
By her teens, Susan "was already a sort of the walking wounded," laying the
groundwork for the later tragedy.[16]

   Clarke did not avoid the prosecution's primary point of attack: she explicitly targeted Susan's carjacking lie, acknowledging the widespread sense that,
with this deception, Susan Smith had personally betrayed untold numbers of
horrified Americans. Susan's lie was "unforgivable," but it was also in keeping with the mentally ill image of Smith. It was, according to Clarke, very
"childlike," representing the rash reaction of a "young mother [who] could
not deal with the horror of what she had done." The source of this incomprehensible behavior was the "mental illness" that led Smith directly to the
water's edge that brisk October night. Clarke characterized the murders as
part of a "failed suicide" plot, listing the various factors which were to serve
as primary evidence for this defense: her father's suicide when Susan was six,
repeated molestation by her stepfather since the age of fifteen, and two suicide
attempts in her teens.[17]

   This trial, then, was not about Smith's sexual dalliances or obsessions. It
was about a damaged girl thrust into motherhood too early, a woman-child
who could not manage her stressors. "Use your common sense," Clarke urged

the jurors. "It was not a boyfriend. . . . Suicide is why we are here." Clarke ended her powerful appeal to the jurors' emotions with dual images of Smith as both angelically maternal and fatally unstable. "She snapped," Clarke concluded. "Everyone has a breaking point. Susan broke where many of us might bend, but I think through the evidence you will see why."[18] Instead of evil, the defense team presented tragedy. Susan Smith was both troubled girl and mentally ill mother.

The state proceeded with their case that afternoon. As the man who single-handedly broke the investigation wide open, Sheriff Wells was something of a star witness for the prosecution, but, as Tommy Pope later ruefully explained, the lawman's testimony was adversarial at best. Indeed, Pope later said that "the back of [his] neck was on fire" as Wells spoke on the stand. The sheriff described a pathetic, pitiable Susan as she confessed to her horrifying crime. In response to his questioning on that ninth day of the investigation, Wells said, "Susan became quiet. She dropped her head, and then she looked back up at me and asked if I would pray with her." Smith put her hands in Wells's, prayed with him, and burst into hysterical tears. Wells told the crowded courtroom that he prayed aloud that "all things would be revealed in time"; then he told Smith quietly, "It's time."[19]

His prayer broke Susan Smith. She blurted out, "My children are not all right," and she asked for his gun in a last desperate suicidal gesture. In the sole company of Sheriff Wells, Smith's words came tumbling out, faster even than she could write them down, detailing how she had wanted to die and wished to save her beloved children the pain of motherlessness by "ending [their] lives together." She told Wells that "she had never felt so low in her life," that she was "depressed," and that she'd intended "to go down that ramp with her children." Sobbing on the floor of the interview room, she looked, Wells testified, "like a child praying at bedtime."[20]

Rather than challenging this damning evidence of Smith's violent crimes, the defense team mined it by spending some time on Smith's written confession. Nine months after Smith confessed to murder in her girlish handwriting, the public got to hear more than the few lines that dealt with Tom Findlay when Smith's defense team asked Wells to read the entire confession for the court. The town's most respected law officer depicted for the court a remorseful, childlike woman who believed her children were better off in heaven. Although he was not asked about it on the stand, Wells later told Rick Bragg that he felt "sorry for [Smith], and [was] disgusted by the men who used her and in their own ways contributed to the tragedy."[21] Without ever delving into Smith's life beyond the nine days of the investigation, Wells established the image of Susan that would dominate the entire trial.

A series of law enforcement officers followed Wells to testify to the various details of the investigation. Then the witness many observers had been waiting for took the stand. Late on the second day of the trial, Tom Findlay, Smith's ex-boyfriend and the so-called "Catch" of Union, was sworn in. In a prosecutorial strategy focused very much on Smith's sexual behavior, Findlay constituted the one-man motive to murder. Amidst Bruck's numerous objections, Pope dragged detail after distasteful detail out of Findlay on the stand. Pope asked Findlay to read aloud his infamous break-up letter to Susan, which listed her children as one reason among many that they could not continue their relationship. The prosecutor repeatedly emphasized Smith's seeming obsession with Findlay. "Evidence" of this obsession included the fact that Smith occasionally went with Findlay and other co-workers to the sole bar in Union for drinks after work, she frequently wore a sweatshirt belonging to him, and she asked David Smith not to get angry if Findlay attempted to contact her during the kidnapping investigation.[22]

Bruck, in his cross-examination, carefully went back over the parts of Findlay's testimony that Pope, and most journalists over the past nine months, had purposefully ignored. Findlay testified to Smith's fear of her sometimes-violent husband, describing an incident in which David Smith had been hiding, uninvited, in Susan's house while Findlay and Susan were talking on the telephone. David "jumped out of the closet," grabbed the phone, and threatened Findlay, who was frightened enough to "start sleeping with a gun under his pillow." Countering the image of Susan Smith as a gold-digging party girl, Bruck established that she had never asked Findlay for money and that there were "multiple reasons for their break-up." In Findlay's estimation, Smith was also a good mother. He testified that Susan loved her children—"her kids were her world"—but he had also noticed on the afternoon of the murders that Susan was "acting suicidal." Bruck ended his questioning by asking Findlay to tell about the night of the boys' disappearance. Findlay told the hushed courtroom that, when he got the late-night phone call asking if he had heard the news about Susan Smith, he immediately thought, "Oh, my God, she's killed herself. . . . Oh, no, I thought, she had taken her life."[23]

Through Findlay, Pope established the "boyfriend motive," although the unhappy bachelor described a Susan Smith who was more sad than sexy. Pope then moved on to witnesses who could establish the more gruesome details of the murders. He called to the stand the diver who discovered the boys' bodies in the car at the bottom of John D. Long Lake, the crime-scene analyst who examined the Mazda after it was pulled from the water, and the forensic pathologist who performed the autopsies on the boys. Repeatedly, Pope tried to go through the shocking physical details of the murders, but Bruck quickly objected on the grounds that the defense did not dispute the cause of death.[24] Bruck's calm manner and his obvious disgust at the prosecution's taste for bloody details positioned him as the voice of decency amidst the angry clamor of the prosecution and the media circus lined up on Main Street.

This defense tactic worked surprisingly well. On the morning of the third day of the trial, July 20, 1995, the State surprised the court by resting their case in the guilt phase. This abrupt ending was primarily due to the judge's prohibition against presenting the more grisly forensic evidence against Smith. The defense proceeded with their witnesses that afternoon, beginning with Pete Logan, the SLED officer "known for his grandfatherly manner" who spent the most time with Susan during the kidnapping investigation.[25] Through Logan, assistant defense attorney Judy Clarke carefully established Susan's victimhood through a series of questions about David Smith. The father of the murdered boys was most certainly a victim in this case, but, as locals were well aware, he was not the perfect husband or father described in the national media. In his testimony, Logan painstakingly detailed a pattern of abuse. In the weeks preceding the murders, David Smith would show up randomly at Susan's house to demand sex and would storm off angrily if she refused. Susan confided to Logan her paranoia that David's jealousy had led him to place a tap on her phone. A Southern Bell employee later took the stand to confirm that Smith had asked that her phone line be checked for a tap the weekend before the murders; no tap or evidence of tampering was found.[26]

Logan also testified that Susan had filed for divorce in August of 1994 when, after four years of fighting and separations, she found out about David's longstanding affair with a Winn-Dixie co-worker. This fact may well have surprised out-of-town observers who had been consuming dramatic exposés about how Susan, not David, Smith had ruined her family by cheating on her spouse. Logan succeeded in adding the crucial image of an abused defendant to the "childlike," hysterical woman described by Wells. She was no merciless killer, he argued. After her confession, he said, Susan Smith exhibited "the greatest level of remorse" Logan had seen in over three decades in law enforcement.[27] Through these witnesses, the defense slowly constructed a new "Susan" out of the community's image of her as a damaged daughter and the expert depiction of her as psychologically traumatized by the men in her life.

The first of several key psychological experts, Carol Allison, a behaviorist who worked for the local branch of the FBI, also testified that afternoon. Allison echoed Wells's description of Susan as "childlike" the day of the confession. Indeed, the federal agent found herself playing an unexpected role: "I was a mother at times. She had collapsed in my lap. Sobbing uncontrollably, telling me what had happened to her children at her own hands, what she had done to them."[28] Smith, according to Wells, Logan, and Allison, was simultaneously a loving mother, a hurt child, and a suicidal depressive the afternoon of her confession.

Allison set the stage for the testimony of Dr. Arlene Andrews, a social worker from the University of South Carolina, who testified later that afternoon. In her assessment of Susan Smith, Dr. Andrews found a surprising amount of clinical depression in the family tree. Susan's maternal grandfather, paternal aunt, father, mother, and older brother had all been treated for depression in the past, an estimate of familial mental illness Andrews deemed "conservative," implying that the family was even more troubled than her complicated genealogical chart indicated.[29]

Dr. Andrews then turned to Susan herself, characterizing her suicide attempts as "childlike" but very serious. According to Andrews, Smith's dysfunctional relationships with both of her fathers caused her teenaged suicide attempts. She linked the first attempt, in which Susan tried to overdose on aspirin at the age of thirteen, to her biological father's suicide and to what a former teacher called Susan's resulting "obsession with the notion of suicide" in her early teens. Andrews linked Smith's second attempt, another overdose, with the molestation by her stepfather. The doctor dismissed Pope's insinuation that, because Susan took aspirin rather than something stronger, the attempt was more a "suicidal gesture," arguing that the staff of the ICU and the Psychology Unit at the local hospital took her very seriously. Pope implied that these "suicidal gestures" were desperate attempts to keep the attentions of several men, not actual death wishes. The doctor refused to budge on this issue under Pope's pressure. His persistent focus on "suicidal gestures" allowed Dr. Andrews to reiterate the seriousness of Susan's suicidality.[30]

Andrews laid the groundwork for the testimony of Dr. Seymour Halleck, a renowned forensic psychiatrist who was on the stand the entire next day. Dr.

Halleck's psychological assessment of Susan—replete with low self-esteem, depression, anxiety, extreme dependence, sexual exploitation, personality and mood disorders, dissociation, and possible auditory hallucinations—provided the court with convincing evidence of Smith's mental instability grounded in authoritative medical language. Dr. Halleck presented his analysis through a timeline of Susan's experiences going back to her early childhood. Halleck told the court that her parents' tumultuous, sometimes violent relationship characterized Smith's formative years. Halleck argued that, like his daughter, Susan Smith's biological father learned to mask his own problems, enabling later tragedy. After Harry Vaughan shot himself shortly after his divorce from Linda, the family explained to young Susan that "her father was in heaven." Halleck indicated that, at an early age, Smith had expressed a wish "to be in heaven with her father, even back then." Bruck paused after this statement from Halleck, letting the implicit reference to Smith's written confession, in which she expressed relief that her sons were with their "Heavenly Father," echo through the minds of the jurors.[31] According to young Susan, suicide was an acceptable option because it led to paradise.

Dr. Halleck moved seamlessly from Harry Smith's suicide to Susan's attempt on her own life at the age of thirteen. Rejecting Pope's assertions that her overdoses were the mere games of an attention-starved teenager, Halleck stated bluntly: "If Susan Smith had walked into my emergency room at the age of thirteen with this history, she either would have been immediately hospitalized, or a very intensive treatment program would have been arranged." Bruck moved the questioning to her molestation by her stepfather a few years later. Halleck informed the court that many victims of incest try to mitigate the trauma of their experiences by redefining the abuse as an "affair." "She feels almost fully responsible," he testified, "and in many ways the family treated her as if she was fully responsible." Susan Smith's other very typical response was to blame herself for what had happened. Smith's second suicide attempt, following an argument with her much-older lover at the age of eighteen, landed her in the hospital, where vomiting was induced to rid her body of a few dozen aspirin. Afterwards, she was "very eager to cover up this event and not make very much of it."[32] Dr. Halleck's testimony made clear that Smith had a decade-long history of failed suicide attempts, a pattern that perhaps made her failure to take her own life when she took her sons' more comprehensible.

This pattern of troubled behavior also indicated key aspects of Susan's everyday behavior, according to Dr. Halleck. Her "incredible need to please" and her loyalty to her family—even her stepfather, the primary source of her teen-aged trauma—made Susan hide her pain with smiles. Bruck gently steered Halleck in the direction of Susan's doomed marriage to David Smith. Halleck narrated a downward spiral in which Susan became "seriously depressed" after she and David separated for the final time just two months before the murders: "She sees herself as a single mother without much money. She is subject to David coming in and out of the house at random, at will, even though there was an official separation. David often comes and insists on having sex, which she complies with, but is in no way a consenting partner. She does not enjoy it."[33] Halleck put Susan's other sexual relationships at the time of the murders in the context of her desperation and confusion following her separation from her husband. Her "pervasive fear of being alone" stemmed from early childhood experiences. Smith told Halleck that she "thought about suicide just about every day" in the late summer and early fall of 1994, but that she tried "espe-cially hard in the community to put up a pretense or façade of being okay."[34]

Finally, Bruck walked Halleck through the night of the murders. That day at work, Susan approached Tom Findlay and confided to him, possibly untruthfully, that she had slept with his father. Several co-workers, includ-ing Findlay, witnessed her erratic, tearful behavior at the Conso plant that afternoon. Susan left work, made dinner for the boys, and called her mother to tell her they were coming over later that evening. At this time, Halleck explained, "Susan [was] frantic." She feared losing her marriage with David and the friendship of Tom Findlay (by that date their sexual relationship had already ended). Her anguish upset her sons, and she and the children cried together, alone in the home she had shared with her abusive husband. She left with the boys, driving "aimlessly" through the quiet town and into the sur-rounding countryside. Crying incessantly, Susan was shaking, biting her nails, and contemplating suicide as she drove through the dark woods surrounding Union. She reached a bridge on the highway and considered flinging herself and the boys into the Broad River, but she decided against it. She kept driving. Inevitably, she reached the turn-off to John D. Long Lake. During this time, according to Halleck, Susan concluded that she "had to die," and she did not want her children to suffer without a mother. She connected this fear to her own fatherless childhood and to the constant conflict between David and her own mother. Halleck emphasized Smith's "strong religious convictions," argu-ing that, cliché or not, she "firmly believed the children would go to heaven."[35]

Bruck asked Halleck about Susan's much-discussed carjacking lie—the public moral failure for which she also seemed to be on trial. Susan's vague answers to Halleck in their counseling sessions indicated to him that she had "dissociated" at the time of the murders: she had blocked out her memory of the children, the car, and the lake. In her dissociative state, she formed an alibi; although she did not remember it, "as she was running up the hill [from the lake], she was making up a story." Susan's lie, Halleck argued, was another kind of nightmare to which she was bound, a "very sensitive and very romantic and gripping story" that had unintended cultural resonance. The carjacking lie was another manifestation of her mental illness rather than an intentionally vicious deception. In Halleck's personal interviews with Smith, she had not tried to gain his sympathy. She consistently "portrayed herself as a bad person, an evil person," to the doctor. Bruck ended with a question about Susan's current mental state, which Halleck unequivocally characterized as "suicidal" and "depressed."[36]

Pope focused his questions in his cross-examination on Susan's sexual history. Honing in on the molestation, Pope tried to paint a picture of Smith as a teenaged seductress. Stating first that he did not "condone" Beverly Russell's actions, Pope asked why Smith might blame herself for the incest. He implied that she crawled into Russell's lap at the age of fifteen, inviting sexual contact. Again, he characterized the abuse as an "affair."[37] Dr. Halleck refused to consider Pope's characterization, focusing instead on Smith's fragile personality and her need to please others at all costs. By this point, Pope's focus on this most famous, sexualized image of Susan Smith seemed almost rote, as if he knew that public perceptions were changing daily with the media coverage of the trial. He led the court through the carjacking lie once more and handed the witness back over to Bruck for his redirect examination.

Bruck followed Pope's lead and questioned Halleck about Susan's sexuality. Susan's sexual activity, according to Halleck, was a direct result of "her early abuse experiences and partly related to her wish to please." Smith constantly gave gifts to the men she dated, yet she could "hardly recall a time that any man had given her anything." Her sexual behavior indicated psychological neediness, not wanton promiscuity. In fact, Halleck testified, she did not even enjoy it: "Most of the time she felt just awful after sex, often cried after sex.[38] Smith's sexual behavior was evidence of her "severe dependent personality disorder," not proof that she was the scheming slut depicted by the prosecution.

Dr. Halleck established Susan's mental illness with the language and authority of a renowned medical specialist. He did not connect Smith's mental illness explicitly with her maternity, which was, according to many witnesses, the only happy aspect of her life. Rather, he, along with other witnesses, linked it to her exploitation by various men. Bruck supplemented Halleck's diagnoses with the very brief testimony of a few local witnesses who had known Smith for many years and had seen her depressive disorder and needy personality in action. Iris Rogers, a family friend who knew Susan in her early childhood, found her to be a "sad" child who was "unhappy," "scared at times," and "stared into space" at a friend's birthday party. Rogers speculated that this early depression was a result of her parents' troubled relationship. Debbie Green, the high-school teacher in whom Smith confided about her stepfather's abuse, said she believed that Smith was suicidal in the tenth grade and that, although she was a good student, she was also the "most troubled" one she had ever taught.[39] The defense then rested their case in the guilt phase.

That night, NBC, for the first time, favored the defense in their coverage. None of the local testimony made the national news that night. Halleck's impact as an expert determined what stuck in the minds of observers across the nation as they, as well as the jurors, decided Smith's culpability that weekend. On NBC's *Evening News*, reporter Bob Dotson described Smith's "failed suicide" attempt as she drove around the night of October 25, 1994. The "graphic defense testimony" included details about "David Smith coming in and out of the house, demanding sex." Television screens across the nation showed headshots of David Smith, Beverly Russell, and Tom and Cary Findlay lined up over a courtroom sketch of Smith looking prim and withdrawn, her face pale and putty above a wide, high-necked collar. Dotson concluded, "She seems much older and heavier than when she was arrested, not a cunning killer."[40] This was a new "Susan," indeed.

That Saturday, after five long days of testimony, the attorneys delivered their closing arguments in the guilt phase. Late that afternoon, after a little over two hours of deliberation, the jurors returned their verdict: Susan Smith was guilty of two counts of homicide, "one for each boy." Few observers were surprised. Judge Howard described the first phase of the trial as essentially a "slow guilty plea"; even the defense team had not challenged Smith's culpability. They knew that their real fight was not the verdict, but the upcoming sentence. The focus immediately became the death penalty, which reporters argued would be an "uphill battle" for the prosecution based on precedent: Union County jurors had never sent anyone to South Carolina's electric chair, and the state of South Carolina had executed only two women in the past century (both in the 1940s).[41]

By all accounts, the penalty phase was the most difficult week of the

Smith trial. After losing the guilt phase, David Bruck and Judy Clarke honed their strategy in the sentencing. They kept expert testimony to a minimum. Their real case now rested with the local representatives of the community who pleaded for Susan's life. Rick Bragg later explained that it was as if the entire community were on trial: "You know, you would interview people at the—I think it was a Wal-Mart, I'm not sure, but you'd interview people in parking lots of grocery stores, you know. And we had—we would—once the trial started, then the dynamic of the town became, was pulled into the court-room—became a part of the testimony. And it was very much like covering—and this sounds cold-hearted, but it's almost like covering a sporting event. You sit in the bleachers, and everything is played out before you. And the social dynamic of the town was drawn into the courtroom in that fashion."[42] In his daily coverage of the trial, Bragg explained that all of the men of Union who had abused Susan Smith emotionally and physically in the past played a key role in this trial: "The community, as much as the jury, is trying those people, even as the outside world judges the town." Union's protectiveness over Susan Smith was, according to Bragg, palpable and perhaps a little bit contagious. "Talking about it after the fact is—you know, it's always easy to talk about," he explained a decade later. "When you're writing it above the machine shop in Union, South Carolina, and you're fighting off ants, it's different."[43]

This reflexive community protectiveness was not enough to save a defendant's life—small-town juries have certainly been known to mete out capital sentences. This was a specific kind of paternal protection, a defensive reaction to both the national vitriol and the local belief that, long before she drove to the lake that fall night, the community had failed Susan Smith. This failure was proved daily in the courtroom as witnesses detailed the various abuses Smith had endured for almost two decades. The defensive tactic of interspersing expert psychological testimony with local voices made Smith's problems more real, more approachable. Neighbors and townspeople translated, in the language of their community, the array of diagnoses detailed by the doctors. The defense team relied on local voices of authority, supplemented by psychological experts, to make their case against the death penalty.

David Bruck took considerable time with his opening statement in the sentencing phase, delivering it in his characteristically calm manner. He began by reassuring the jurors that the defense did not question the guilty verdict of the previous weekend. The power given the jurors in this capital punishment case, Bruck implied, was the power to play God and end lives, but the question was not whether Susan Smith should be punished. She was already being punished; she already lived "in a lake of fire" in her prison cell, ruminating over her sons. The jurors knew by this point about Smith's history of depression and suicidal tendencies, which were only exacerbated by her crimes, imprisonment, and trial. Reminding them of her suicidal tendencies, Bruck told the jurors, "her life is over and death would be a relief."[44]

Bruck asked his listeners not to let the carjacking lie and their own personal senses of betrayal cloud their judgment of the tearful young woman seated before them. Echoing Dr. Halleck, he argued that the lie itself was a manifestation of her mental instability. To hear Smith's lie was to glimpse her mental illness. To focus on it, as the prosecution had in the guilt phase with their poster-board calendar of the nine deceitful days, was to ignore a lifetime of psychological traumas—"the twenty-three year story that led to the water's edge that night." Bruck argued that the prosecution's new focus in the sentencing phase—the memory of Michael and Alex and their father's enormous grief—made understanding Susan Smith's past even more imperative.[45]

Bruck acknowledged that the Smith case, "in its very nature," roused extreme emotions, but he urged the jurors not to act in anger. "Grief is not a monopoly of the prosecution's side," he said, justifying the numerous local witnesses he would question in the coming days. The jury was charged with deciding "if there [was] any value in Susan," and with making "the best decision for the family of Michael and Alex Smith; the best decision for the prosecution; the decision for Susan; and the best decision for [their] community of Union."[46] This, then, was what the entire trial would hinge upon: would this strategic combination of local and psychological authority save Susan Smith's life?

The state proceeded with their witnesses that afternoon, calling a series of people who underscored points already made in the guilt phase about Smith's "strange and inappropriate" behavior during the kidnapping investigation. In all likelihood, Pope used these repetitive witnesses to take up the afternoon so that David Smith and the state's forensic experts would have the entire following day for testimony. Pope relied heavily upon victim impact statements to make his case for the death penalty, a strategy reflective of changes in criminal trials in the late twentieth century. Elayne Rapping argues that there was a major shift from "defendant-centered" to "victim-centered" trials, so that, by the 1990s, the impact of the crime on its victims—defined broadly as anyone related to or familiar with the victim(s) of a violent crime—was more important to the outcome of a trial than the mentality of the perpetrator. To this end, "victim impact statements," or prepared testimony in which friends and family members of the victim tell the jury how their lives have been negatively altered by the crime, began to take precedence in trials, especially in penalty phases. The use of these statements to make the case for harsher punishment of criminals indicates, in Rapping's estimation, a "reactionary, often even bloodthirsty," attempt at getting revenge.[47] Victim impact statements are generally graphic and emotional. The Smith trial was no exception.

If there was a point during which the prosecution could have stemmed the rising tide of sympathy for Susan Smith, it would have been David Smith's day on the stand. By all accounts, David's testimony was the most emotional of the trial. Spectators, jurors, and attorneys wept openly, prompting Judge William Howard to call a recess. Some media outlets featured a return to the "boyfriend motive" as part of their public display of sympathy for the anguished father. Through tears, David listed many of the things he had looked forward to teaching his sons, describing Michael as a "daddy's boy" who was "very protective" of his little brother Alex. Pope walked him through the agony of the investigation and the searing revelation of Smith's confession. David, frequently pausing to weep on the witness stand, showed the jury "tear-smudged" pictures of their two little boys. "All my hopes, all my dreams that I had planned for the rest of my life came to an end that day," he sobbed. "I don't know what I'm supposed to do without my kids." One female juror reportedly wept, and, along with the rest of the courtroom, Susan Smith shed tears as she "rocked in her attorney's arms."[48]

David Bruck declined to cross-examine David Smith, an empathetic move that won points for the defense even as every heart in the courtroom went out to the father. He later explained to reporters that Susan Smith had asked him "not to hurt David anymore" by questioning him, and he granted her request. As David Smith exited the witness box, Bruck softly wished him luck, and the tear-stained witness thanked him. But the David Smith of the trial coverage was not the same distraught father that the public remembered weeping over his boys' single coffin. Media accounts of his testimony, including Rick Bragg's in the *New York Times,* listed David's physical abuse of Susan in which he, by his own admission, "chased," "tackled," and "dragged her out of bed and onto the porch" on separate occasions. Few reporters failed to mention Smith's lucrative book deal for a memoir of his life with Susan. Locals were eager to get David's side of the story, too. The book arrived in bookstores the very week of his appearance on the witness stand. Kerhulas Books on Main Street received

150 copies the day before David testified and another 250 on the day of his court appearance; by noon, only 6 copies remained. Observers speculated that the grieving father had, like the media that had overtaken Union, capitalized on the tragedy when he "pocketed some $20,000."[49] Although some locals said they understood why he might capitalize on the tragedy, the prosecution's star witness in the sentencing phase received a less than laudatory reception in the national media, even as journalists acknowledged his singular grief.

After David Smith testified, Tommy Pope presented his coup de grâce: reenactment videos of the drowning of the boys. Weeks before, the prosecution had staged a reenactment with divers and a car with "childs'-eye-view" cameras in it in order to recreate the crime. Although Bruck argued against its admission until he "was blue in the face," the judge allowed the video to be entered into evidence and viewed in the courtroom. A forensic pathologist and a SLED examiner explained the manner of death in detail before the viewing. The recreation, Bruck argued, was incredibly misleading. He later revealed that the viewing of the videos was one of the points at which he truly worried that the jury might give Susan Smith the death penalty.

> To present this whole thing in brilliant sunshine, as if that's what Susan saw as she did it, just completely misrepresents, you know, the total blackness, physical and emotional, in which this occurred. But . . . you see the divers all clinging to the car as it's sinking, and you think how easy it would have been to rescue the children even when the car had gone into the lake. You know, none of that is true, but it makes it look that way. So in a way, I thought it was one of those very accurate recreations that was actually a complete distortion of the crime. And the judge had been inclined to keep it out, and in the end he let it in. It was . . . it was pretty gruesome to watch. You know, you see the water rising over the camera, it makes you just feel like you're drowning.[50]

The defense did not dispute the facts of the crime at all, but the courtroom viewing of the video, timed carefully to follow David Smith's testimony, could have proved devastating to the defense.

After emotionally exhausting everyone in the courtroom, the prosecution rested that afternoon. The next morning, people lined up outside the courtroom to hear the defense present the final case against the death penalty; about one hundred spectators were already waiting outside in the ninety-degree heat before the court's 9:30 opening time. Even with seating for two hundred, some were left waiting outside hoping to get a seat after the lunch recess. Although many observers drove in from out of town to see the famous trial in action, the gallery was generally filled with Union folks and reporters.[51] That day, a series of townspeople testified to Susan Smith's girlishness, her teenaged depression, her love for her sons, and her piety. They spoke to the court about Christian forgiveness, laying groundwork for the afternoon testimony of Beverly Russell.

Guilt and grief were written on his face as Russell took the stand. The shamed community leader asked his neighbors for that most difficult kind of mercy: for Susan and for himself. If there was any doubt about the veracity of the sexual misconduct charges against Beverly Russell, he erased it with his tearful testimony. He described the act in biblical terms, arguing tearfully that the town was reaping the tragedy that he had sown years before. On the stand, Russell read aloud a letter he had written to Susan in prison on Father's Day, a few weeks before her trial began. In it, he took the responsibility for Susan's crimes: "I must tell you how sorry I am for letting you down as a father. I had responsibilities to you in which I utterly failed. Many say this failure had nothing with October 25th [the day Susan killed her sons]. But I believe differently. Of course had I known at the time what the result of my sin would be, I would have mustered the strength to behave according to my responsibilities. . . . When I came into the family, you leaned on me and looked to me for support and love. . . . To see unfolding before our eyes the principle of reaping and sowing. . . . I want you to know that you don't have all the guilt in this tragedy."[52] The positioning of Susan Smith as a victimized little girl completed the cycle of sins: Russell sinned against her, and she sinned against her sons. Both had sinned against the community. But, Bruck explained later, prompted by the tragedy in which he believed he had a hand, Russell finally "did what a father should do" by revealing his sins to his neighbors.[53]

Smith's former math teacher testified that day, as well. Kay Dillard was one of the teachers in whom Susan Smith confided when her stepfather began sexually abusing her during her junior year of high school. Dillard helped Smith find a local pastor to talk to about the abuse, and they kept in touch after Smith graduated from high school. She described Smith as a "great," "loving" mother of "happy, well-adjusted children" who "lit up when she came to get them." Dillard told the court that Susan's sons were her life and that she "always thought Michael and Alex would be her salvation." The teacher and friend argued that a part of her would die if the jury sentenced Smith to death, because in her heart, she would "have to live with maybe if [she'd] done this or that," she could have prevented the crime. There was, according to Dillard, a direct link between the prior depression and abuse and the murders. Reverend Tom Currie took the stand later that day and made the same connection. The respected minister described the letter he had written to Tommy Pope months before, asking that he not seek the death penalty, which would only bring more "trauma to the community."[54]

After this stirring local testimony, the defense put on the stand Dr. David Heatherly, who played a unique crossover role as both a local and an expert witness. Dr. Heatherly was a respected family therapist. Unlike some of the other experts, he had actually known Susan Smith as a girl. He was able to introduce the court personally to Susan as a depressed teen: he had treated Smith in 1987 after she came forward about her stepfather's sexual abuse. Heatherly firmly fused the troubled, sweet child of local testimony with the more recent psychological assessments of the criminal mother. Her father's suicide caused Susan to "stop growing emotionally," so that her psychological growth was stunted at the level of an eager-to-please little girl. According to Heatherly, Smith's traumatic youth and her untreated "adjustment disorder with a depressive mood" bred her unintentional criminal behavior—an opinion he carefully couched in moral, rather than medical, terms. "Susan is not an evil person," he explained. "A lot of things happened that placed her in that situation."[55]

This "sweet," "needy" girl depicted by Heatherly was not some distant "Susan" of the past. She was currently under constant "mental observation and suicide watch" in prison, according to one of her prison guards who took the stand after Heatherly. Bruck's decision to follow Heatherly, who knew Susan as a very troubled teen, with Officer Mungo, who knew her as a suicidal prisoner, posited a direct line of causation between these two stages of Smith's life—a connection that eclipsed her teenaged love affairs, her failed marriage, and Tom Findlay and positioned her squarely as a victim. As Mungo implied when she spoke of Smith's reliance on the Bible behind bars, she was a victim searching for salvation.[56]

Finally, the defense questioned Reverend Toni White, a chaplain from a neighboring town who counseled Susan in prison in the months before her trial. Reverend White, who served as Susan's prison chaplain, told the court in no uncertain terms that Smith was, in many respects, still a child: "The thing that strikes you about Susan is that she is very childlike, although she is certainly a woman. But she has a certain vulnerability about her. . . . What I find is that she herself is very easily manipulated." The chaplain testified that Susan felt extremely remorseful about the murders, and echoed local witnesses' charge that capital punishment would just cause more pain for the community.[57] White tied together the many themes of the defense: victimization by the men in Susan's life, the expert medicalization of her past experiences, community guilt for her troubled past, religious forgiveness, and the necessity of future community protection of this wounded girl in the form of a life sentence.

Closing arguments took up the entire last day of the trial. Prosecutor Tommy Pope seemed to take a cue from the defense and emphasized the jurors' roles as guardians of their community. Pope appealed directly to the jury's sense of their wronged community, calling Michael and Alex "Union boys" who would never grow up to play football for Union High, or teach local children, or parent their own sons. He urged the jurors to act on their sense of outrage and betrayal: "So what you have to do now is speak, the twelve of you, as the voice of this community," and publicly state the value, in terms of Smith's life, of Union's lost boys.[58] Pope's statement was direct, energetic, and brief. The jurors, he implied, knew what they had to do to protect their community.

In his closing argument, in a voice so quiet that the jury initially complained of not being able to hear him, David Bruck used the images provided to him by the people of Union to make the final case for the defense. His ninety-minute summation rested upon the idea of Christian forgiveness, psychological illness, and community responsibility for this fatally lost young woman. Although the judge could not allow Bruck to tell the jury how a death sentence for Susan would weigh on him personally, he nevertheless spoke the language of the community. Punishment, he argued, was not really the issue in this phase of the trial; God was already torturing Smith for her sins. Of Smith's personal hell, he said evenly, "This young woman is in the lake of fire. That is the remorse, the grief, the shame she feels. And it's not going to go away any time soon. That is her punishment if you show her what is sometimes called mercy." Bruck led the jury through the chronology of Susan's life, replete with family suicide, depression, incest, and abuse at the hands of her husband. Smith was constantly troubled, "so dependent on her mother, just like a little kid."[59]

In a few minutes, Bruck argued, the jury would decide the fate of this suffering young woman, and when they did, he wanted them to know they were not the first to attempt such a judgment. Referencing the Bible upon which they had all sworn, Bruck told the story recorded by "a court reporter named John" about the "death penalty proceeding in the Gospel." Jesus confronted a crowd, waiting with stones in hand, who had gathered to kill an adulterous woman. Despite their clamor, and the fact that she was guilty of adultery, John stopped them with the words: "He that is without sin among you, let him first cast the stone at her." Bruck told the jury that these people, who dispersed at John's words and left the woman unharmed, must have wondered if they had done the right thing by following their hearts. "In other words," Bruck explained, "each of you have a stone." The choice the jury was to make was between heeding the angry crowds and stoning the offending woman, or listening to the local, medical, and religious authorities in the courtroom who urged them to take responsibility for the young woman who had been abused repeatedly in their midst.

Susan Smith's mental state, Bruck argued, was the jury's responsibility. He asked them to extend to Susan the community protection they had failed to provide in the past.

> Despite everything that you've heard, I'm going to ask you to watch over Susan too. She doesn't know that she can go to the people who care about her. That, as you heard, is part of what is wrong with her. That is part of her illness. She said in her confession, "I never felt so lonely and so sad in my entire life." Her judgment is impaired, but yours is not. So this time you go to her.
>
> She will be all alone again soon. . . . She will be all alone soon to resume her awful, awful struggle with suicide. Just do this for her. Don't leave her just yet. Stay with her just a little while. Watch over her.[60]

With these words—the last spoken in the courtroom before the judge's sentencing instructions to the jury—the defense offered the compelling vision of an abused daughter, not a violent woman. Judge Howard delivered his instructions, and the twelve men and woman adjourned to decide the fate of the nation's most famous mother.

7

FROM "MONSTER" TO "MENTALLY ILL"

OR TWO AND a half hours, the jury of nine men and three women argued over how to properly punish Susan Smith. The facts of the crime were undisputed; instead, they went over the haunting traumas from Smith's past one last time. Angry words were exchanged; several jurors cried; and when they passed around the Maxwell House coffee can in which they slipped their votes, one man initially held out for the death penalty. Robbie Christian, a thirty-one-year-old textile worker and father, later showed reporters the packet of antacids he'd had in his pocket the entire trial. "I've been eating these every day," he explained unhappily. His inner conflict as a juror stemmed from his belief that, even after she let go of the emergency brake, Susan Smith could have saved her sons by following them into the water. To Christian, those crucial seconds when she decided to run up the hill rather than wade into the lake made all the difference. In the end, however, his fellow jurors reported having "little trouble" convincing Christian that capital punishment would not be just, and that such a sentence would benefit no one. "Let her live and let her conscience guide her," explained juror John Dunn, who worked at the local Chevy dealership. As the Clerk of Court read the verdict, Bruck held Susan Smith close to him. She closed her eyes as her family burst into tears and hugged their friends and neighbors.[1]

With their unanimous decision that Susan Smith should serve a life sentence for her crimes, the "trial of the century in the Carolinas" came to an end. Although she was found guilty, the sentence of life in prison can be seen as a "win" for the defense because they successfully avoided the death penalty. Judge Howard thanked the jury, telling them how "proud" the "community" was of their service. "Under our system," he told them, "the jury becomes not just the fact finders but the soul searchers, if you will, of the community."[2] As Howard formally sentenced Susan Smith to life in prison a few minutes later, "thunder rolled outside and rain poured as a summer storm cloud passed over," perhaps signaling a fresh start for the community and its infamous daughter.[3]

Observers and journalists streamed out of the courtroom and into the steamy summer rain, and the town breathed a collective sigh of relief. Reactions on Main Street were largely subdued, although speculation about why the jurors saved Smith's life circulated immediately. Their decision was not based on pity, but rather on justice. Judge Howard believed that the defense portrayed her convincingly as a child "who never matured emotionally" due to the various traumas in her life. When a child commits a crime, society inevitably looks to the parents; David Bruck later argued that "many people carried these burdens of doubt and guilt" so heavily that each local who testified "thought maybe it was something that they had done." Tommy Pope agreed, calling it "Union's case," a "truly unique" trial that drew in "the whole fabric of the community." The facts, jurors believed, showed that the "mistreatment by her stepfather, Beverly Russell, and others" played a role in her crimes. "I just feel really bad for Susan Smith because of the way that she's been treated, the way that men used her," one juror told the Rock Hill Herald. Juror Deborah Benvenuti, a dry cleaner whose own daughter had been sexually assaulted in the past, agreed that the jury was swayed by Smith's "rough life." Beverly Russell, they believed, "bore great responsibility for her actions." Benvenuti explained, "He was supposed to have been a father figure. . . . he should have been punished for what he did to her." In the end, Bruck believed, "the jury realized that she truly could have been any of their daughters."[4]

In fact, according to the exit interviews of jurors, it was not just Beverly Russell who deserved punishment in this trial. All of the community adults who failed young Susan bore responsibility. "There are lot more people in this case who should have been punished," argued juror Leroy Belue, a local butcher. "She never received the help she should have." Juror Michael Roberts, a productions manager at a local textile plant, later summed up the sense of community guilt, saying simply, "It's a reflection on the parents when the kid goes wrong." He told the Charleston Post and Courier: "If anybody hears a cry for help from somebody young, they need to take it seriously. . . . She had asked for help, but nobody knew the seriousness of it." Over a decade later, a spokesperson for the Union County Chamber of Commerce agreed: "Had it not been for what the jury perceived as the failure of the system as a young person, Susan would have gotten the death penalty." Some locals went even further, arguing that Smith's abusers should have been the ones on trial. Dot Frost of Union placed the blame squarely on the shoulders of a society that did not extend aid to the troubled teenager: "They should go get the ones that hurt her—and they hurt her like hell."[5]

Over the next few days, Union tried its best to return to normal. The media abandoned the town, returning Main Street to an avenue of empty storefronts and few pedestrians. Although the vans, scaffolding, and wires were gone, the clamor for blood could still be heard in some of the national headlines. Despite the mitigating evidence provided by the defense, *Newsweek* reported after her trial that 65 percent of readers believed that Susan Smith should have received the death penalty for her crimes. But most of the media had toned down their angry rhetoric, and reports reflected the fact that Union was in a forgiving, and a forgetting, mood. The following Sunday, Reverend Tom Currie reiterated the defense team's closing argument, inviting the innocent among his parishioners to cast the fabled stones.[6] No one did. In Union, the Susan Smith drama had transformed from the sickening case of an evil mother to the troubling story of an abused daughter during the nine months between the murders and the trial. Paradoxically, given the nature of this crime, their narrative was more about fathers and daughters than it was about mothers and sons. This local version of Smith fed directly into the other important image of her at her trial: the mentally ill mother. This final image called upon the controversial legal script of psychological victimization. Together, these two scripts formed a new "Susan," one that fit a neotraditional narrative of female immaturity and mental instability.

This image saved Smith's life, and it wholly dictated the way that Union viewed its most famous resident. Its staying power in the national media, however, was limited, possibly because most reporters left Union immediately after Judge Howard announced Smith's sentence. Because he hung around Union for a few days, gauging the reactions of the community, it was Rick Bragg of the *New York Times* who elevated Sheriff Howard Wells to the status of nationally known father-hero in a lengthy profile published the week after the sentencing. Wells is many things in this account: a local leader, a national hero for solving the crime, an impeccable, by-the-book lawman. But he is, above all, an ideal father, the kind of protector that Susan Smith never had. Bragg described for readers how Wells, the "killer's only confidant," played the role of confessor to Susan Smith when she finally broke down after nine long days of lies. He "held her and prayed with her," and then he "tricked her with a small lie of his own," explaining to Smith that the scene of the alleged carjacking was under drug surveillance, and they knew her Mazda had never even come close to that intersection that night. This piece of false information, meant to elicit a confession from Smith, worked; Wells's "lie and a prayer" captured a killer and ended the nationwide manhunt, making him a national hero and a model for other law enforcement officials.[7]

When he spoke publicly of Smith's confession after the trial, Wells described a delicate parallel investigation in which officers searched for the alleged carjacker while simultaneously turning their suspicion on the family and especially on Susan Smith, the only "witness" to the crime. A bond developed between the "weeping mother and a doubting sheriff." Although the media offered a host of other images, Wells told Bragg that he was aware of Smith's mental fragility from the very beginning.

> Mr. Wells says he has no doubt that he and other investigators walked a tightrope with Mrs. Smith's mental state and that as the inquiry closed around her, she planned to kill herself. For nine days she lived in a hell of her own making, surrounded by weeping, doting relatives she had betrayed in the worst way. "She had no one to turn to," he said.
>
> So although he was her hunter, he also became the person she could lean on, rely on, trust.

It was a role he served in the community, as well. Locals told Bragg that they liked Wells because he was "one of them." He had worked in the mills with people like Susan Smith's father, but he had bridged the historical divide between mill and town by serving as a law enforcement officer. Bragg clearly admired his multifaceted role in Union's society: "He knows what it feels like to work eight hours a day in the nerve-straining clatter and roar of the textile mills that dominate Union's economy," and he had worked as a deputy and a wildlife officer before being elected sheriff.[8]

According to Bragg, Wells's pivotal paternal role in this case was one he often sought. Because they had no children of their own, the Wellses were godparents to the children of friends and neighbors, including, incredibly, Susan's brother Scotty Vaughan's children. "The Smith case," wrote Bragg, "pitted a man who wants children against a woman who threw hers away." Throughout the investigation and the trial, Wells was visibly protective of Susan Smith, often shielding her from the waiting media cameras with his own jacket. Wells believed a trial would be damaging to Union, and he personally asked the prosecutor to avoid it after Pope announced his decision to seek the death penalty. He later explained: "I am a mirror image of the people I represent. Government leaders, professional people, people from all walks of life, clergy. . . . You have a person who had confessed, who is willing to plead guilty, so why go through with it? It will be bad for this community." The good sheriff spoke for his community, and many observers clearly admired his role in the case. Bragg wrote in the idiom of the community, and through his profile of their haloed sheriff, he disseminated the local, paternal vision of Smith as a damaged daughter one last time.[9]

Although some media outlets still clung to the *Peyton Place*–Southern Gothic narrative of the small town's secrets and "down-home dirty laundry," most had altered their opinions in response to the two fused images—Smith as troubled daughter, and Smith as mentally ill mother—that characterized the trial. Surprisingly, it was NBC, the network that consistently provided the most sensationalized television coverage throughout the trial, that best encapsulated Union's perspective in the immediate aftermath of the trial. Although the headline, for good measure or just lack of imagination, called the case "Southern Gothic" one last time, Bob Dotson's final report from Union was sympathetic rather than sensational. Dotson argued that it was more than just guilt over the airing of its secrets, or instinctive protection of one of its own citizens, that kept the tiny town of Union from sentencing Susan Smith to death. Union might never be the same again, because the community had failed to protect the children in their midst—and they meant Susan Smith, not just her sons: "For a month its secrets were broadcast in unflinching graphic detail, the town's problems laid bare, and worst of all, in this close-knit village where most everyone is related, no one kept Susan Smith from being sexually abused as a child."[10]

In this report, Dotson rightly argued that the Smith trial was a battle of images: was Susan Smith a scheming vixen, or was she a spiraling victim? Some legal experts argue that the latter is always the more likely option when the defendant is female. This is the key to the "chivalry hypothesis," in which women are perceived as receiving more lenient treatment throughout the legal process. This hypothesis is dubious as a general criminological rule, and at any rate, there are major exceptions. If a woman commits a crime that is traditionally considered to be a masculine act, or if she commits a crime that goes against the culture's notions of proper womanhood, the "chivalry hypothesis" no longer applies. Ann Jones, who wrote the definitive book on female murderers in the United States, found that "traditionally masculine offenses," like homicide, generally incur harsher sentences for women. And when that homicide further violates our notion of "what women are supposed to do" by involving violence toward children, there really is no rulebook. A review of the trials of filicidal women in the United States reveals erratic legal punishments. No trend, and certainly no "chivalry," is discernible.[11]

Jones's findings reveal the flip side of the legal "chivalry": the "evil woman hypothesis," in which women who step out of their proper gender roles in any way are rewarded with *harsher* legal punishment than men who commit similar crimes, violent or not. Conformity to gender roles appears to have some benefits in the legal process. When courts do treat women more leniently, scholars argue that the lighter sentence is often based on the "paternalistic attitudes of prosecutors and judges who strongly believe that women are the weaker sex and should be afforded protection." If, for example, the offending woman is a wife or "especially a mother," juries almost cannot help but to consider these roles when judging her. Jurors supposedly judge evidence, but often they are actually "studying character." This explains the prosecution's enormous interest in Susan's sex life, which had nothing to do with her guilt or innocence. Indeed, capital punishment can be seen in this case as having a gendered social and political purpose: serious punishment of "fallen" women, argues one legal theorist, "has always been integral to enforcement of the boundaries of the 'good' girls' and women's place in patriarchal society."[12]

Although they are slightly off the mark when applied to the Smith case, these two criminological models—chivalry and the "evil woman hypothesis"—are instructive. Simply put, regardless of her actual crime, if a female defendant can be made to conform to the cultural ideals of femininity, it appears that she is more likely to escape harsh punishments. In the context of the New Right 1990s, conformity to female ideals meant playing the part of the "new mom," a virtually impossible role for Susan Smith to recapture. Impossible, that is, if Smith were in her right mind. The successful portrayal of Smith as mentally ill (and thus deserving of some leniency) required that she appear to be a girl who had tried desperately to stay within the boundaries of proper femininity (although the various abusive men in her life pushed her far beyond those boundaries). The only remaining way to position Smith within the bonds of appropriate womanhood was to depict her as a fragile, weak victim who, rather than seeking to do away with her children, had in fact been trying to save them from her own life of misery.[13]

This timely expert positioning of Smith was a legal strategy that would not have been likely to work in previous decades. By the 1990s, a new legal discourse had developed that called for leniency in punishments of psychologically disturbed individuals. Scholar Elayne Rapping first discovered the existence of this legal "narrative battleground" while watching the televised trial of the Menendez brothers, who murdered their parents in California in 1989. The defense team in the case challenged the prosecution's personal attack on the brothers as spoiled brats or "bad seeds."

> The defense—in the persons of two impressive female attorneys—managed, without really challenging "the facts" of the prosecution case, to present a wholly different narrative, this one based on a whole *different* set of relevant facts (the evidence of child abuse) and an oppositional set of ideas about gender and generational violence within the patriarchal family (ideas feminists made public). . . . The defense did this by masterfully reorganizing jury *perceptions* not only of what facts might be in question in the case but of what narratives and assumptions about the patriarchal family the jury should be using to gauge the guilt of the defendants.[14]

Rapping explains that "the Menendez defense centered largely on issues of emotional, physical, and sexual child abuse by a brutally authoritarian patriarch," showing a clear indebtedness to "issues of gender, race, family dysfunction and abuse, gay rights, and other issues politicized by the sixties' social movements." The brothers' defense team created a "counternarrative" in which the perpetrators were also the victims of the very people they killed. Their first trial ended with a hung jury, split precisely along gender lines, with female jurors sympathizing with the allegedly abused boys. Rapping argued that those who did not watch the trial on television were "outraged" that the boys were not found guilty, but those who did watch it, "especially women and college students—came to see a situation that looked very different from the one they had originally assumed—once the issue of sexual abuse became a central theme."[15]

This intricate process of the "reorganization of jury perceptions" played a critical role in the Susan Smith trial. Some legal experts derided this approach as the "abuse excuse." Dick Harpootlian argued during the first week of Smith's trial that psychiatric experts can often be "about as valuable as somebody reading Tarot cards."[16] To keep a narrow focus on Smith's violent crime, the prosecution needed to focus solely on the day that Smith reported being carjacked, but they ventured further into the past when they delved into her sexual history. This proved to be a miscalculation that opened the door for all sorts of expert witnesses to speculate on her long-term mental state before the guilt phase was even over (this kind of expert testimony generally characterizes the sentencing phase, when the defense attempts to establish mitigating factors to avoid the death penalty). Smith's defense team, on the other hand, consistently emphasized facts of her life stretching all the way back to the age of six, when her father killed himself. This lengthier narrative made her crimes the endpoint of a very long history of abuse and depression rather than the rash violence of a spurned woman. For the Menendez brothers, the strategy ultimately resulted in guilty sentences, followed by life imprisonment rather than the death penalty. The use of this "counter-narrative" in their famous, televised trial resulted in unprecedented public debating of a new legal strategy.

At the same time, Rapping also charts the rise of a new "law and order" mentality that called for harsher criminal punishments centered on a heroic, protector role of the state (as represented by law enforcement officials and prosecutors). Gone was the defense attorney hero of yore. As seen on the televised trials on CourtTV and prime time reality shows like *Cops*, 1990s viewers were in the mood for revenge than rehabilitation. The mood was exemplified in the popularity of *America's Most Wanted*, an interactive tabloid-type show that asked for viewers' aid in locating violent criminals. Rapping argues that this kind of television show created an "us and them" mentality: "they" were the "dark armies of anti-social predators," while viewers were "good solid citizens" and "middle-class families" united in their "fear of crime." American television's longest-running crime drama, *Law & Order*, featured a similar divide between criminals and "regular" people, portrayed through the perspective of law enforcement and state prosecutors. The title of this show alone exemplifies the state-as-hero mentality.[17]

More than just idle entertainment, these shows reflected the New Right mentality that underwrote the exoneration of Bernie Goetz, the paranoia of the Willie Horton ad, and Dan Quayle's response to the Los Angeles riots in 1992. In politics, "law and order" meant more diligent law enforcement and stricter sentencing, and in the 1980s and 1990s, the phrase was a racist code that positioned African American men as social predators. The language translated into legislation after the GOP swept Congress in 1994. "America Fights Back," the subtitle added to *America's Most Wanted* in 1995, could, in fact, have served as a subheading in the GOP's "Contract with America"—one of the major components of the agenda was the "Take Back Our Streets Act," which proposed tougher punishments like "three strikes, you're out," laws.[18]

Thus, Susan Smith murdered her sons in an era during which Americans lauded "tough on crime" television and supported "law and order" legislation. "Law and order" neoconservatives attacked the "abuse excuse" as touchy-feely, soft-on-crime psychobabble. This legal strategy was a gamble in a southern courtroom in 1995. The focus on abuse and past traumas in legal defense was seen as a politically liberal strategy—and worse, it was seen as feminist. A link between past abuse and criminal insanity had worked its way into public consciousness from a decidedly feminist perspective as the defense that would come to be known as "battered women's syndrome." Francine Hughes, the first woman to successfully use this defense, killed her abusive husband in his sleep in 1977. After hearing graphic testimony of abuse, the jury found her not guilty by reason of temporary insanity.[19] The fourteen years of abuse of Francine "excused" her violence as self-defense, but more importantly, the verdict represented a serious social recognition of the patriarchal offense of domestic violence and the psychological trauma it incurs.

Although, by the 1990s, most Americans were probably not familiar with the intricate details of the Francine Hughes case, many were well versed in the trial through its televised version, *The Burning Bed* starring Farrah Fawcett. Originally conceived of as a feminist defense that challenged patriarchal violence within the home, the "abuse excuse" of "battered women's syndrome" was quickly transformed along new sexist lines. Elayne Rapping argues that, in the award-winning 1984 television movie, the feminist elements of this defense were "seriously contained, watered down, and 'declawed.'" Instead of an abused wife and mother fighting against the patriarchal system that allowed domestic violence to function invisibly, the movie had a new hero: Hughes's attorney, a "middle-class, white, straight male authority." Fawcett's Hughes complemented her paternal protector as a "perfect mother" and an "upwardly mobile aspirant to middle-class respectability."[20]

The "abuse excuse," then, can become something entirely different when it is deployed in the protection of a woman. Legal theorist Wendy Chan argues: "Male defendants' pathological personalities do not diminish their choice-making activity; it simply places limits on how well they can make these choices. Unlike the reports in cases involving female defendants, psychiatric reports of male defendants provide lengthy lists of the defendants' symptoms and how they acted during their mental illness, stressing what they *did or could not do* rather than *what happened to them*."[21] Robbed of its feminist elements, the "abuse excuse" defense is not the liberal or progressive strategy attacked by "law and order" conservatives in cases like that of Susan Smith. In fact, this defense fits squarely within neotraditional models of womanhood.

Especially in cases of maternal filicide, we can chart an alternative legal trend, one that got national press with the Smith trial. A key difference between the use of this "abuse excuse" strategy in Smith's defense and its use in the Menendez trials or in "battered women's syndrome" trials was that Smith did not commit the violent act against her abusers—she did not lash out violently at her stepfather or her estranged husband. Her crime was inherently maternal because her victims were her own children. In the context of the New Right 1990s, these two issues—the perpetrator's maternity and her own victimization—combined with developing ideas within criminology to result in the new American image of the mentally ill mother.

The timing of the Susan Smith case is immensely important. Had she committed this crime in previous years, it is likely that she would not have garnered nearly as much media attention.[22] We have seen how public representations shifted rapidly from the "sexpot on trial" to the suicidally depressed young girl. But why did they change? The answer lies within the cultural politics of gender, which were, as we have seen, undergoing a reformulation in the late twentieth century. American culture was still in the throes of the New Right "backlash" against feminism, characterized primarily by the rise of political neoconservatism and the patriarchal discourse of "family values." Mothers were a primary point of attack, and images of ideal maternity were a key means of social control.

Regardless of the social, political, and cultural images bombarding them daily, American women knew well the tension between the institution, experiences, and popular images of motherhood. Longtime critics of the constraining institution, feminists decided to capitalize on the underground complaints that ran counter to the "new momism." Ann Snitow formally reopened the conversation by responding to the "rising national babble of pronatalism in the 1980s" with her 1992 review of feminist theories of motherhood. Women, she argued, had absolutely nothing to gain from the contemporary idealization of motherhood.[23] In 1994, several authors in *Feminist Studies* heeded her call with an issue devoted to "Scenarios of the Maternal," agreeing with Snitow that the institution needed major examination and revision.[24]

Some observers applied this critique of motherhood to the Susan Smith case when they wrote to editors in response to the media coverage, voicing their concerns about the modern institution of motherhood. These women were, so to speak, the popular voice of the nascent discursive change. But theirs were by no means the dominant voices, and the sensational, sexualized images of America's most famous infanticidal mother resurfaced not long after Smith was sentenced and transferred to prison in Columbia. Post-trial coverage of Susan Smith traffics only in sensationalism; gone were the complex psychological analyses that characterized her trial. Popular memory has reverted to a default "Susan," the class-climbing, oversexed single mother of the "boyfriend motive."

Headlines like ""Murderous Mom Susan Smith Still Enthralls Nation" and "Continuing Saga of Sex, Murder, and Racism: Susan Smith Still Scheming in Prison" appeared periodically in the late 1990s. In 2000, Smith received quite a bit of coverage when it was discovered that she had had intimate relations with two different prison guards. For many, this seemed to be further proof that she was the scheming slut of the "boyfriend motive," although one could just as easily read her behavior as being in keeping with her long history of coercive and/or abusive relationships with men. Tabloids declared that she was pregnant as a result of these "consensual" liaisons (she was not); the *Weekly World News* reported that Smith was pregnant with twins, but that she planned to commit suicide before their birth to replicate her previous crime. A year later, the same publication doctored her mug shot to make it appear as if fellow inmates had beaten her. More recently, there was a flurry of coverage when Smith reportedly placed a personal advertisement online through a site that links inmates to pen pals. Ironically, even as a more empathetic image of maternal violence worked its way into the mainstream culture, popular representations of Susan Smith reverted to the original "boyfriend motive" of early post-confession coverage. As recently as the fall of 2011, Susan Smith graced the cover of the tabloid the *Globe* along with Charles Manson, Sirhan Sirhan, and the "Son of Sam Killer" under the headline: "Outrage! Keep These Monsters Caged."[25]

But by the turn of the twenty-first century, as Susan Smith adapted to her new antidepressants and learned to cope in prison, a more sympathetic alternative reading started to become a familiar refrain, and it spanned the academic disciplines. Psychologists, sociologists, historians, and literary scholars all chimed in, publishing text after text targeting the "cultural contradictions" of motherhood and calling for more realistic images of, as well as real socioeconomic aid for, American mothers.[26]

At the same time, criminologists began to correct the "stag effect" in their overwhelmingly male-centered field. Ann Jones connected the two topics of female criminals and feminism most explicitly, arguing in her groundbreaking 1996 work on female murderers that "the same social and legal deprivations that compel some women to feminism push others to homicide." Jones argued that her violent subjects were not deviant aberrations; rather they were representative women on the margins who "made plain the fabric of society."[27]

Jones did not explicitly apply her feminist criminological model to the crime of filicide, but the academic debate of which she was a part culminated in a complete revision of the prevailing narrative of maternal violence. The specifics of this particular crime made it a tricky one to redefine. There was the overall context of the cultural idealization of the relationship between mother and child, and there was the unavoidably incendiary problem of the victims, who were, by definition, defenseless and innocent. In a comprehensive study of maternal filicide in 1997, criminologist Ania Wilczynski argued that infanticide by males fit within the general framework of patriarchal power over the family, but for women "filicide reflects their simultaneous position of power and powerlessness."[28] This problematic duality combined with the New Right obsession with motherhood to redefine maternal filicide along the lines suggested several years earlier by Susan Smith's defense team.

One post-trial avenue of feminist legal analysis focuses on Smith's suicidality, a symptom of her depression that resulted from her abuse. Although Pope and many outside observers consistently dismissed Smith's self-destructiveness as contrived, suicidal ideation is actually quite typical in infanticidal mothers. This conclusion, made by criminologists interested in gender and crime, confirms that many mothers who kill express a warped sense of what is best for their children. Suicidal mothers in many cases practice "altruistic infanticide" in which the "child was seen as a dependent of and extension of the offender, without a separate personality or independent right to life." These "extended suicide" infanticides often feature no evidence of hostility or prior child abuse, and these mothers overwhelmingly express "strong religious views"—in other words, they think they are sparing their children further pain by sending them to heaven.[29]

The overwhelming media scrutiny and her inability to testify at her own trial obscured Susan Smith's own words, which, as we have seen, seemed to uphold this "altruistic" reading of her motive. In her written confession of November 3, 1994, she expressed acute anxiety over motherhood as well as suicidal tendencies. She began by describing her own depressive state: "When

I left home on Tuesday, Oct. 25, I was very emotionally distraught. I didn't want to live anymore! I felt like things could never get any worse." She continued: "As I rode and rode and rode, I felt even more anxiety coming upon me about not wanting to live. I felt I couldn't be a good mom anymore but I didn't want my children to grow up without a mom. I felt I had to end our lives to protect us all from any grief or harm." Smith then described her thoughts at the lake—those moments that constituted "malice aforethought" for the prosecution: "When I was @ John T. Long Lake, I had never felt so scared and unsure as I did then. I wanted to end my life so bad and was in my car ready to go down that ramp into the water and I did go part way, but I stopped. I went again and stopped. I then got out of the car and stood by the car a nervous wreck. Why was I feeling this way? Why was everything so bad in my life? I had no answers to these questions. I dropped to my lowest when I allowed my children to go down that ramp into the water without me." Smith wrote that she was a "mental case" who "could not believe" what she had done. She considered going into the water after her children, but it was "too late." She expresses profound remorse, but also a kind of relief for her children.

> I love my children with all my [heart symbol]. That will never change. I have prayed to them for forgiveness and hope that they will find it in their [heart symbol] to forgive me. I never meant to hurt them!! I am *sorry* for what has happened and I know that I need some help. I don't think I will ever be able to forgive myself for what I have done. My children, Michael and Alex, are with our Heavenly Father now and I know they will never be hurt again. As a mom, that means more than words could ever say.

Susan Smith's confession, written in her childish, loopy handwriting, replete with heart symbols and overpunctuation, reads like the diary of a very sick girl, one whose love for her children, paradoxically, led to their murders.[30]

In 2001, scholars Cheryl Meyer and Michelle Oberman revisited the Smith case. In their review of the case, they acknowledge the "boyfriend motive," but their real concern was the depth of Smith's mental illness: "Would Susan Smith have had a mental illness, according to the *DSM-IV* [the APA's guide to official diagnoses]? . . . Clearly, she was and had been depressed and suicidal most of her life. She was likely grappling with depression the day she killed her children and has continued to grapple with it in prison following their murder. She has been on multiple suicide watches. She would certainly meet the criteria for at least one clinical disorder, depression. However, by all accounts Susan also had some features of dependent personality disorder, including a history of an excessive need to be taken care of and fears of separation."[31] Meyer and Oberman represent the authoritative fields of psychology and the law, respectively, and the expert testimony at Susan Smith's trial clearly convinced them. But it would take another infanticidal mother in the headlines for their analysis to become the reigning understanding of maternal filicide.

In June 2001, Andrea Yates systematically drowned all five of her children in the bathtub of her suburban Texas home. When she finished the deed, she called 911 and told the operator what she had done, sparking a media frenzy that would span her two homicide trials of 2002 and 2006. The day after the murders, Rusty Yates, Andrea's husband, scripted what quickly became the dominant narrative of the case. Rusty informed the media of Andrea's "postpartum depression" following the birth of their last two children. Crying and holding a portrait of his family, he assured the public that Andrea loved her children and that she was ill, not evil: "Everyone who knows her knew she loved the kids. She is a kind, gentle person. What you see here and what you saw yesterday, it's not her." The coverage of the Yates case was fundamentally different from the treatment of other cases of maternal filicide. In direct contrast to the early coverage of the Susan Smith drama, in which the story was about the mother's sexuality, coverage of Andrea Yates's crime immediately focused on the mother's psychology. Her case was, from the beginning, about "a mother and her sickness."[32]

When Andrea Yates killed her children, postpartum depression was not the well-known disorder that it would become. Mothers, of course, knew about it, as did healthcare professionals, but it was not the cultural phenomenon, or the "widening crisis," that it has been perceived to be since the horrific details of the Yates case hit newsstands across the country. Yates exhibited symptoms of the most severe form of postpartum mental illness, postpartum *psychosis* (which affects roughly one to four out of every thousand new mothers), but her case quickly became shorthand for the much less severe postpartum *depression* (which affects between 5 and 20 percent of new mothers) in the extensive media coverage of the case.[33]

The widespread sympathy for Andrea Yates and the subsequent support for her insanity defense were not inevitable. We have seen how the public tried, and virtually burned at the stake, other mothers for similar crimes. It is true that Yates did not lie or try to cover up her crime, so that element of public outrage was understandably absent. Yates's immediate confession, however, is not what saved her from public culpability. If anything, the details of her crime were more graphic, and the number of her victims far greater, than in other famous infanticide cases. Yet even articles that included the gory details were generally sympathetic. Yates was, from the outset, "mad" and not "bad," "nuts" rather than a "slut."[34]

Many reports depicted Yates as almost representative, a tragic spokeswoman of the hidden pathologies of motherhood. One journalist argued that "mental illness is often the backdrop of this most baffling of crimes," quoting an expert who estimated that, of the few hundred mothers who kill their children each year, roughly half of them are found to be mentally ill. The reporter depicted Yates's extreme symptoms as typical of infanticide cases, which "pit sympathy against revulsion": "A severely depressed mother, planning to commit suicide, might kill her children first to avoid traumatizing them—then face a jury after her suicide fails. Or a psychotic mother may believe that her children have been marked by the devil and must be sacrificed, or may entertain a distorted Christian hope that death will free the children's souls from earthly troubles. Yates may have been both suicidal and psychotic, and experts identify postpartum depression as a likely root cause."[35] This broad definition of postpartum depression slips easily between two very different crimes: from the suicidal, altruistic model, which Susan Smith vaguely described in her written confession, to the severe, hallucinatory infanticide committed by Andrea Yates. This, then, was how the American public had come to understand infanticide at the beginning of the twenty-first century.[36] The possibility of maternal mental illness was suddenly front-page news, with all media outlets, from the New York Times to the tabloids, weighing in on the "new" crisis.

By the time of Yates's first trial, in the winter of 2002, journalists were well versed in postpartum depressive disorders, having reported on them for eight months in the course of covering the Yates case. Media reports focused on the psychological testimony in the trial, and especially on Yates's satanic hallucinations. One forensic psychologist testified that Yates believed that cartoon characters were telling her she was a "bad mother," and that Satan had been telling her to kill her children for some time before she actually did it. Yates told the doctor she was guilty and she needed "to be punished." The doctor concluded, in an oft-repeated sound bite, "Of all the patients I've treated for major depression with psychotic features, she was one of the sickest."[37]

However, under Texas's narrow insanity standards, all that mattered was whether Yates knew what she was doing was wrong at the time of the crime. Using this definition, the jury in her first trial rejected her insanity plea, found her guilty, and sentenced her to life in prison. A public outcry ensued. The spokesman for the National Mental Health Organization deemed the verdict a "travesty"; added Yates's brother sadly, "A sick person has been sent to prison for forty years." The case was clearly not over. Three years later, the judge decided to overturn her conviction and award her a new trial on the basis of false testimony from the one expert witness who testified that Andrea Yates was sane. One Texas woman applauded the judge's decision, explicitly blaming the cultural idealization of motherhood that allowed Yates to be isolated in her home with her children and her madness: "The 'caretaker syndrome,' which tethered her to pills, blind obedience and a selfishness that ignored her fragile mind and body, was to everyone's advantage except her and her five children." Another Houstonian echoed this opinion, arguing that "sanity [had] prevailed at last" in the decision for a new trial.[38]

Although her trials spanned over four years, periodic updates kept Yates in the public eye as her lawyers prepared for a second trial. People magazine described "her private hell" on the eve of the third anniversary of the children's deaths: Yates was rushed to the hospital, displaying symptoms of severe depression, "psychotic episodes," and self-starvation. Newsweek reported that she spent much of her time staring "out the window of her cell" and was often confused, like when she asked a visiting lawyer who was babysitting her children. Her doctors reported that her mindset changed daily. She was often unsure of her past, but when her medications worked, her mind was clear, triggering overwhelming memories of her crime.[39]

The intervening years between Yates's two trials for the deaths of her children witnessed the cultural ascendance of postpartum depression. Concern about the illness was no longer the province of medical or legal professionals; it became something of a celebrity cult and even a political issue. Incredibly, the popular television show Desperate Housewives was initially conceived as a response to the Yates trial. In the years since its 2004 debut, creator Marc Cherry has often repeated his startling inspiration for the show. While watching the coverage of the 2002 Andrea Yates trial, he reported that his mother "took her cigarette out of her mouth and said, 'I've been there.'" She explained how hard it had been for her to raise three young children while their father was in graduate school. Cherry wrote the show around the idea that a "perfectly sane, rational woman could have the life she wanted, being a wife and mother . . . and still have moments of insanity." Although the actual televised product hardly resembles its tragic inspiration, what we witnessed on this show and through other pop cultural outlets was the slow dissemination of a more complicated psychological discourse of motherhood.[40]

Suddenly, in the wake of Yates's first trial, a much-needed corrective to the beatific, "mommy myth" media profile appeared in the form of female celebrities who revealed their own struggles with maternal depression. Timing, again, was key. Marie Osmond published a book about her struggle with postpartum depression in May 2001, just weeks before the Yates murders, to little fanfare. The overwhelming media coverage of postpartum depression surrounding the Yates case, however, soon ensured that celebrity reports of maternal depression were front-page news. Perhaps most famous was Brooke Shields's chronicle of her own depression after the birth of her first child, complete with inner rage, failure to bond with her newborn, and suicidal thoughts. Shields's book, *Down Came the Rain: My Journey Through Postpartum Depression*, was the subject of much media attention almost as soon as it was published in May of 2005. Oprah Winfrey devoted an entire show to Shields's story that summer, and Shields got even more press when she was attacked by actor Tom Cruise for taking antidepressants to treat her depression. Media outlets from *People* magazine to the *New York Times* devoted serious coverage to this argument, which otherwise might have been viewed as mere celebrity gossip. Shields seems to have set off a wave of like-minded confessions. Courtney Cox-Arquette, the television actress, and Carnie Wilson, the singer, both went public with their postpartum depression in the summer of 2005, one year before Yates's second trial.[41]

Maternal mental illness was making headlines that summer, but it was not just a temporary pop cultural phenomenon. Volumes have been written on the subject in the past few years. Amazon.com alone currently lists almost four thousand titles on the subject of postpartum depression; the vast majority of these, including *Postpartum Depression for Dummies,* have been published since Andrea Yates's first trial. The *Journal of the American Medical Association* issued a report about the illness in 2002 and again in 2006, deeming it a "major public health problem." At the same time, feminists and other American mothers continued writing about motherhood in general. Susan Douglas and Meredith Michaels published their influential study of the "new momism" in 2004, just a few months before Andrea Yates's conviction was overturned.[42]

One month after the judge ordered a new trial for Andrea Yates, *Newsweek* did a feature entitled "The Myth of the Perfect Mother: Why It Drives Women Crazy." The cover illustration depicted a glowing, serene mother holding a perfect, smiling baby. The mythical mom had eight arms, each holding something different: the baby, toys, an exercise weight, a frying pan full of bacon, a telephone, and a high-heeled shoe. The message of the image was clear, and just in case it was not, the cover also promised a column by Anna Quindlen entitled "Why Mothers Shouldn't be Martyrs." Inside, readers found the feature story about "Mommy Madness," which profiled *Perfect Madness,* a new book that called for social aid to mothers in the form of family-friendly corporate policies and high-quality, affordable day care. By the end of the year, the new discourse of motherhood had entered the realm of politics: New Jersey legislators pondered a bill mandating that healthcare professionals provide information on postpartum depression to pregnant women and screen new mothers for the illness. Even Texas, a state not known for its legal leniency (but perhaps reeling from the negative press surrounding Andrea Yates's first trial), considered a bill in 2009 that would recognize "postpartum mental illness" as a legitimate legal defense for women.[43] The Good Mother had suffered a blow (albeit not a fatal one), and the acknowledgment that mothering was a difficult task that could be more stressful than fulfilling had gone mainstream.

By the beginning of Yates's second trial in the summer of 2006, postpartum depression had become a full-blown cultural phenomenon. During her second trial, Yates was not the front-page national news that she had been during her first trial. Hers was now a familiar story, and most observers expected that she would be found insane. The verdict was not a foregone conclusion, although many journalists expressed surprise when the jury deliberated for twelve hours over three days. This was far longer than in the first trial, and the questions the jurors sent out all addressed issues of mental illness. When jurors finally arrived at the unanimous decision of not guilty by reason of insanity, Harris County prosecutors blamed the new discourse of motherhood, citing "a growing public sentiment in the past five years that seemed to support her insanity plea." Yates's attorney, George Parnham, called the verdict a "watershed event in the treatment of mental illness."[44] Many journalists heaved a sigh of relief that justice had finally been served, and Andrea Yates was committed to the care of a Texas mental health institution, where she will likely remain for the rest of her life.

The postpartum image clearly represented some feminist progress over some of the new sexist representations examined thus far. The mentally ill mother did not fit neatly into the age-old Madonna/whore dichotomy of the "new momism" versus the devil in the shape of a woman. Although the National Organization for Women lauded the final Yates verdict, and mothers across the nation expressed their empathy, we should be careful about declaring this new image of maternity, and of female criminality, a feminist victory.[45] It echoes Union's own infantilized vision of Smith as well as paternalistic scholarly models of female criminality. More importantly, like so many new sexist models, the image called upon traditional ideas about womanhood, violence, and the female body while wearing a progressive, even a feminist, mask.

Although many criminologists, legal scholars, feminists, and mothers viewed this image as a promising challenge to the constraining logic of the "new momism," this specifically female kind of mental illness has clear sexist historical precedents. Historians of infanticide argue that, prior to the twentieth century, society generally viewed infanticide as an act of desperation based on socioeconomic circumstances, committed most often by exploited slave or servant women. The best-known American example is the former slave Margaret Garner, whose violence against her children was immortalized in Toni Morrison's prize-winning novel *Beloved*. At the end of the nineteenth century, however, the new science of psychology advanced the "medical model" of behavior and with it a new focus on the deviant female body. Societal motives were out, and gender-based psychiatric motives began to explain a range of human behavior. Hence, Americans became familiar with the specifically female psycho-medical diagnoses, like the Victorian hysteria epidemic (literally, "womb disease"), premenstrual syndrome, menopause, and most recently, postpartum depression.[46]

These medical labels redefined exceedingly normal female experiences as mental illnesses. The diagnoses, according to historians, explained female criminal behavior as well, an application that subtly indicates an "official," legal belief that, because all women suffer from these disorders, they therefore all have the potential for insanity.[47] This psychological focus on the gendered body, promoted most famously by Freud, has been codified in legal understandings of child murder by females over the course of the twentieth century, culminating in the discourse du jour of postpartum mental illness.

We saw key parts of this evolution enacted in the Smith trial. According to Dr. Halleck's very persuasive testimony, Susan Smith killed because she was depressed and "out of control"—an image that calls upon historical ideas of female nature as weak willed, hysterical, and vulnerable. To be sure, experts did not argue that Smith's depression was a biological disorder from which all women might suffer; its etiology was based on male victimization. But that understanding of infanticide was not far off. It only took ten years for that image of violent maternity to transform into one that is based solely on uniquely female biology. The rhetoric of postpartum depression and the biology of motherhood posits all women as potentially, even probably, mentally ill at certain points in their lives. Hormones—not the impossible idealization of motherhood, the condemnation of the millions of mothers who do not meet the stringent criteria of the "new momism," or the dire lack of social support experienced by so many mothers—are to blame.

Although this kind of analysis of maternal crime was new to the United States at the end of the twentieth century, over twenty nations around the globe already recognized maternal filicide as a distinct form of homicide deserving of different legal treatment. Certain Western nations "medicalized" infanticide in the early twentieth century by "positing a causal relationship between pregnancy, childbirth, and subsequent maternal mental disorder." In 1922 and 1938, Great Britain enacted statutes defining maternal infanticide as distinct from other kinds of homicide "due to the impact of pregnancy and birth upon the mother's mental status." According to these statutes, mothers who can prove that they suffered from a postpartum mental disorder at the time of the crime are charged with manslaughter, not murder, and they generally receive probation and psychiatric treatment rather than prison time. At least twenty-two other nations followed suit in the twentieth century.[48]

Despite these historical and international precedents, until the end of the twentieth century, legislators and legal theorists in the United States resisted this gendered, biological model of motive. But by the 1990s, it was on the legal radar. Although it received very little press in the United States, there was something of a test case of infanticide statutes two years after Smith murdered her sons. In 1996, a British woman named Caroline Beale killed her newborn in a New York City hotel room. 60 Minutes said Beale's case "sparked a transatlantic furor that called into question the way American law deals with infanticide." In her home country, Beale was seen as a "tragic victim" deserving of "sympathy and a psychiatrist." In the United States, she was a "cold-blooded monster." After spending eight months in Riker's Island, Beale was returned to England, where she was convicted of manslaughter. She received five years of probation and lengthy psychiatric treatment.[49] If she had been tried in the

United States, her punishment could have ranged anywhere from probation to capital punishment.

To be clear, Susan Smith's crimes did not fall within general international legal standards regarding infanticide, most of which extend the postpartum period to one year (Smith's younger son was fourteen months old). Nor was Smith's defense firmly based on ideas about the female body. "Postpartum depression" was not in the popular lexicon at the time, and her lawyers did not suggest the diagnosis in the courtroom. And at any rate, this was a strategy that was not likely to succeed in the United States in the early 1990s.

Instead, Bruck and his assistants had to combine the criminological trends—the traditional view of women as weaker and less prone to violence, the "abuse excuse" strategy, and international precedents for maternal violence—into a composite defense based on Smith's distinctly female psychology. The experts in the Smith trial consistently offered a gendered reading of her psychological state in which she epitomized feminine victimhood and mental instability. Dr. Halleck's assessment of Susan indicated that her mental instability stemmed from external traumas—in each case, her mistreatment by the men in her life. The overwhelmingly masculine sources of Susan Smith's traumas, rather than her crimes, positioned her as a distinctly female victim. It was derided as the new-fangled "abuse excuse," but this defense actually has a long history for female defendants. The only thing new about it was its application to a filicidal mother.[50]

Smith's alleged mental illness stemmed from past and ongoing abuse; Yates's, on the other hand, seemed to a have a wholly biological etiology. The new popular analysis of maternal filicide in the twenty-first century was eerily reminiscent of biological ideas about the female capacity for mental illness dating back to the Victorian era. The coverage of the Yates case made the new pathologization of motherhood explicit. The recognition that good mothers could, under certain circumstances, hurt their children was indeed a corrective to the "new momism." Yet diagnosing Yates with a peculiarly female mental illness also made her less dangerous. She was not just any mother, she was one suffering from a grave disorder. Discussions of her case almost always called her illness "depression," even though Yates suffered from the much more severe postpartum *psychosis*. In the past decade, studies have repeatedly shown that this diagnosis of postpartum depression is often available only to white, middle- and upper-class mothers, even though poor and minority mothers are astronomically more likely to suffer from it.[51] The diagnosis, then,

replicates the new sexism and racism of the "mommy myth." In fact, it rei-
fies the "new momism" itself: certain neoconservative ideals of motherhood
could remain intact if all violent mothers who otherwise fit the ideal were
partitioned off as insane.

In a very short time, the way that Americans responded to and represented
infanticide by certain mothers had changed dramatically. Andrea Yates's story
was tragic and puzzling, but in contrast to the actions of previous infanticidal
mothers such as Susan Smith, hers did not result in widespread condemnation. Instead of lurid headlines and angry sound bites, readers and viewers consumed volumes of reports about a seemingly new mental illness, and it soon
became clear that it was plaguing many mothers, not just the homicidal Yates.

This image of hormonal violence is obviously gendered, and it represents
a new way of viewing mothers in American culture. But this transformation
of the "new momism" produced an image in keeping with the New Right cultural prescriptions for female behavior. By excusing the acts of certain kinds
of mothers, the new image protects cultural idealization by masking the fact
that motherhood can be problematic for all women, especially those mothers
who lack social and economic support. This "new" illness, postpartum depression, plagues many new mothers.[52] Despite epidemic levels, the rhetoric of
postpartum depression implies that mothers who struggle need to seek out
their own help, an individuating, self-help, gendered message that falls right in
line with the new sexism. Yet the percentage of new mothers who suffer from
postpartum depression indicates that the problem might not be individual. It
might, in fact, be social.

Legal scholar Wendy Chan argues that "the reliance on individualistic
explanations by the legal and medical profession has not been helpful since
they pathologise women's behaviour and fail to explain why so many women
defendants share such similar circumstances." The diagnosis of postpartum
psychological disorders individualizes women, although estimates of its
frequency indicate that it is a fairly normal experience. Between 5 and 20
percent of all new mothers reportedly suffer from postpartum depression in
this culture, and doctors caution that it is drastically under-reported. Recent
clinical studies suggest that a full two-thirds of women who kill their children may be suffering from a postpartum mental illness.[53] The numbers of
women who suffer from the disorder seem to grow every time a new study
is published.

Scholars have reconceived other so-called "female maladies" to account for women's shared experiences. Naomi Wolf argues that our ideas about anorexia, for instance, need to be placed in their historical context: "Victorian female hysteria, mysterious at the time, makes sense now that we see it in the light of the social pressures of sexual self-denial and incarceration in the home. Anorexia should be simple to understand. What hysteria was to the nineteenth-century fetish of the asexual woman locked in the home, anorexia is to the late twentieth-century fetish of the hungry woman."[54] Uniquely female psychological disorders, according to Wolf, are part and parcel of patriarchy. These diagnoses mask the problems of gender inequality. When a woman murders, our immediate reaction is to ask how she could have done such a thing, and our answer now often centers on postpartum mental illness. But we might be asking the wrong question. "Given the enormous costs of being born female," writes crime scholar Meda Chesney-Lind, "the real question, as a review of the history of women's crimes illustrates, is not why women murder, but why so few murder."[55] At the end of the twentieth century, in reaction to these crimes, we developed a way to understand some of these offending women—if they meet the proper race, class, and marital requirements—that does not require revision of the primary institutions of patriarchy.

Although white, middle-class, Good Mothers who violently violate the neo-traditional rules of maternal behavior pose challenges to family-values politics, in the twenty-first century these women have instead been incorporated into the new sexist code. Laura Briggs has argued that the Victorian label of "hysteria" served to delineate between the "civilized" upper-class white women who allegedly suffered from it and the many minority, immigrant, and poor women to whom the diagnosis was completely unavailable. The same is true of the diagnosis of postpartum depression one hundred years later: mothers who fall outside of the ideal due to race, class, and/or marital status—exactly those mothers who lack "social support" and who are more likely to experience postpartum depression, according to the U.S. National Institute of Health—are those who are least likely to be able to get adequate health care, to be diagnosed by a mental health professional, and to seek treatment.[56] The diagnosis serves to protect the "new momism" by ascribing Good Mothers' violent behavior to mental illness. At the same time, crimes committed by other mothers are just seen as deviant behaviors in need of harsh legal punishment.

Roughly five hundred children are killed by their parents in the United States each year. Sentences for the very same crime can range from outpatient psychiatric treatment and probation to capital punishment. Ann Jones argues that "women who kill find extreme solutions to problems that thousands of women cope with in more peaceable ways from day to day."[57] But this is not how we think of infanticidal mothers in this culture; they are either incomprehensibly evil or absolutely insane. There is a discernible script for how we make sense of maternal filicide within courtrooms, as seen in mentally ill "Susan" and the obviously psychotic Andrea Yates of her second trial. Yet many Americans, if asked, would insist that there is a vast difference between Susan Smith, the "slut," and Andrea Yates, the "nut."

In this book, I argue that these judgments are clearly historically contingent. In the case of Susan Smith, the primary lens through which we read her was neoconservatism. By the time Andrea Yates made headlines—indeed, the reason that *she* made headlines, rather than any one of the hundreds of other filicidal mothers in 2001—the new sexist code had been altered ever so slightly to allow for violent mothers with postpartum insanity. But these mothers had to meet certain requirements. They had to be white, middle-class, married—they had to be family-values-type good girls. This shift in perspective required that Susan Smith be recast as evil incarnate yet again, and she stood in stark contrast to Andrea Yates, who was clearly a mother in need of psychiatric help for her postpartum mental illness. Every time a white mother is accused of killing her children, this image of Susan Smith rears its ugly head. David Smith, her ex-husband, appeared on CNN's "Dr. Drew" show on June 16, 2011, to spell out the similarities between Susan Smith and the nation's most recent famous mother accused of murder, Casey Anthony. Among those similarities, he listed "partying," extramarital affairs and sexual activity, and "selfishness." "Partying, lying, partying, lying—lies, lies, lies seem to be at the center of all of this," Dr. Drew concluded. Sociopath or psychopath—Dr. Drew seemed unwilling to make a final diagnosis—but the implications were clear: Susan Smith was a compassionless monster.[58] And this image of Smith has endured in popular culture, eclipsing all others.

EPILOGUE: THE NEW "NEW MOMISM"

ECAUSE THIS IS a book about representations of women, rather than women themselves, I have found myself in the ironic position of feeling like a part of the system that actually silences these marginal figures. Susan Smith never gave an interview after her arrest, even once the trial was over, the gag order was lifted, and she was behind bars for decades to come. She did not testify in her own defense. Bill Howard, the judge at her trial, described her as "very much a mystery," even to those present in the courtroom; she spoke only to affirm that she understood the charges against her, and she generally displayed a flat, dissociated affect during the trial.[1] Once she stopped lying, she has had no public voice. She is like a screen on which any of us can project our own beliefs, which is why there have been so many "Susans" in the headlines in the past two decades. To remedy this, my original plan for this Epilogue was to give Susan Smith a space to speak for herself.

I have been in written contact with Susan Smith, off and on, for seven years. When I first started this project as a doctoral dissertation, I wrote her a letter in prison. Ms. Smith agreed to answer the questions I sent her, and she signed the required consent form. She writes me short notes every now and then from her cell at Leath Correctional Institution in South Carolina. She has large, loopy, girlish handwriting, and she often punctuates sentences with smiley faces (even before "emoticons" became popular). In her letters, she is always polite, even sweet—she drew me a picture of Mickey Mouse when I had to flee Hurricane Katrina. Even though we'd just begun our correspondence at the time, she expressed what sounded like genuine relief that I had evacuated New Orleans safely, and she assured me that she had donated what little money she could to help the victims. She is well aware of the many negative images of her, and she was clearly cautious with me, as well. She asked that I be "patient" with her, and she told me that she is "proud" of me "for getting this far with [my] education." Many of her letters are signed, "May God bless you! Love, Susan."[2]

Through this correspondence and from some of her current friends and acquaintances, I know something of what Susan Smith's life behind bars is like. After her trial, she was on suicide watch in a solitary cell for two months, and then she was moved to the prison general population without incident. She tried to make some friends, or pen pals, by posting an advertisement on "WriteaPrisoner.com," but her posting caused such a sensation that the site crashed and she removed her query.[3] When I first contacted her, she was taking a psychology course and was concerned about doing well on her final exam. Her friend, Reverend Tom Currie, indicated to me that she has taken other college courses while behind bars. A former fellow inmate told me that Susan Smith was on the board for program affairs at the prison, and that she was involved in other activities at Leath. Smith also apparently gets quite a bit of mail. As is to be expected, she has "good days and bad days like everyone else," and she often feels "down" and "overwhelmed" by "issues" from her past. I know from her friend and chaplain that she has thought quite a bit about postpartum depression, but, unfortunately, I do not know this from Susan Smith herself. Over the course of our several-year correspondence, she never answered the questions I sent her, and she never invited me to the prison for an in-person interview. But she mentioned the questions in every single letter. I learned quickly that if a few months went by and I did not hear from her, things were not going well, and she would write me when she was feeling up to it. In a Christmas card from 2006, she wrote: "Things have been rough for me. . . . I haven't forgotten you so please don't think that. . . . Don't give up on me yet!"[4]

I did not give up on Susan Smith, but unfortunately, it seems that she gave up on me. She did consider giving me more access; I know that she asked a visitor, Reverend Bob Cato, about me. She wanted to know if I seemed like a "good, honest person," and he answered in the affirmative. She indicated tacit approval to Cato, who is currently working on a book about postpartum depression from a Christian perspective, when she told him: "These are stories that need to be told." And she gave permission to Reverend Toni White, her chaplain in prison, to participate in an interview with me.[5] But she never answered the questions that I sent her over six years ago.

It is, of course, completely understandable that Susan Smith would be unable to deal with answering questions about her infamous crime from a virtual stranger. Frankly, I was surprised that she agreed to correspond with me so readily, given the fact that she does not give interviews from prison. And in retrospect, looking over her letters, I am, to my surprise, somewhat relieved that she did not answer my questions. Like the good doctors at her trial argued, Ms. Smith does come across as childlike, earnest, and eager to please; had she answered my questions fully, I might have felt like some kind of academic vulture, or at the very least, given her long history of emotional instability, I might have felt manipulative. I know some readers will find this naive. Prosecuting attorney Tommy Pope warned me years ago that Susan was very good at this game, and that she would try to play me just like she did the media.[6] Maybe he's right. At any rate, it is interesting that these two images—childlike victim or scheming criminal—are the two that still seem to surround Susan Smith, despite the many others that made headlines during her year of fame.

When I first set out to write this book, I also planned to include an "eighth Susan" in which I examined the contemporary feminist response to her case. I was well versed in the second-wave feminist critique of motherhood that characterized the 1970s, a vibrant, complex analysis of the wide variety of maternal experiences, including violence. According to Adrienne Rich and other feminists of the 1970s, motherhood, as both "experience and institution," was fraught with peril in modern America. Rich, of course, loved her children, but she also wrote frankly about negative, even violent, feelings toward them. "My children cause me the most exquisite suffering," she told readers on the very first page of her widely read *Of Woman Born* (1976): "It is the suffering of ambivalence: the murderous alternation between bitter resentment and raw-edged nerves, and blissful gratification and tenderness. Sometimes I seem to myself, in my feelings toward these guiltless tiny beings, a monster of selfishness and intolerance. Their voices wear away at my nerves, their constant needs, above all their need for simplicity and patience, fill me with despair at my own failures, despair too at my fate, which is to serve a function for which I was not fitted. And I am weak sometimes from held-in rage."[7] Rich's admissions of failure, anger, and unsuitability for the impossible job of ideal motherhood prefigured Susan Smith's own written confession. The primary reason for Smith's crime, according to her written confession, was her failure as a mother: "I felt I couldn't be a good mom anymore, but I didn't want my children to grow up without a mom. I felt I had to end our lives to protect us all from any grief or harm."[8]

In *Of Woman Born,* Rich recounts a discussion of a local infanticide case with a group of female friends in 1975: "We talked of poetry, and also of infanticide, of the case of a local woman, the mother of eight, who had been in a severe depression since the birth of her third child, and who had recently murdered and decapitated her two youngest, on her suburban front lawn."

Some of the women in the group had written letters protesting the local media coverage of the case. They all felt a "direct connection with her desperation." Rich wrote that "every woman in that room who had children, every poet, could identify with her."[9]

This was decidedly *not* the kind of conversation that American mothers were having, at least not publicly, about Susan Smith almost twenty years later. The 1970s—the decade during which Susan Smith was born—represented a distinct cultural moment in which American women, if not the American public in general, mined maternal ambivalence with the intent of tearing down the impossible prescriptions that required mothers to devote their entire beings, without complaint, to their children. Rich was literally writing the "unspeakable" when she described the darker side of maternity in modern America.

When I began this project, I did not realize just how distant that cultural moment actually was by the mid-1990s. That era summarily ended with the meteoric rise of the New Right in the 1980s. Even if women like Adrienne Rich did not speak for all American mothers, she was, at least, getting published in the 1970s. I was unprepared for how difficult it was to find feminist voices within the cacophony of pronatalism in the 1990s. To my dismay, that eighth, feminist "Susan" essentially did not exist, or at least the feminist reaction at the time of her national fame was so under-reported as to be virtually invisible.

The few published feminist responses to Susan Smith at the time of her crime had to reach back to Adrienne Rich in the 1970s as a reference point, so scarce were the feminist analyses of motherhood from the 1980s and early 1990s. Just a month after Smith's confession, one columnist argued that Susan Smith was "within the spectrum, not off the spectrum, of motherhood": "Those of us who look deeply enough at our own experience will know better. She belongs to the center, not the border. She is like a lot of other women. . . . [She] walked up to the brink of her limitation and shook hands with it. God save her soul. She is still one of us."[10] A small but distinct minority agreed. Newspaper editors published the letters of a handful of mothers confessing similar feelings of wanting to hurt themselves or their children, or both. *Time* magazine reportedly received "hundreds" of letters of concern for Susan Smith, including one in which a Virginia mother described her trip to the doctor to address her "overwhelming urge to kill her three young children" and herself. *Los Angeles Times* columnist Lynn Smith received so many letters from mothers expressing similar impulses that she wrote a column describing resources where these women could get help. The national shock and outrage notwithstanding, Susan Smith was clearly "not alone with her demons" as a mother, argued one reporter the week of Smith's confession.[11]

For several years, as I read the trial transcripts, combed through the media coverage, and conducted interviews, I sought contemporary feminist views to the "seven Susans." I found so few—they are all cited in the previous paragraph—that I was forced to conclude that the neoconservative politics of gender had thoroughly saturated American culture. In terms of motherhood, these ideas prevailed until the turn of the twenty-first century.

If anything good came from Andrea Yates's crimes, it was that American mothers began to speak honestly about their experiences. Perhaps the best articulation of the new discursive possibilities for motherhood came from Anna Quindlen in *Newsweek* in response to the Andrea Yates case. Quindlen called upon the "insidious cult of motherhood" as the motive for Yates's crime. She explained that though she, like the rest of the world, was horrified by Yates's behaviors, she understood the impulses behind them.

> But there's another part of my mind, the part that remembers the end of a day in which the milk spilled phone rang one cried another hit a fever rose the medicine gone the car sputtered another cried the cable out "Sesame Street" gone all cried stomach upset full diaper no more diapers Mommy I want water Mommy my throat hurts Mommy I don't feel good. Every mother I've asked about the Yates case has the same reaction. She's appalled; she's aghast. And then she gets this look. And the look says that at some forbidden level she understands. The look says that there are two very different kinds of horror here. There is the unimaginable idea of the killings. And then there is the entirely imaginable idea of going quietly bonkers in the house with five kids under the age of 7.[12]

Mothers across the country responded to Quindlen's "forbidden" admission that Yates's crime was "almost unimaginable—but not quite." One reader called it "women's dirty little secret," while others acknowledged that they, too, had suffered as new mothers, and not only from postpartum depression.[13]

Although Quindlen clearly spoke for many mothers, the problem remains. The opportunity to aggressively challenge our culture's idealization of motherhood lies dormant. We now live in a culture that acknowledges, through the new dialogue of postpartum mental illness, that primary caretakership does not come "naturally" to all new mothers and that it can be a difficult, even unmanageable, experience. Yet this more complex analysis of motherhood has ended up replicating many of the tenets of the recent new sexism, in addition to calling upon overtly sexist, historical politics of gender. There is a way to respond to maternal filicide that does not reinscribe inequalities of gender, and the voices that have dared to argue this publicly—from Adrienne Rich to Anna Quindlen—are few and far between, silenced by a neoconservative culture.

Susan Smith committed a horrifying crime, and she told a terrible lie. She was (and sometimes still is) a tabloid sensation. But her significance lies in the fact that she became the cipher for all manner of new racist and new sexist images. Some of these images had been a part of the neoconservative pantheon since at least the 1970s. Others were of more recent vintage, but only one, the mentally ill Good Mother, was a brand-new invention. Representations of Susan Smith reflected the New Right 1990s, not some timeless truths about filicide or infanticidal women. Making sense of mothers like Smith within a new sexist framework required this new image of the mentally ill mother, which became the postpartum depressive mother by the twenty-first century.

In the neoconservative mind, the United States of the past fifty years is, like Susan Smith, "in a lake of fire." The prescribed remedy is white masculine redemption, and a large part of that redemption centers on the idealized female role of mother. Although neoconservative "macho politics" reigned supreme during the past decade, it remains to be seen how the new sexism will fare in the twenty-first century (although Sarah Palin's "Mama Grizzly" rhetoric, Michelle Bachman's paeans to wifely submission, and the recent resurrection of the "mommy wars" in the 2012 presidential campaign indicate that it's not going anywhere any time soon).[14] Mothers resist the "new momism" daily, yet the new sexist code of which it is a key part is entrenched. Unless we understand its intricate workings through our culture, it will continue to function as a neotraditional norm that manipulates American women through unachievable prescriptions, guilt, and condemnation.

NOTES

INTRODUCTION

1. Rick Bragg, "An Agonizing Search for Two Boys," *New York Times*, October 28, 1994; Gary Henderson, interview, Spartanburg, SC, November 3, 2006; *NBC Evening News*, November 3, 1994.

2. Richard Whitt, "Gingrich Fires Back Over His Susan Smith Remarks," *Atlanta Journal and Constitution*, November 19, 1994; Molly Ivins, "Gingrich's Comments on Killings Despicable," *Austin American-Statesman* (TX), November 29, 1994.

3. *NBC Evening News*, November 7, 1994.

4. Glenn Feldman, "The Status Quo Society, the Rope of Religion, and the New Racism," in *Politics and Religion in the White South*, ed. Glenn Feldman (Lexington: University Press of Kentucky, 2005), 302.

5. Marjorie J. Spruill, "Gender and America's Right Turn," in *Rightward Bound: Making American Conservative in the 1970s*, ed. Bruce J. Shulman and Julian E. Zelizer (Cambridge, MA: Harvard University Press, 2008), 71–72, 79–80.

6. Linda Gordon, *Heroes of Their Own Lives: The Politics and History of Family Violence* (New York: Viking Press, 1988), 3; Judith Stacey, *In the Name of the Family: Rethinking Family Values in the Postmodern Age* (Boston: Beacon Press, 1996), 49, 43.

7. Arlene Skolnick, "Talking about Family Values After 'Family Values,'" *Dissent* 57, no. 4 (Fall 2010): 96; Matthew D. Lassiter, "Inventing Family Values," in *Rightward Bound: Making America Conservative in the 1970s*, ed. Bruce J. Shulman and Julian E. Zelizer (Cambridge, MA: Harvard University Press, 2008), 13–28.

8. Kenneth L. Karst, *Law's Promises, Law's Expression: Visions of Power in the Politics of Race, Gender, and Religion* (New Haven, CT: Yale University Press, 1993), 2, 1, 8; Alan Crawford, *Thunder on the Right: The 'New Right' and the Politics of Resentment* (New York: Pantheon Books, 1980), 107, 78; Amy Ansell, *New Right, New Racism: Race and Reaction in the United States and Britain* (New York: New York University Press, 1997), 92.

9. Lassiter, "Inventing Family Values," 16; Skolnick, 96; Stacey, 2, 7, 9

10. This is a cultural system that scholars, particularly those who study modern Islamic cultures, identify as a "neopatriarchy." See Hisham Sharabi, *Neopatriarchy: A Theory of Distorted Change in Arab Society* (New York: Oxford University Press, 1988).

11. Gill Jagger and Caroline Wright, eds., *Changing Family Values* (New York: Routledge, 1999), 8; Gail Bederman, *Manliness and Civilization: A Cultural History of Gender and Race, 1880–1917* (Chicago: University of Chicago Press, 1995), xi.

12. Linda K. Kerber coined the phrase "republican motherhood" in her groundbreaking *Women of the Republic: Intellect and Ideology in Revolutionary America* (Chapel Hill: University of North Carolina Press, 1980). For an overview of the role of mothers in the developing ideology of the "separate spheres" of the industrial age, see Jeanne Boydston, *Home and Work: Housework, Wages, and the Ideology of Labor in the Early Republic* (New York: Oxford University Press, 1994). Linda Gordon analyzes the images of motherhood that characterized the development of the American welfare system in *Pitied But Not Entitled: Single Mothers and the History of Welfare,*

1890–1935 (Cambridge, MA: Harvard University Press, 1998). Ruth Feldstein deconstructs the mid-century assumptions that "bad mothering" resulted in widespread social problems in *Motherhood in Black and White: Race and Sex in American Liberalism, 1930–1965* (Ithaca, NY: Cornell University Press, 2000). Elaine Tyler May critiques 1950s nostalgia in her analysis of family images and ideals during the Cold War in *Homeward Bound: American Families in the Cold War Era* (New York: Basic Books, 1988). More recently, media studies scholars Susan Douglas and Meredith Michaels studied the "new momism" of the 1980s and 1990s in *The Mommy Myth: The Idealization of Motherhood and How It Has Undermined All Women* (New York: Free Press, 2004).

13. For the historiography of the gendered images of lynching, particularly the "black beast rapist," see: Jacquelyn Dowd Hall, "'The Mind That Burns in Each Body': Women, Rape, and Racial Violence," in Ann Snitow, Christine Stansell, and Sharon Thompson, eds., *Powers of Desire: The Politics of Sexuality* (New York: Monthly Review Press, 1983); Joel Williamson, *The Crucible of Race: Black-White Relations in the American South Since Emancipation* (New York: Oxford University Press, 1984); Jacquelyn Dowd Hall, *Revolt Against Chivalry: Jessie Daniel Ames and the Women's Campaign Against Lynching* (New York: Columbia University Press, 1993); W. Fitzhugh Brundage, *Lynching in the New South: Georgia and Virginia, 1880–1930* (Urbana: University of Illinois Press, 1993); Glenda Gilmore, *Gender and Jim Crow: Women and the Politics of White Supremacy in North Carolina, 1896–1920* (Chapel Hill: University of North Carolina Press, 1996); Martha Hodes, *White Women, Black Men: Illicit Sex in the Nineteenth-Century South* (New Haven, CT: Yale University Press, 1997); Glenda Gilmore, "Murder, Memory, and the Flight of the Incubus," in David S. Cecelski and Timothy B. Tyson, eds., *Democracy Betrayed: The Wilmington Race Riot of 1898 and Its Legacy* (Chapel Hill: University of North Carolina Press, 1998); Stephen Kantrowitz, *Ben Tillman and the Reconstruction of White Supremacy,* especially chapter 5, "The Mob and the State" (Chapel Hill: University of North Carolina Press, 2000); Lisa Lindquist-Dorr, *White Women, Rape, and the Power of Race in Virginia, 1900–1960* (Chapel Hill: University of North Carolina Press, 2003): Crystal Feimster, *Southern Horrors: Women and the Politics of Rape and Lynching* (Cambridge, MA: Harvard University Press, 2009).

14. For more information on the role of race and the new racism in neoconservative politics, see: Thomas Byrne Edsall and Mary D. Edsall, *Chain Reaction: The Impact of Race, Rights, and Taxes on American Politics* (New York: W. W. Norton & Co., 1991); James M. Glaser, *Race, Campaign Politics, and the Realignment in the South* (New Haven, CT: Yale University Press, 1996); Ansell; Feldman, ed., *Politics and Religion in the White South*; Kevin Kruse, *White Flight: Atlanta and the Making of Modern Conservatism* (Princeton, NJ: Princeton University Press, 2005); Matthew Lassiter, *The Silent Majority: Suburban Politics in the Sunbelt South* (Princeton, NJ: Princeton University Press, 2006); Bruce J. Schulman and Julian E. Zelizer, eds., *Rightward Bound: Making America Conservative in the 1970s* (Cambridge, MA: Harvard University Press, 2008).

15. For information on the sexualization of female criminals, see: Helen Birch, ed., *Moving Targets: Women, Murder, and Representation* (Berkeley: University of California Press, 1994); Patricia Pearson, *When She Was Bad: Violent Women and the Myth of Innocence* (New York: Viking Press, 199); Nancy D. Campbell, "States of Secrecy: Women's Crimes and the Practices of Everyday Life," *Journal of Women's History* 10, no. 3 (Autumn 1998): 204–14. For general criminology on female murderers, see: Ann Jones, *Women Who Kill* (Boston: Beacon Press, 1996); Coramae Richey Mann, *When Women Kill* (Albany: State University of New York Press, 1996); Meda

Chesney-Lind, *The Female Offender: Girls, Women, and Crime* (Thousand Oaks, CA: SAGE Publications, Inc., 1997); Ania Wilczynski, *Child Homicide* (London: Greenwich Medical Media, Ltd., 1997); Cheryl L. Meyer and Michelle Oberman, *Mothers Who Kill Their Children: Understanding the Acts of Moms from Susan Smith to the "Prom Mom"* (New York: NYU Press, 2001).

16. Lance Morrow, "Yin and Yang, Sleaze and Moralizing," *Time*, December 26, 1994.

17. The historiography of mill culture and economics was something of a cottage industry during the second half of the twentieth century. See: J. K. Morland, *Millways of Kent* (Chapel Hill: University of North Carolina Press, 1958); Mimi Conway, *Rise Gonna Rise: A Portrait of Southern Textile Workers* (Garden City, NY: Anchor Press, 1979); David Carlton, *Mill and Town in South Carolina, 1880–1920* (Baton Rouge: Louisiana State University Press, 1982); Jacquelyn Dowd Hall, James Leloudis, Robert Korstad, Mary Murphy, Lu Ann Jones, and Christopher B. Daly, *Like a Family: The Making of a Southern Cotton Mill World* (Chapel Hill: University of North Carolina Press, 1987); Douglas Flamming, *Creating the Modern South: Millhands and Managers in Dalton, Georgia, 1884–1984* (Chapel Hill: University of North Carolina Press, 1992); Bryant Simon, *A Fabric of Defeat: The Politics of South Carolina Millhands, 1910–1948* (Chapel Hill: University of North Carolina Press, 1998); Timothy Minchin, *Hiring the Black Worker: The Racial Integration of the Southern Textile Industry, 1960–1980* (Chapel Hill: University of North Carolina Press, 1999); George Waldrep, *Southern Workers and the Search for Community* (Urbana: University of Illinois Press, 2000).

18. Florence King, "In the Dark," *Oxford American*, October–November 1996, 10. For the basic historiography of southern "distinctiveness," see: John Egerton, *The Americanization of Dixie: The Southernization of America* (New York: Harper & Row, 1974); Fred Hobson, *Tell About the South: The Southern Rage to Explain* (Baton Rouge: Louisiana State University Press, 1983); Peter Applebome, *Dixie Rising: How the South Is Shaping American Values, Politics, and Culture* (New York: Times Books, 1996); Carl N. Degler, *Place Over Time: The Continuity of Southern Distinctiveness* (Athens: University of Georgia Press, 1997); James Cobb, *Away Down South: A History of Southern Identity* (New York: Oxford University Press, 2005); Matthew D. Lassiter and Joseph Crespino, eds. *The Myth of Southern Exceptionalism* (New York: Oxford University Press, 2010).

19. For more feminist legal theory, see: Martha A. Fineman and Isabel Karpin, eds., *Mothers in Law: Feminist Theory and the Legal Regulation of Motherhood* (New York: Columbia University Press, 1995); Martha A. Fineman and Martha T. McCluskey, eds., *Feminism, Media, and the Law* (New York: Oxford University Press, 1997); Karen J. Maschke, ed., *Feminist Legal Theories* (New York: Garland Publishing, Inc., 1997); Wendy Chan, *Women, Murder, and Justice* (New York: Palgrave, 2001); Jayne Huckerby, "Women Who Kill Their Children: Case Study and Conclusions Concerning the Differences in the Fall from Maternal Grace by Khoua Her and Andrea Yates," *Duke Journal of Gender and Law Policy* 10, no. 147 (2003): 149–72. For legal theories of the role of images and narratives in popular understandings of the law, see: Ron Christensen, *Political Trials: Gordian Knots in the Law* (New Brunswick, NJ: Transaction Books, 1986); Susan Sage Heinzelman, "Women's Petty Treason: Feminism, Narrative, and the Law," *Journal of Narrative Technique* 20, no. 2 (Spring 1990): 89–106; Janet Malcolm, *The Journalist and the Murderer* (New York: Alfred A. Knopf, 1990); Patricia Williams, *The Alchemy of Race and Rights: Diary of a Mad Law Professor* (Cambridge, MA: Harvard University Press, 1991); Peter Brooks and Paul Gerwitz,

Law's Stories: Narrative and Rhetoric in the Law (New Haven, CT: Yale University Press, 1996); George H. Taylor, "Transcending the Debate on Legal Narrative," *University of Pittsburgh School of Law Working Paper* 11 (April 2005): law.bepress.com/pittlwps/papers/art11 (accessed August 15, 2011).

20. *NBC Evening News,* July 29, 1995.

21. Reverend Toni White, interview, West Columbia, SC, July 15, 2005. Because postpartum depression is a relatively recent diagnosis, there are no major historical analyses of it, although there is an evolving body of scholarship from other fields. See: Velma Dobson and Bruce Sales, "The Science of Infanticide and Mental Illness," *Psychology, Public Policy, and Law* 6 (2000): 1098–1112; Michele Connell, "The Postpartum Psychosis Defense and Feminism: More or Less Justice for Women?" *Case Western Law Review* 53, no. (2002): 143–69; Connie Huang, "It's a Hormonal Thing: Premenstrual Syndrome and Postpartum Psychosis as Criminal Defense," *Southern California Review of Law and Women's Studies* (Spring 2002); Deborah Denno, "Who Is Andrea Yates? A Short Story about Insanity," *Duke Journal of Gender Law and Policy* 10, no. 1 (Summer 2003); Michael L. Perlin, "She Breaks Just Like a Little Girl: Neonaticide, the Insanity Defense, and the Irrelevance of 'Ordinary Common Sense,'" *William and Mary Journal of Women and the Law* 10, no. 1 (Fall 2003); Becky L. Jacobs, "PMS: Perpetuating Male Superiority," *Texas Journal of Women and the Law* 14, no. 1 (Fall 2004); Cristie L. March, "The Conflicted Treatment of Postpartum Depression Under Criminal Law," *William Mitchell Law Review* 32, no. 1 (November 2005); Ruta Nunacs, *A Deeper Shade of Blue: A Woman's Guide to Recognizing and Treating Depression in Her Childbearing Years* (New York: Simon & Schuster, 2006); Lindsey C. Perry, "A Mystery of Motherhood: The Legal Consequences of Insufficient Research on Postpartum Illness," *Georgia Law Review* 42 (Fall 2007): 193–226; Lisa S. Segre, Michael W. O'Hara, Stephan Arndt, and Scott Stuart, "The Prevalence of Postpartum Depression: The Relative Significance of Three Social Status Indices," *Social Psychiatry and Psychiatric Epidemiology* 42, no. 4 (2007): 316–21; Vue Yang, "Postpartum Depression and the Insanity Defense: A Poor Mother's Two Worst Nightmares," *Wisconsin Journal of Law, Gender, and Society* 24, no. 229 (Spring 2009).

22. Suzanne Fields, "It's Personal Responsibility, Stupid," *Washington Times,* November 10, 1994; Chris Elder, "Feminists Must Unite Behind Susan Smith," *Greensboro News & Record* (NC), November 11, 1994.

CHAPTER ONE

1. All of the information about Smith's life comes from Linda Russell (with Shirley Stephens), *My Daughter, Susan Smith* (Brentwood, TN: Authors' Book Nook, 2000), 97–98, 102, 107–11, 128.

2. *NBC Evening News,* October 26, 1994.

3. Rick Bragg, "Police Say Woman Admits to Killings as Bodies of 2 Children Found Inside Her Car," *New York Times,* November 4, 1994; Clif Leblan and Twila Decker, "Parents of Missing Boys Plead Again for Their Return: 'No One Can Understand the Pain,'" *Peoria Journal Star,* November 2, 1994.

4. Douglas and Michaels, 3–4. Philip Wylie famously coined the term "momism" in his 1942 *Generation of Vipers,* in which he argued that excessive mothering led to an overattachment of

America's sons to their mothers, resulting in not just emasculation, but pervasive cultural decline: "The mealy look of men today is the result of momism and so is the pinched and baffled fury in the eyes of womankind" (*Generation of Vipers* [Normal, IL: Dalkey Archive Press, 1996], 210).

5. Diane Eyer, *Motherguilt: How Our Culture Blames Mothers for What's Wrong with Society* (New York: Times Books, 1996), 7.

6. U.S. Census Bureau, "Fertility of American Women, 1994," www.census.gov/hhes/fertility/data/cps/1994.html (accessed August 1, 2011); U.S. Census Bureau, "Fertility of American Women, 2002: Population Characteristics," www.census.gov/prod/2003pubs/p20-548.pdf (accessed August 1, 2011); U.S. Department of Health and Human Services, "Poverty Guidelines," *Federal Register* 59, no. 28 (February 10, 1994): 6277–78; Douglas and Michaels, 3.

7. *NBC Evening News,* October 26, 1994.

8. Gary Henderson, "Yellow Ribbons Fly for Union Children," *Spartanburg Herald-Journal,* October 28, 1994; *ABC Evening News,* October 27, 1994.

9. Russell, 182–83.

10. David Bruck, interview, July 29, 2005.

11. Russell, 211, 228.

12. Gary Henderson, *Nine Days in Union: The Search for Michael and Alex Smith* (Spartanburg, SC: Honoribus Press, 1995), 7.

13. Amy Birnbaum, interview, October 3, 2007; Twila Decker, interview, July 27, 2007. Jeanne Boylan, a sketch artist associated with the case, cites CBS reporter Randall Pinkston's early suspicion in her *Portraits of Guilt: The Woman Who Profiles the Faces of America's Deadliest Criminals* (New York: Pocket Books, 2000), 174. Reporter Bob Dotson also confessed to early suspicion of Smith's story (telephone interview, November 4, 2006). David Bruck, Smith's defense attorney, told me that the local police were suspicious of Smith immediately: "You know, she took law enforcement in for all of about ten minutes. They knew, right that night at the house where she rang the doorbell, that there was something fishy about this, but they couldn't say so, and the rest of country got all hooked in. . . . They didn't think she had murdered the children, but they thought she had hidden them or done something that was, that she knew where they were" (interview).

14. Gary Henderson, interview, November 3, 2006.

15. Eric Klinenberg, *Heat Wave: A Social Autopsy of Disaster in Chicago* (Chicago: University of Chicago Press, 2002), 107.

16. Gary Henderson identified the family's "home base" as Smith's parents' home in his very first article on the case ("A Mother's Frantic Call: I Love Y'all," *Spartanburg Herald-Journal,* October 27, 1994).

17. Richard Gruneau and Robert A. Hackett, "The Production of Television News," in *Questioning the Media: A Critical Introduction,* ed. John Downing, Ali Mohammadi, and Annabelle Srebeny-Mohammadi (London: Sage Publications, 1990), 285; Sari Thomas, "Myths In and About Television," in Downing et al., 331.

18. Douglas and Michaels define a "media panic" as a news peg that identifies "a person or a group, an event or a condition, as a profound, deeply destructive threat to society," and they argue that the panic over "childhood perils" increased after the mid-1980s (88–90).

19. Paula Fass, *Kidnapped: Child Abduction in America* (New York: Oxford University Press, 1997), 7; Douglas and Michaels, 93. Sociologist Barry Glassner calls these kinds of reports "pseudodangers" that "represent further opportunities to avoid problems we do not want to confront," such as, for instance, the fact that most child abuse, including child homicide, occurs within the home, perpetrated not by a stranger, but by a relative (*The Culture of Fear: Why Americans Are Afraid of the Wrong Things* [New York: Basic Books, 1999], 8, 31).

20. Susan Faludi, *Backlash: The Undeclared War Against American Women* (New York: Crown Publishers, Inc., 1991), 32–34; Ben J. Wattenberg, *The Birth Dearth* (New York: Pharos, 1989).

21. Douglas and Michaels, 92–93.

22. David Smith (with Carol Calef), *Beyond All Reason: My Life with Susan Smith* (New York: Pinnacle Books, 1995), 61.

23. *NBC Evening News,* October 27, 1994. It is difficult to imagine that local sources told national reporters about Susan Smith's job at the Winn-Dixie, where she had worked several years prior to the murders, but not about her current job at the Conso plant, where she had worked for over two years.

24. *NBC Evening News,* October 27, 1994.

25. Faludi, *Backlash,* 92, 117–23; Allison Morris and Ania Wilczynski, "Rocking the Cradle: Mothers Who Kill Their Children," in Birch, ed., *Moving Targets,* 198–217; Molly Haskell, "Hollywood Madonnas," *Ms.,* May 1988, 84–87.

26. Stacey, 6; Alexander Cockburn, "Out of the Mouths of Babes: Child Abuse and the Abuse of Adults," *The Nation,* February 12, 1990, 190–91; Russell Watson, "What Price Day Care?" *Newsweek,* September 10, 1984; Douglas and Michaels, 241; James Warren, "The Latest Harmful Drug of the '80s: Day Care?" *Chicago Tribune,* November 11, 1987. Douglas and Michaels quantified the day-care hysteria by counting articles in the *New York Times.* In 1980, there were approximately 50 articles about day care, "most of them innocuous and emphasizing the undersupply." By 1984, when the McMartin case made headlines, there were 240 (Douglas and Michaels, 95). For some background on the McMartin case, see Dorothy Rabinowitz, *No Crueler Tyrannies: Accusation, False Witness, and Other Terrors of Our Times* (New York: Free Press, 2003), viii–ix. Several of the child victims in the case have since recanted the accusations (Katherine Ramsland, "The McMartin Nightmare and the Hysteria Puppeteers: The True Victims," www.trutv.com/library/crime/criminal_mind/psychology/mcmartin_daycare/9.html [accessed July 26, 2010]).

27. Faludi, *Backlash,* 42; Douglas and Michaels, 88.

28. See Henderson, *Nine Days in Union,* 31, and Henderson, "'We Are Not Ruling Out Anything: Children Pray for Playmates," *Spartanburg Herald-Journal,* October 29, 1994.

29. *Ms.,* "Special Mothers' Issue," May 1988.

30. Anne Summers, "Editor's Essay: Mothers and Us," *Ms.,* May 1988, 4.

31. Barbara Ehrenreich, "The Heart of the Matter," *Ms,* May 1988, 20–21; Phyllis Chesler, "What Is a Mother?" *Ms.,* May 1988, 36–39.

32. Kathy Dobie, "Cherryl's Story," *Ms.,* "Special Mothers' Issue," May 1988, 42.

33. The scene on the next page of the ad depicts a young woman, the only African American in all eight pages, holding two cats in her lap. The copy argues that "it doesn't have to be an either/or decision." In the middle of the "Special Mothers' Issue," this copy perhaps had special meaning to the magazine's largely middle-class readers, bombarded as they were with the

1980s image of the full-time, careerist supermom who somehow managed to "have it all-in-one" (achievable "at Chevrolet," argued the fine print on that page). The last double-page image of the advertisement showed the only man in the ad; he is in a power suit, smiling, being hugged from behind by his equally ecstatic wife, also in a suit. "The advantage of being in control," reads the copy. In smaller print, the ad continues: "Taking matters into your own hands is an idea you wholeheartedly embrace. It lets you do what you want, when you want—while having as much fun as you want." These statements are about Chevy's "rack-and-pinion steering," but in this context and with this audience, they could just as easily be about women's life choices. The final page of the Chevy spread is slightly subtler. It features no large copy, just a sleeping child and the Chevy logo: "The Heartbeat of America" (Chevrolet advertisement, *Ms.*, "Special Mothers' Issue," May 1988, 45–52).

34. Edith Fierst, "Careers and Kids," *Ms.*, "Special Mothers' Issue," May 1988, 62.

35. Ibid., 64; Eyer, 8.

36. Louis Genevie and Eva Margolies, *The Motherhood Report: How Women Feel About Being Mothers* (New York: Macmillan Publishing Co., 1987).

37. David R. Francis, "Changing Behavior of Married Working Women," *National Bureau of Economic Research Digest,* November 2005, www.nber.org/digest/nov05/w11230.html (accessed August 1, 2011); Ann Snitow, "Feminism and Motherhood: An American Reading," *Feminist Review* 40 (Spring 1992): 40.

38. With an audience of twenty million viewers, weekly and monthly newsletters, two *New York Times* bestsellers, and planned expansions into the remainder of the English-speaking world, Dr. Laura was the most recognizable global voice of the "mommy myth" in the 1990s (Douglas and Michaels, 309–11; "Dr. Laura's Spiritual Journey Takes Turn," *WorldNet Daily,* www.wnd. com/?pageId=20212 [accessed July 4, 2011]; Craig Hamilton, "The Conscience of America," *What Is Enlightenment? Magazine* [Fall–Winter 1997], www.enlightennext.org/magazine/j12/laura. asp#at [accessed July 4, 2011]). In fact, she is still at it: in the spring of 2009, she published *In Praise of Stay-at-Home Moms.* In this latest tome, Dr. Laura expressed pity for working mothers and stated that she is as "happy as peach pie" that the 2009 recession forced women out of the workforce and back into the home (Sandy Maple, "Dr. Laura Schlesinger on Working Moms," www. parentdish.com/2009/05/13/dr-laura-schlessinger-on-working-moms/ [accessed July 4, 2011]).

39. Dobie, 44 (photograph and caption).

40. *ABC Evening News*, October 28, 1994; Russell, 89.

41. "'Ten Most Wanted' Deadbeat Dads," *Atlanta Journal Constitution*, June 24, 1994; "2 on Deadbeat Dad Poster Are Located," *Atlanta Journal Constitution*, August 24, 1994.

42. Editor, "Rewriting the Role of the Welfare System," *Atlanta Journal Constitution*, April 19, 1994; Susan Thomas, "From the Culture of Poverty to the Culture of Single Motherhood," *Women & Politics* 14, no. 2 (September 1994): 65–97.

43. Decker-Davis, interview; *CBS Evening News*, October 28, 1994. Rick Bragg of the *New York Times* argued that Decker-Davis was a primary voice in this coverage; in fact, he said that many other reporters "just kind of borrowed from her" (Bragg, interview, July 27, 2005). Decker-Davis agrees: "I definitely think the national media followed our newspaper on this story. We had the contacts with the local authorities and had all the sources. We also had loyal readers who would prefer to talk with reporters from their hometown newspaper."

44. Henderson, *Nine Days in Union,* 28; *ABC Evening News,* October 28, 1994; *CBS Evening News,* October 28, 1994; *NBC Evening News,* October 28, 1994; *CBS Evening News,* October 29, 1994. ABC's Mike von Fremd said in his report that night that the "new" information was from the local media. South Carolina journalist Gary Henderson remembers that the local and national media worked in tandem, with the national media often following the lead of local reporters (*Nine Days in Union,* 13).

45. Henderson, "Yellow Ribbons Fly for Union Children"; Bragg, "Agonizing Search."

46. Bragg, "Agonizing Search"; *CBS Evening News,* October 28, 1994; *NBC Evening News,* October 28, 1994. Gary Henderson of the *Spartanburg Herald-Journal* was not surprised to see Bragg in Union; Bragg had won awards a few years earlier for a piece he wrote on Mother's Day, so Henderson surmised that this apparent case of besieged southern maternity warranted Bragg's attention (*Nine Days in Union,* 42).

47. All of the background information about the investigation of Susan Smith comes from Russell, 162–66, 174–78, 189, 193.

48. The October 29, 1994, issue of the *Union Daily Times* is missing from their archives. Maria Eftimiades cites this article in her book on the case (*Sins of the Mother: The Heartbreaking True Story Behind the Susan Smith Murder Case* [New York: St. Martin's, 1995], 84); Bragg, "Sense of Dread Now Pervades Frantic Search," *New York Times,* October 31, 1994; *NBC Evening News,* October 29, 1994.

49. Bragg, "Sense of Dread." The nightly news programs of the three major television networks did not report on Smith's job at the Conso plant at all during the investigation, although they talked to plenty of locals who knew this information. Her occupation did not routinely make the national news until after her confession.

50. *NBC Evening News,* October 31, 1994.

51. Ibid.

52. Chris Burritt, "Parents' Emotional Plea to Missing Boys: 'Be Brave, Hold on to Each Other,'" *Atlanta Journal Constitution,* November 1, 1994; *NBC Evening News,* November 2, 1994. Police originally interviewed Sinclair as part of the routine investigation—he was, after all, part of Smith's alibi. His statement on the tabloid news program *A Current Affair* that Monday (six days after the boys went missing) that "the truth would come out" interested the media, and it caught the attention of Sheriff Wells. Sinclair later clarified that he meant that he knew law enforcement would do a good and thorough job with the investigation, not that he knew the "truth" or anything about the crime at all (*A Current Affair,* FOX, October 31, 1994; Russell, 207).

53. Russell, 223. This information did not leak to the media until after Smith's arrest. Gary Henderson literally smacked his forehead and called himself "stupid" for not checking out the stoplight during the investigation. "I could've busted the case wide open," he told me, shaking his head and smiling ruefully (interview). Bob Dotson of NBC, on the other hand, knew this information early on in the investigation; his brother-in-law, who worked for ATF in Charlotte, North Carolina, at the time, told him about the light in confidence. He could not publicize the information, but he believes he was the first national reporter to clearly show his own suspicion because of this confidential information (interview).

54. Russell, 223.

55. "Parents Aching to Hug Sons Again," *Spartanburg Herald-Journal,* November 2, 1994.

The family spokesperson told reporters that Susan and David Smith did not have the "emotional strength" to face the media (Burritt, "Parents' Emotional Plea").

56. Les Timms III, "Mother Made Impassioned Plea on National Media Hours Before Arrest," *Union Daily Times*, November 4, 1994; *NBC Evening News*, November 2, 1994.

57. *NBC Today Show*, November 3, 1994. Susan and David Smith were interviewed live via satellite on ABC, CBS, and NBC.

58. There are several websites that purport to contain Susan Smith's entire written confession, but many of them are excerpted and contain typos and/or misinformation. Gary Henderson included a copy of Smith's handwritten confession in the appendix of *Nine Days in Union* (117–18).

CHAPTER TWO

1. Dotson, interview.

2. Tom Teepen, "Baby-killing Mother Plays the Race Card," *Charleston Gazette* (WV), November 8, 1994. Historian Glenda Gilmore realized as much when she saw the composite sketch of the alleged carjacker on the news. In an essay about the "black beast rapist" and the Wilmington, North Carolina, riots of 1898, she described her realization. Although the initial reports of carjacking on the radio frightened Gilmore, her feelings changed when she watched the news that night: "Susan Smith was lying, I realized in a rush. For I had 'seen' this man before, in sources almost one hundred years old" ("Murder, Memory, and the Flight of the Incubus," 74).

3. Feldman, "The Status Quo Society," 302.

4. Paul Harvey, "Gods and Negroes and Jesus and Sin and Salvation: Racism, Racial Interchange, and Interracialism in Southern Religious History," in *Religion in the American South: Protestants and Others in History and Culture,* ed. Beth Barton Schweiger and Donald G. Mathews (Chapel Hill: University of North Carolina Press, 2004), 291.

5. Jacquelyn Dowd Hall, "'The Mind That Burns,'" 334; Williamson, 117; Hodes; Brundage, 10.

6. Brundage, 117; Hall, "'The Mind That Burns,'" 329–49; James McGovern, *Anatomy of a Lynching* (Baton Rouge: Louisiana State University Press, 1982), 66; Southern Commission on the Study of Lynching, *Lynchings and What They Mean* (Atlanta: Southern Commission on the Study of Lynching, 1931), 44–45; Arthur Raper, *The Tragedy of Lynching* (Chapel Hill: University of North Carolina Press, 1933), 12–13; Ralph Ginzburg, ed., *One Hundred Years of Lynchings* (Baltimore: Black Classic Press, 1962), 221–23; Williamson, 185–89; Kantrowitz, 163.

7. For estimated numbers, see: Clarence A. Bacote, "Negro Proscriptions, Protests, and Proposed Solutions," in *The Negro in the South since 1865,* ed. Charles E. Wynes (University: Alabama University Press, 1965), 158; Hall, "'The Mind That Burns,'" 334. The majority of male victims were accused of murder or complicity therein. Historian Glenda Gilmore points out the misuse of rape statistics in turn-of-the-century North Carolina; a rise in reported rapes could be taken as proof of a "black beast rapist" rampage, but for one problem: the attorney general's record of these cases does not list the race of the rapists (*Gender and Jim Crow,* 86). Likewise, prior to the Wilmington race riot of 1898, there was no "appreciable increase" in rapes or attempted rape ("Murder, Memory, and the Flight of the Incubus," 75). Historian Joel Williamson points out that

the numbers were unknown at the time: "In the 1890s, when lynching was most prevalent, no one really knew how many rapes or attempted rapes there had been, or how many lynchings, or that the whole distressing process would end this side of disaster" (118). The "Southern rape complex" required little actual proof in numbers. For information about Ida Wells-Barnett and Jessie Daniels Ames's critiques of the "rape myth," see Jacquelyn Dowd Hall's "'The Mind That Burns'" and *Revolt Against Chivalry*. In the 1890s, Wells-Barnett wrote that only about a third of lynchings "were even purportedly in retaliation for acts of rape or attempted rape" (Kantrowitz, 164; see also Alfreda Duster, ed., *Crusade for Justice* [Chicago: University of Chicago Press, 1970]). She also famously challenged the "rape myth" on the grounds that it served as a cover for white male violence against African American women. In her famous 1895 tract, she listed several female victims of lynching. Historian Crystal Feimster has since counted at least 130 African American women who fell prey to lynch mobs between 1880 and 1930.

. 8. Wilbur J. Cash, *The Mind of the South* (New York: Vintage Books, 1941), 117; Williamson, 214.

9. Gilmore, "Murder, Memory, and the Flight of the Incubus," 89, 75; Hall, "'The Mind That Burns,'" 332; Williamson, 129. Pamela Haag points out that with black male/white female relations, consent was considered "impossible," but when black women were involved, consent was assumed. She quotes a contemporary sociologist, Lester Ward, who explained the four laws of consent, or "acceptable" rape: first, "the women of any race will freely accept the men of a race which they regard as higher"; second, "the women of any race with vehemently reject the men of a race which they regard as lower than their own"; third, "the men of any race will greatly prefer women of a race which they regard as higher"; and fourth, "the men of any race, in default of women of a higher race, will be content with women of a lower race" (*Consent: Sexual Rights and the Transformation of American Liberalism* [Ithaca, NY: Cornell University Press, 1995], 143).

10. James Goodman, *Stories of Scottsboro* (New York: Vintage Books, 1995), 1–2, 11.

11. Richard Wright, *Native Son* (New York: Harper & Row Publishers, 1940); Stephen J. Whitfield, *A Death in the Delta: The Story of Emmett Till* (Baltimore: Johns Hopkins University Press).

12. Eldridge Cleaver, *Soul on Ice* (New York: Mass Market Paperbacks, 1970); Jennifer Auther, "'He Was a Symbol': Eldridge Cleaver Dies at 62," CNN, May 1, 1998. The real irony here is that, after fulfilling all manner of white fears during his militant phase, Cleaver went on to become a born-again Christian, an anti-communist, and a Republican (Auther).

13. Malcolm Gladwell, *The Tipping Point: How Little Things Can Make a Big Difference* (New York: Little, Brown, and Co., 2000), 133–135.

14. Elayne Rapping, *Law and Justice as Seen on Television* (New York: New York University Press, 2003), 61.

15. "Your Car or Your Watch," *Economist,* September 14, 1991; John Hurwitz and Mark Peffley, "Public Perceptions of Race and Crime: The Role of Racial Stereotypes," *American Journal of Political Science* 41, no. 2 (April 1997): 375–401; Tom Wolfe, *The Bonfire of the Vanities* (New York: Bantam Books, 1988); U.S. Department of Justice, "National Crime Victimization Survey: Carjacking, 1993–2002," bjs.ojp.usdoj.gov/content/pub/ascii/c02.txt (accessed August 15, 2011).

16. Wendy Kozol, "Fracturing Domesticity: Media, Nationalism, and the Question of Feminist Influence." *Signs* (Spring 95): 660.

17. Susan Fraiman, "Geometries of Race and Gender: Eve Sedgewick, Spike Lee, and Charlayne Hunter-Gault," *Feminist Studies* 20, no. 1 (March 1994).

18. Tali Mendelberg, "Executing Hortons: Racial Crime in the 1988 Presidential Campaign," *Public Opinion Quarterly* 61, no. 1 (Spring 1997), 134–57. Video of the ad is available online at www.youtube.com/watch?v=Io9KMSSEZoY (last accessed July 4, 2011).

19. Feldman, "The Status Quo Society," 309; Mendelberg, 137.

20. Constance L. Hays, "Boston Agonizes Over Street Violence," *New York Times*, October 28, 1989; David Mehegan, "He's Turned the Stuart Case into Fiction," *Boston Globe*, July 11, 2006.

21. Judy Rakowsky, "Jury Clears Officers in Stuart Case: Victory Claimed for Police in Handling of 1989 Probe," *Boston Globe*, July 8, 1995; Kozol, 646. Nikki Giovanni reportedly called the Simpson case a "Scottsboro Redux" (Abigail Thernstrom and Henry D. Felter, "From Scottsboro to Simpson," *Public Interest* 122 [January 1, 1996]).

22. Anna Brown, "Search Widens for Carjacking Suspect," *Union Daily Times*, October 26, 1994; *NBC Evening News*, October 26, 1994. "Tobaggans," or knit winter caps, are more commonly known as "sleds" outside the South.

23. Gilmore, "Murder, Memory, and the Flight of the Incubus," 74, 90.

24. The fetishized photo of the boys acquired even more significance after Smith's confession. When Sheriff Howard Wells announced that he had arrested Susan Smith for the murder of her children, he wore the picture of them over a yellow ribbon on his lapel (*NBC Evening News*, November 3, 1994). With one exception, the photo has graced the cover of every book published about the case (Eftimiades; Henderson, *Nine Days in Union;* Andrea Peyser, *Mother Love, Deadly Love: The Susan Smith Murders* [New York: HarperCollins, 1995]); Smith [with Calef]. Prosecutor Tommy Pope still had the picture on display in his office over a decade after the trial, or at least he did the day that I interviewed him (interview, York, SC, July 19, 2005).

25. Ron Rosenbaum, "Staring Into the Heart of the Heart of Darkness," *New York Times*, June 4, 1995; Peyser, 90.

26. David Hancock, "A Tale of Two Kidnappings: Media Questioned about the Why's of Who's News," CBSNews.com, www.cbsnews.com/stories/2002/06/20/national/main512915 .shtml (accessed July 4, 2011). This problem again made headlines as this book went to press. In October 2011, Margaret Hartmann of Jezebel.com highlighted the disparity in media coverage of the case of infant Lisa Irwin of Missouri and that of Jahyssye Shockley, a five-year-old African American girl from Arizona. Irwin made the cover of *People,* while Shockley received only local and statewide media coverage. Hartmann argues that, while the "missing white woman" syndrome' is certainly real," there are other factors that might explain the difference in coverage ("Is Racism Behind the Underreporting of a Missing Black Girl?" Jezebel.com, October 27, 2011, jezebel.com/5853792/is-racism-behind-the-underreporting-of-a-missing-black-girl [accessed November 1, 2011]).

27. Bruck, interview; Charles L. Warner, "Oprah Winfrey Brings Show to Buffalo," *Union Daily Times*, November 7, 1994; *The Oprah Winfrey Show,* ABC, November 8, 1994. Many locals disagreed with this statement, arguing that they would have acted the same way regardless of the race of the children and their mother. Reverend A. L. Brackett argued that the boys were thought of as the "children of the country," and that black and white alike searched the local woods for them. Like many others, Brackett firmly believed that the boys had been kidnapped right up until

Smith's confession. On the other hand, he believes that the media paid such attention to this case because "a black was involved" in Smith's carjacking lie, so race was a factor (interview, Union, SC, July 20, 2005).

28. Lindquist-Dorr, 99; Kozol, 278. Historian Stephen Kantrowitz found a case with this class and gender dynamic in his research on former South Carolina governor and senator Ben Tillman: "When Jake Davis, a black man, was lynched for allegedly attempting to rape the wife of a 'respectable' white Abbeville man, a reporter noted that Davis had 'committed an assault on a white woman in this community a few years ago, but as her character was questionable he was allowed to go unpunished.'" Likewise, Tillman pardoned another convicted rapist on the grounds of his victim's "questionable character" (Kantrowitz, 170). Wendy Kozol argues that this question of a female victim's "suitability" was a problem at the end of the century as well. Comparing the "Central Park Jogger" case, in which a wealthy white woman was the victim, and the "Glen Ridge Rape" case, in which a mentally retarded, white, high-school girl was gang-raped by her classmates, she finds that the media coverage indicated that the rape of the "brilliant investment banker" was somehow more "heinous." The perpetrators in the "Central Park Jogger" case were minorities, while in the Glen Ridge case, they were middle-class, all-American, football-playing white teenagers. This may well account for some of the discrepancies in the media coverage of the respective victims. See Bernard Lefkowitz, *Our Guys: The Glen Ridge Rape and the Secret Life of the Perfect Suburb* (Berkeley: University of California Press, 1997).

29. Judy Rakowsky, "Carjacking Mystery Stuns SC Community," *Boston Globe*, October 30, 1994.

30. *CBS Evening News*, November 2, 1994.

31. Chris Burritt, ""Mother Charged with Murder: The Unraveling Life of Susan Smith," *Atlanta Journal Constitution*, November 6, 1994; Chris Burritt, "Blacks See Mother's Story as Just Another Outrage," *Atlanta Journal Constitution*, November 4, 1994; Eftimiades, 175. Edwards continued his diatribe to Eftimiades: "No black person does something like that. We know we're ninety percent of the prison population, we been ninety percent since 1776. We know when we go down to that prison for certain crimes, we going to be taken care of. It ain't going to be tomorrow, it's going to be as soon as we get down there. One's bothering children, bothering old women, messing with the women. You going to get it, that's all. Any black guy would have to be completely out of his mind to commit such a crime. You see me? Big old black guy with two white kids? No, no" (94).

32. *Nightline*, November 3, 1004; Don Terry, "A Woman's False Accusation Pains Many Blacks," *New York Times*, November 6, 1994; *NBC Evening News*, November 4, 1994.

33. *Nightline*, November 3, 1994.

34. Gary Lee, "Black Residents Angered By Reaction 'to False Story; 'No One Has Rushed Forward to Apologize,'" *Washington Post*, November 7, 1994. Reverend Brackett said that the local police only seriously questioned three African American men, and that they did so on tips from other African Americans (interview). These locals' words inspired the Cornelius Eady poem, "Next of Kin." Eady writes of the men the police questioned during the investigation: "The black man in town / They thought looked like me, / Without the dreamed-up cap / And wardrobe. / The police have him now. / . . . I whisper *we're innocent* / Into his ears. / He looks so much like me, / We could be brothers. / Already, folks / May have their doubts: / He's poor enough. / Where has

he been? / He has his needs. / What do they know? / Neighbors call him *quiet,* / A new knot of stress / On the tongue. / It's been a hard week / To be black in Union, S.C." (*Brutal Imagination: Poems* [New York: G. P. Putnam's Sons, 2001], 39–40).

35. Charles Sennott, "Case Confirms Some Fears of Racism in SC Town," *Boston Globe,* November 6, 1994; "The Kidnapping of Trust," *Boston Globe,* November 5, 1994. Cynthia Tucker of the *Atlanta Journal Constitution* argued that Smith's confession struck a different "chord" with African Americans, who may have even felt relief. "Black experience has taught that black men can be accused of—sometimes executed for—crimes they did not commit," and this may well have been the outcome if Smith had not confessed ("Hysteria Slows Search for Any Lasting Solutions," *Atlanta Journal Constitution,* November 11, 1994).

36. Harpo Productions, Inc., *The Oprah Winfrey Show,* November 8, 1994.

37. Rick Bragg, "Police Say Woman Admits to Killings"; McElroy Hughes, interview, Union, SC, July 16, 2006.

38. Hughes, interview; Peyser, 88–90. Hughes argues that race relations in Union are still conflicted. He operates a makeshift African American history museum in the basement of his church in downtown Union, but he has had trouble getting the local schools to approve class visits. He does acknowledge some progress—for instance, he said, a white women (me) coming to interview an African American man on his terms represents real change (although he also later admitted that a combination of my persistence and his belief that I was a black woman led him to grant the interview). Growing up, he said, black men "did not have the liberty to look a white woman in the eyes," but we have both been "liberated," so perhaps the culture is "on the right path racially" (interview).

39. Tom Teepen, "Baby-killing Mother Plays the Race Card," *Charleston Gazette* (WV), November 8, 1994; Jan Glidewell, "Racial Hoax Shows Our Inner Bias," *St. Petersburg Times* (FL), November 20, 1994; Edward Pratt, "Please Find Another Scapegoat," *Advocate* (LA), November 14, 1994; "Significant Contrast," *Augusta Chronicle* (GA), November 14, 1994; Adam Pertman, "Mother Held in SC Killings" *Boston Globe,* November 4, 1994; "Susan Smith's Betrayal," *Washington Times,* November 6, 1994; Jerry Adler and Ginny Carroll, "Innocents Lost," *Newsweek,* November 14, 1994; Pamela Warrick, "Exposing the Big Lie," *Los Angeles Times,* August 29, 1995; Kevin A. Ross, "Letter to the Editor: Drowning Case Embitters U.S. Race Relations," *New York Times,* November 11, 1994. Many have questioned the credibility of Murray and Hernstein's research; in addition to disputing some of their findings, FAIR (Fairness and Accuracy In Reporting) traced their research funding to a eugenics organization (Jim Naureckis, "Racism Resurgent," *Extra!* January–February 1995, www.fair.org/index.php?page=1271 (accessed August 1, 2011).

40. Glidewell, "Racial Hoax Shows Our Inner Bias"; "Significant Contrast," *Augusta Chronicle* (GA), November 15, 1994; Burritt, "Blacks See Mother's Story as Just Another Outrage'; "Smith's Allegation Angers Black Mother," *Greensboro News & Record* (NC), November 16, 1994; "Stereotyping, Black and White," *Times-Picayune* (LA), November 9, 1994; "Saving Grace in Smith Tragedy," *Atlanta Journal Constitution,* November 9, 1994. The *Union Daily Times* reported that Wells received "mountains of mail" commending him on his professionalism conducting what could have been a controversial investigation (Anna Brown, "Sheriff Getting Mountain of Mail Concerning Case," *Union Daily Times,* November 17, 1994).

41. Richard Lacayo, "Stranger in the Shadows," *Time,* November 14, 1994.

42. Ibid.

43. *NBC Evening News,* November 8, 1994; Russell, 251; William Raspberry, "Apology Eases Pain of False Accusation," *Tampa Tribune,* November 10, 1994.

44. Sam Venable, "Rev. Jesse Jackson Should Hush, Leave Union, SC, Alone," *Knoxville News-Sentinel* (TN), November 13, 1994.

45. Douglas and Michaels, 165; Burritt, "Blacks See Mother's Story as Just Another Outrage"; Teepen, "Baby-Killing Mother Plays the Race Card"; Henderson, interview; Henderson, "'Hideous' Scene Ended Ordeal," *Spartanburg Herald-Journal* (SC), November 5, 1994.

46. This was a particularly interesting news peg given the history of images of African American mothers in the South. The "black beast" myth was peculiar to African American men; in general, black women were not seen as predatory to southern whites, although historian Crystal Feimster has unearthed some instances in which turn-of-the century media accounts portrayed African American women as monsters in order to justify a lynching after the fact (166). The majority of African American women were seen as harmless by whites, for a very practical reason: this image would have challenged the racist and sexist labor structure of the South. Up to 90 percent of African American women worked in white homes and often cared for white children in the first half of the twentieth century, a working relationship that has recently gotten a lot of press coverage because of the summer 2011 film *The Help.* See the Association of Black Women Historians' "Open Statement" regarding the film at www.abwh.org/index.php?option=com_content&view=article&id=2:open-statement-the-help&catid=1:latestnews (accessed October 20, 2011). At any rate, in order for the economic exploitation of black female domestic workers to continue unabated, these women had to be seen as unthreatening. For background on African American female domestic workers, see Tera Hunter's *To 'Joy My Freedom: Southern Black Women's Lives and Labors* (Cambridge, MA: Harvard University Press, 1997) and Jacqueline Jones, *Labor of Love, Labor of Sorrow: Black Women, Work, and the Family, from Slavery to the Present* (New York: Basic Books, 1985).

47. "Family Apologizes to Union Blacks for Smith's False Claim," *Atlanta Journal Constitution,* November 9, 1994; Tom Currie, interview, July 11, 2005. Clearly, this begs the question; as Helan Page pointed out in *American Anthropologist,* Smith's lie simply underscored the "racial knowledge" of the "plausibility" of black male criminality that she had "internalized" ("Black Male Imagery and Media Containment of African American Men," *American Anthropologist* 99, no. 1 [March 1997]: 101).

48. *Nightline,* November 3, 1994; Larry Timbs, "To Print or Not to Print an Alleged Victim's Claims," *Editor and Publisher* 127, no. 51 (December 17, 1994). Wilder explained that they did not print the composite sketch because the attacker was black, saying that if Smith had blamed a "pointed-ear Vulcan," they would have run that information if it would help find the children.

49. Bob Cato, interview, Laurens, SC, January 11, 2006.

50. Brackett, interview; Charles Warner, "Mother's Actions Not Seen as Racially Motivated," *Union Daily Times,* November 4, 1994; Anna Brown, "Forum Planned for Citizens to Voice Feelings on Case," *Union Daily Times,* November 5, 1994.

51. Eftimiades, 223. Rev. Brackett told me that Jackson called him because he wanted to help: "He was willing to come in, to do whatever that he could, to help with the healing process—and

Jessie did us a lot of good. He came in and he went to—he came to this church, and he addressed the local leaders, religious and city and county officials, and then he went to the high school, where I imagine 1,500 or more kids filled the auditorium, and he addressed them and he, you know, Jessie can excite as nobody else can. He did a lot of good" (interview).

52. *CBS Evening News,* November 4, 1994.

53. Allan Charles, *The Narrative History of Union County, SC,* 3rd ed. (Greenville, SC: A PRESS Printing Co., 1997); Allen Charles, interview, Union, SC, November 2, 2006. Mac Johnson, formerly of the Union County Chamber of Commerce, agreed that "mixed couples" existed in Union, but the "taboo" against it was probably only amongst the "older crowd" (Peyser, 84). "Much has been made of the lynching of blacks, especially for the crime of raping white women," he wrote in the county's only official history. "But either there was very little lynching done in Union County or the newspapers refused to report it." Indeed, the Union newspaper explicitly condemned lynching during the Jim Crow era, "with possibly the exception of rape" (Charles, *The Narrative History of Union County, SC,* 319).

54. Kantrowitz, 156, 165; "Statistics on Lynching in the United States and South Carolina," www.sciway.net/afam/reconstruction/lynching.html (accessed July 5, 2011); Fox Butterfield, *All God's Children: The Bosket Family and the American Tradition of Violence* (New York: Harper Perennial, 1995), 49, 56; Kantrowitz, 177.

55. A historical marker acknowledging Earle's murder was erected in February 2011 ("Willie Earle Memorial," WSPA News, www2.wspa.com/news/2011/feb/24/willie-earle-memorial-04953-vi-72200/ [accessed August 15, 2011]). For information on the Orangeburg Massacre, see Jack Bass and Jack Nelson, *The Orangeburg Massacre* (Macon, GA: Mercer University Press, 1996). For reports on the flag controversy of 1994, see: "South Carolina G.O.P. Backs Rebel Flag," *New York Times,* August 11, 1994; "March of Opponents of Confederate Flag," September 4, 1994; Jerelyn Eddings, "Business Takes on the Confederate Flag," *U.S. News & World Report,* December 5, 1994. The controversy still plagues South Carolina: in the summer of 2011, the NAACP asked Governor Nikki Haley to remove the flag from a monument outside the statehouse, where it has been on display since its relocation in response NAACP protests in 2000 ("Nikki Haley Asked by NAACP Head to Remove Confederate Flag by South Carolina Statehouse," *Huffington Post,* July 26, 2011, www.huffingtonpost.com/2011/07/26/nikki-haley-confederate-flag_n_910392.html [accessed August 15, 2011]).

56. Peyser, 83–84.

57. Ibid.

58. Kevin Kingsmore, interview, Moore, SC, November 3, 2006; Michael Roberts, interview, Buffalo, SC, November 4, 2006; Phil Hobbs, interview, November 16, 2006. The quotes about local racism came from, respectively: Kingsmore, interview; Hobbs, interview; Tom Currie, interview; Thom White, interview, Union, SC, July 19, 2005.

59. Torance Inman, interview, Union, SC, June 18, 2007.

60. Bragg, interview. CBS's Amy Birnbaum told me about another reporter "scoffing" at the prosecution's decision to seek capital punishment, "saying this jury would never hang a young blond mother, one of their own" (interview).

61. *NBC Evening News,* July 22, 1995; Charles L. Warner, "Racism Issue Takes Up Much of 'TalkBack' Time," *Union Daily Times,* July 18, 1995.

62. Cynthia Tucker, "The Painful Legacy of Susan Smith," *New Orleans Times-Picayune* (LA), November 14, 1994.

63. Kozol, 646.

64. The disappearance of the racial angle from the media did not go unnoticed by media consumers, particularly African Americans. In fact, the racial dynamics of the Smith case became the subject of two acclaimed works in the ensuing years, Cornelius Eady's *Brutal Imagination,* a book of poems, and Richard Price's *Freedomland* (New York: Random House, 1998), a popular novel that became a not-so-popular film in 2006 (Joe Roth, dir., *Freedomland,* Revolution Studios, 2006).

CHAPTER THREE

1. "A Saving Grace in Smith Tragedy," *Atlanta Journal Constitution,* November 9, 1994; Daniel Maier-Katkin, "Infanticide By Mothers Is a Common Form of Homicide," *Greensboro News & Record* (NC), November 27, 1994; Harrison Ranie, "A Mother, Two Kids, and the Unthinkable," *U.S. News and World Report,* November 14, 1994; "Children: Nothing Is More Important," *Virginian-Pilot* (Norfolk), November 24, 1994; Bella English, "Mothers Wonder: How?" *Boston Globe,* November 5, 1994; Henderson, interview; *NBC Evening News,* November 4, 1994. Veteran *New York Times* reporter Rick Bragg said he believed Smith up until the moment of her confession, but he was always plagued with a "nagging doubt." He ignored the doubt, because "it was all too awful otherwise" (interview). CBS producer Amy Birnbaum remembers thinking of her own toddler when she heard about Smith's confession; fearing she could no longer cover the story objectively, she called her boss to see if she could be replaced in Union (interview).

2. Deborah Halter, "Susan Smith Becomes the Moral Scapegoat of a Nation," *Arkansas Democrat-Gazette,* November 13, 1994; Charles M. Sennott, "In SC, Fury Over Deaths," *Boston Globe,* November 5, 1994. Smith's crimes met two of the criteria for capital punishment: there was more than one victim, and both victims were children (Pope, interview).

3. Henderson, interview.

4. Maralee Schwartz and Kenneth J. Cooper, "Equal Rights Initiative in Iowa Attacked," *Washington Post,* August 23, 1992.

5. Russell, 113.

6. Ibid., 122.

7. Annalee Newitz, "Murdering Mothers," in *"Bad Mothers": The Politics of Blame in Twentieth-Century America,* ed. Molly Ladd-Taylor and Lauri Umansky (New York: NYU Press, 1998), 340.

8. Elizabeth Kastor, "The Worst Fears, the Worse Reality: For Parents, Murder Case Strikes at Heart of Darkness," *Washington Post,* November 5, 1994.

9. Elizabeth Simpson, "Susan Smith Case Awakens Fear of the Enemy Within," *Virginian-Pilot,* November 13, 1994; Adler and Carroll, "Innocents Lost"; *NBC Evening News,* November 5, 1994; Timms, "Mother Made Impassioned Plea"; Bragg, "Police Say Woman Admits to Killings." *People* reporter Maria Eftimiades recounted Susan's paeans to motherhood in her diary after Michael's birth in 1991: "I was so happy. I had given birth to the most beautiful boy in the world. When he was put in my arms for the very first time, I forgot all about my other pains. He really lifted my spirits and touched my heart" (Eftimiades, 45).

10. Rick Bragg, "Life of a Mother Accused of Killing Offers No Clues," *New York Times*, November 6, 1994.

11. Timms, "Mother Made Impassioned Plea."

12. Bob Herbert, "The Ugliest of Stories, with Coverage to Match," *Tampa Tribune*, November 13, 1994.

13. Smith, 145. *Time* reported that Susan's most recent ex-boyfriend also turned over a copy of the letter during the initial investigation (Nancy Gibbs and Kathy Booth, "Death and Deceit," *Time*, November 14, 1994).

14. South Carolina v. Smith, 2685. The full text of Findlay's break-up letter is available online at crime.about.com/od/murder/a/susan_smith_4.htm.

15. "Crowd at Court Hearing Jeers Murder Suspect," *Charleston Gazette* (WV), November 5, 1994.

16. Ann Jones, 3.

17. The Equal Opportunity Employment Commission opened for business less than two weeks before the Crimmins case made headlines. See U.S. Equal Employment Opportunity Commission, "A 'Toothless Tiger' Helps Shape the Law and Educate the Public," www.eeoc.gov/eeoc/history/35th/1965-71/index.html (accessed July 5, 2011); "Roosevelt Finds Sex Discrimination in Jobs Is Big Problem; Appoints Seven Key Aides," *New York Times*, July 21, 1965; "Women Complain of Bias on Jobs," *New York Times*, July 26, 1975; Kenneth Gross, *The Alice Crimmins Case* (New York: Alfred A. Knopf, 1975).

18. Ann Jones, 277; Gross, 19, 33; "'Sexpot' on Trial," *CourtTV's Crime Library*, www.crimelibrary.com/notorious_murders/family/crimmins/8.html. The site is "The Crime Library," run by the popular cable television station CourtTV, now known as "TruTV." (www.trutv.com/library/crime/notorious_murders/famous/downs/index_1.html [accessed July 5, 2011]).

19. "Shock and Aftermath," *CourtTV's Crime Library*, www.crimelibrary.com/notorious_murders/family/crimmins/15.html (accessed July 5, 2011). Her case inspired two true-crime books, two novels, two plays, and three films, one of which starred Tuesday Weld "at her most glamorous and vulnerable" as Alice Crimmins ("Genesis of a Sensation," *CourtTV's Crime Library*, www.crimelibrary.com/notorious_murders/family/crimmins/1.html). The books include: Gross's *The Alice Crimmins Case*; George Capozi Jr.'s *Ordeal By Trial* (New York: Walker & Co., 1972); Dorothy Uhnak's *The Investigation* (New York: Pocket Books, 1978); and Mary Higgins Clark's *Where Are the Children?* (New York: Mass Market Paperbacks, 1992). The plays are: John Guare, *The Landscape of the Body* (New York: Grove Press, 1977), and Neal Bell, *Two Small Bodies*, which also opened in 1977. The films are: *A Question of Guilt* (Robert Butler, director, Polygram Video, 1978); *Where Are the Children?* (Bruce Malmuth, director, Columbia Pictures, 1986); and *Two Small Bodies*, based on Neal Bell's play (Daniel Zuta Filmproduktion, 1993).

20. Ann Rule, *Small Sacrifices* (New York: Signet Books, 1987).

21. "Diane Downs," *The Oprah Winfrey Show*, September 26, 1988. The media revived the story again in 2005 when an Oregon file clerk came forth with the startling information that he fell in love with Downs after her appearance on *Oprah* and was in the process of hatching yet another elaborate escape plan with her (Phil Stanford, "Diane Downs' Love Slave," *Portland Tribune* [OR], 2005).

22. S. Bryan Hickox, producer, *Small Sacrifices*, Anchor Bay Entertainment, Inc., 1989. The

film was nominated for several awards, including three Emmys and two Golden Globes, and it won a Peabody (www.imdb.com/title/tt0098352/awards [accessed July 5, 2011]).

23. Alan O'Connor, "Culture and Communication," in Downing et al., 35.

24. Anthony's defense team borrowed the Susan Smith script again when they introduced the idea that Anthony's father had repeatedly molested her in the past as a potential mitigating factor for her dishonesty (Warren Richey, "Casey Anthony Murder Trial: What did her 'Bella Vita' tattoo mean?" *Christian Science Monitor*, June 14, 2011).

25. Adler and Carroll, "Innocents Lost"; Gibbs and Booth, "Death and Deceit."

26. Abigail Trafford, "The Medea Syndrome," *Washington Post*, November 8, 1994; Mary McGrory, "We're Not Talking Crime, More Like Raw Evil," *Charleston Gazette* (WV), November 9, 1994.

27. Don Melvin, "A Mom's New Love Often Tied to Child Killings," *Atlanta Journal Constitution*, November 4, 1994. And it was not just "new" lovers that sparked infanticide; Melvin detailed the case of Martha Ann Johnson, who allegedly murdered her four children over the course of five years to "get her husband to return" after fights.

28. *CBS Evening News*, November 4, 1994; Tom Currie, interview; Hickox, *Small Sacrifices* (film). Like the "Long Island Lolita" Amy Fisher and prostitute/serial killer Aileen Wuornos, Smith became, in public representations, a "sex kitten in the slammer" almost overnight (Elizabeth Wurtzel, *Bitch: In Praise of Difficult Women* [New York: Random House, 1998]), 3. Wurtzel argues in her discussion of the Amy Fisher case: "You see, Amy is not, I don't think, one of those girls who would inevitably become a sex object, a wild thing. She was apparently shy—all the news accounts seem to agree on these few facts—and she was not one to play with alcohol or drugs. But more to the point—and I feel like somebody needs to say this—she was no great beauty" (114). In other words, the sexualization of certain female criminals has little to do with looks or behavior. Regardless, sex reigned in the headlines, especially the tabloids, which featured "Baby Killer Susan Smith's X-Rated Secret Life" and "Story that Could Blow Lid Off Tiny Town: Susan Smith's Many Lovers" ("Tabloids Tell Different Story of Smith Trial," *Union Daily Times*, July 17, 1995). The minute details of these images have remarkable staying power; Dr. Allan Charles of USC-Union mentioned the hot tub in his interview with me ten years after the trial.

29. *CBS Evening News*, November 3, 1994.

30. Douglas and Michaels, 93; U.S. Department of Health and Human Services, Administration for Children and Families, "Survey Shows Dramatic Increase in Child Abuse and Neglect, 1986–1993," press release, September 18, 1996, www.prevent-abuse-now.com/stats.htm#Increase (accessed July 5, 2011); "Third National Incidence Study of Child Abuse and Neglect," www.healthieryou.com/cabuse.html (accessed July 5, 2011); Kastor, "The Worst Fears, the Worse Reality." There are problems with these estimates, especially the idea of "likelihood"—in raw numbers, women abuse more than men because more women are caregivers. But if you do the numbers for likelihood of women caregivers versus male caregivers, a male caregiver is at least twice as likely to abuse a child ("Statistics—Male versus Female: Who Is More Likely to Perpetrate Child Abuse," *Liz Library Online*, www.thelizlibrary.org/site-index/site-index-frame. html#soulhttp://www.thelizlibrary.org/site-index/site-index [accessed July 5, 2011]). Thirty to 40 percent of child-abuse perpetrators are "mothers acting alone" (Jeanne Flavin, *Our Bodies,*

Our Crimes: The Policing of Women's Reproduction in America [New York: New York University Press, 2009], 30).

31. *NBC Evening News,* November 18, 1994.

32. Rebecca Ann Schernitzski, "What Kind of Mother Are You? The Relationship Between Motherhood, Battered Woman Syndrome and Missouri Law," *Journal of the Missouri Bar* 56, no. 1 (January–February 2000), www.mobar.org/journal/2000/janfeb/scher.htm (accessed February 20, 2011); Michelle S. Jacobs, "Requiring Battered Women Die: Murder Liability for Mothers Under Failure to Protect Statues," *Journal of Criminal Law and Criminology* 88, no. 2 (Winter 1998): 579–660.

33. David Van Biema and Ratu Kamlani, "Parents Who Kill," *Time,* November 14, 1994; "Susan Smith's Betrayal"; Don Melvin, "Parents as Killers a Familiar Refrain in Recent Years," *Atlanta Journal Constitution,* November 4, 1994.

34. Schernitzski; Zile and her husband were convicted of first-degree murder, and she is now serving a life sentence without parole in Florida (Jacobs, "Requiring Battered Women Die," 583

35. Dan Quayle maintained that his real target was not single mothers but absent fathers, and the idea of forcing a nuclear family structure played a large role in the welfare reforms passed while Smith awaited trial. As John Fiske argues, "The problem is that Murphy Brown, as a woman-mother, does not have a man" (*Media Matters: Everyday Culture and Political Change* [Minneapolis: University of Minnesota Press], 39).

36. Brackett, interview; Shelley Levitt and Don Sider, "Portrait of a Killer," *People,* November 21, 1994. Susan Smith appeared on the cover of *Time* accompanied by the headline, "How Could She Do It?" on November 14, 1994. The image is available online at www.crimerant.com/wp-content/uploads/2006/09/susan%20smith.jpg (accessed July 5, 2011).

37. Elizabeth Gleick and Lisa H. Towle, "It Did Happen Here," *Time,* December 19, 1994; Letter to the Editor, "Fathers Should Have Equal Rights," *The Advocate* (LA), November 19, 1994. Reverend Bob Cato told me about a phone call he got from a group called Men Without Children, which he described as an organization dedicated to the issue of "mothers who had abused kids in the absence of fathers." The caller was very angry in his defense of David Smith: "He really went off, talking as if David could walk on water" (interview).

38. Ansell, 92. Video of the ad is available online at www.youtube.com/watch?v=KIyewCdXMzk (accessed July 5, 2011). Some credit the ad with "destroying" Gantt's campaign (William Saletan, *Bearing Right: How Conservatives Won the Abortion War* [Berkeley: University of California Press, 2003], 120).

39. Ansell, 197, 206.

40. Quoted from *Dateline* on *NBC Evening News,* November 15, 1994.

41. "Dan Quayle vs. Murphy Brown," *Time,* June 1, 1992.

42. Quoted in Fiske, 28.

43. Katha Pollitt, "Subject to Debate," *The Nation,* March 27, 1995. In her book on the Smith case, journalist Andrea Peyser argued that in Union, "the most dangerous place for women and children is in the home." In 1994, by the time Smith killed her sons, Union County had recorded sixty-two incidents of domestic violence, and the county's last two homicides were related to domestic violence as well: one women was later acquitted of killing her abusive husband, and one man was convicted of killing his wife in a "religious rage" (83).

44. Eftimiades, 38; Charles M. Sennott, "SC Tragedy Has Roots in Troubled Life," *Boston Globe*, November 6, 1994.

45. Sennott, "SC Tragedy Has Roots in Troubled Life." False information with dubious sources abounded in these first few weeks of coverage. The most sensational example was probably the *Newsweek* report that Susan Smith watched her sons struggle as her car sank (Adler and Carroll, "Innocents Lost"). Smith's lawyer, David Bruck, was tipped off about this misinformation before it was published and tried to run interference, but to no avail; *Newsweek* simply printed his protest alongside the misinformation (interview).

46. Smith, 49–50.

47. Kristen Luker, *Abortion and the Politics of Motherhood* (Berkeley: University of California Press, 1984), 205.

48. C. Dianne Horton, "Death and the Mother's Choice" (Editorial), *Arkansas Democrat-Gazette*, November 17, 1994; "Tell Us What You Think: TV Turned Tragedy into Ratings Circus" (Letters to Editor), *Atlanta Journal Constitution*, November 17, 1994; David Kirk, "Why Doesn't Nation Mourn for Those Aborted?" (Letter to the Editor), *News and Record* (NC), November 19, 1994; Judy House, "Anti-Abortion Advocates Should Redirect Energies" (Letter to the Editor), *Greensboro News and Record* (NC), November 20, 1994.

49. Chris Elder Liberty, "Feminists Must Unite Behind Susan Smith" (Letter to the Editor), *News and Record* (NC), November 11, 1994.

50. William Saletan has documented this slow but steady erosion of rights in his *Bearing Right*.

51. Ellen Willis, "Abortion: Is a Woman a Person?" in *Powers of Desire: The Politics of Sexuality*, ed. Ann Snitow, Christine Stansell, and Sharon Thompson (New York: Monthly Review Press, 1983), 473. William Saletan argued similarly in his analysis of the "rape and incest" exception in anti-abortion rhetoric: "Every woman who seeks an elective abortion sees it as an escape from the unwanted consequences of intercourse. If you grant abortions to rape survivors but not to other women, you're enforcing the unwanted consequences of sex on women who choose to have intercourse while sparing other women those same consequences. In short, you're punishing women for having sex. You can't claim that you're just letting nature take its course, since you're disrupting nature by letting rape survivors abort their pregnancies. You, not nature, are deciding which women are entitled to abortions and which aren't" (158).

CHAPTER FOUR

1. Charles M. Sennott, "Bid to Climb Social Ladder Seen in Smith's Fall to Despair," *Boston Globe*, November 8, 1994.

2. Leora Tanenbaum, *Slut! Growing Up Female with a Bad Reputation* (New York: Seven Stories Press, 1999), xvi.

3. Dorothy Allison, *Two or Three Things I Know for Sure* (New York: Dutton Books, 1995), 36.

4. Dorothy Allison, *Skin: Talking About Sex, Class, and Literature* (Ithaca, NY: Firebrand Books, 1994), 15, 153. Allison's most celebrated novel, *Bastard Out of Carolina*, is centered on the themes of motherhood, sexuality, class, and violence (New York: Penguin Books, 1992). Allison knowingly exploits stereotypes of class as Bone, the young female narrator, muses upon

the cultural trappings of being "trash" in the modern South. Specifically, the men drink, fight, and dominate their families, while the women, despite a down-home air of nurturance, allow violence to flourish in their modest households. In the end, Bone's mother abandons her, leaving town with her pedophilic and incestuous husband, but not before she procures for her daughter a "clean" birth certificate that is not labeled "Bastard." But this is no simple morality tale of child abandonment; Bone's mother professes her love to the end, and Bone forgives her. According to Bone, her actions are part of the long saga of her experiences as a poor southern woman: "Who had Mama been, what had she wanted to be or do before I was born? Once I was born, her hopes had turned, and I had climbed up her life like a flower reaching for the sun. Fourteen and terrified, fifteen and a mother, just past twenty-one when she married Glen. Her life had folded into mine. What would I be like when I was fifteen, twenty, thirty? Would I be as strong as she had been, as hungry for love, as desperate, determined, and ashamed?" (309).

5. McGrory, "We're Not Talking Crime, More Like Raw Evil"; Dreiser is quoted in Nancy McIlvaine Donovan, "Susan Smith: An 'American Tragedy' Narrative Retold," *Dreiser Studies* 34, no. 1 (Summer 2003): 58–59.

6. Theodore Dreiser, *An American Tragedy* (New York: Signet Classics, 1964), 607. Donovan, 59. Dreiser considered several other cases, even writing the draft of a novel about one, before he settled on the Gillette/Brown case. See Craig Brandon, *Murder in the Adirondacks: An American Tragedy Revisited* (Utica, NY: North Country Books, 1986), 332–35; 142–72.

7. Donovan, 59; Douglas and Michaels, 263–64.

8. "American Tragedy: How Could She Have Done It?" *Roanoke Times* (VA), November 9, 1994.

9. Douglas and Michaels, 3.

10. Smith, 83; Funding Universe, "Conso International Corporation: Company History," www.fundinguniverse.com/company-histories/Conso-International-Corporation-Company-History.html (accessed August 15, 2011); "Koni and Cary Findlay: A Passion for Art, Education, and Action," www.ringling.edu/index.php?id=2146 (accessed August 15, 2011); "The Cliffs Residents Raise $50,000 for Local North Carolina Charities," *AshevilleNC.com*, July 29, 2009, www.ashevillenc.com/local_scoop/categories/non-profit (accessed August 15, 2011); "South Carolina Plantations: Fair Forest Plantation, Union County," south-carolina-plantations.com/union/fairforest.html (accessed August 15, 2011); Smith, 83–84.

11. Charles, *The Narrative History of Union County, SC*, 452b; Hughes, interview; South Carolina Plantations, "Fairforest Plantation—Union County," south-carolina-plantations.com/union/fair-forest.html (accessed February 20, 2011); Sennott, "Bid to Climb Social Ladder."

12. Levitt and Sider, "Portrait of a Killer"; Sennott, "Bid to Climb Social Ladder"; Marc Peyser and Carla Koehl, "No Vacancy," *Newsweek*, July 10, 1995; "Smith Case Reveals Dark Side of Union," *Charleston Post & Courier* (SC), January 1, 1995. *Time* magazine did the math: Smith took home $1,096 a month, but her $344 mortgage, $300 in day care—plus car payments, utilities and other costs—added up to $1,284. She was apparently still in debt from the hospital delivery of Alex fourteen months before the murders (Gibbs and Booth, "Death and Deceit").

13. Russell, 22–37.

14. Russell; Smith, 19.

15. Russell, 68.

16. Smith, 51.

17. Ibid., 71.

18. All of the background on Linda Russell and Susan's childhood is from Russell, 22–37, 73–96.

19. Gordon, *Pitied But Not Entitled,* 258.

20. Robert Asen, "Women, Work, Welfare: A Rhetorical History of Images of Poor Women in Welfare Policy Debates," *Rhetoric and Public Affairs* 6, no. 2 (2003): 294.

21. Ibid., 301.

22. Ibid., 295

23. Asen, 303; Douglas and Michaels, 185; Patricia Hill Collins, *Black Feminist Thought: Knowledge, Consciousness, and the Politics of Empowerment* (New York: Routledge, 2000), 84.

24. R. Kent Weaver, Robert Y. Shapiro, and Lawrence R. Jacobs, "The Polls—Trends: Welfare," *Public Opinion Quarterly* 59 (1995): 606–27.

25. Asen, 305.

26. William J. Clinton, "Remarks to the Governor's Leadership Conference in New York City," October 19,1994, www.presidency.ucsb.edu/ws/?pid=49326#axzz1hmkyILoj.

27. Although Martin Carcasson argues that Clinton consistently tried to construe the welfare system, rather than welfare recipients, as the primary problem, the president clearly trafficked in the new sexist and new racist imagery of welfare ("'Ending Welfare as We Know It': President Clinton and the Rhetorical Transformation of the Anti-Welfare Culture," *Rhetoric & Public Affairs* 9, no. 4 [Winter 2006]: 667).

28. Eyer, 14.

29. Quoted in Fiske, 68–69.

30. Charles Murray, *The Bell Curve: Intelligence and Class Structure in American Life* (New York: Simon & Schuster, 1994), 190.

31. Dan Fost, "The Lost Art of Fatherhood," *American Demographics,* March 1996, findarticles.com/p/articles/mi_m4021/is_n3_v18/ai_18056285/ (accessed July 5, 2011).

32. Most Democrats recognized Clinton's racial posturing for what it was: safe national politics. Alexander Lamis quotes an African American politician from Detroit on this: "As a politician, I understand why Clinton is playing down [overt policy commitments to the black community]. It's because he is trying to reach white middle America. I'm not bothered by his strategy, I think the strategy is paying off. . . . I am bothered by the racism of this country that forced him to do that" ("The Two-Party South: From the 1960s to the 1990s," in *Southern Politics in the 1990s,* ed. Alexander Lamis [Baton Rouge: Louisiana State University Press, 1999], 35).

33. *NBC Evening News,* November 7, 1994; Richard Whitt, "Gingrich Fires Back Over His Susan Smith Remarks," *Atlanta Journal Constitution,* November 19, 1994.; *NBC Evening News,* November 7, 1994; "American Tragedy: How Could She Have Done It?" *Roanoke Times* (VA), November 9, 1994.

34. *NBC Evening News,* November 7, 1994.

35. David E. Rosenbaum, "Republicans Offer Voters a Deal for Takeover of House," *New York Times,* September 28, 1994.

36. Ed Gillespie and Bob Schellhas, eds., *Contract with America: The Bold Plan by Rep. Newt Gingrich, Rep. Dick Armey, and the House Republicans to Change the Nation* (New York: Times

Books, 1994), 7. The full text of the contract is also available online: www.house.gov/house/
Contract/CONTRACT.html.

37. Ibid., 65; 17; 67–68.

38. Gwendolyn Mink, "Violating Women: Rights Abuses and the Welfare Police State," *Annals of the American Academy of Political and Social Science* 577 (September 2001): 79-93."

39. Feldman, "The Status Quo Society," 308.

40. Dr. Win Pound, "TV Turned Tragedy into Ratings Circus," *Atlanta Journal Constitution,* November 17, 1994.

41. Jo-Ann Clegg, "Susan Smith Should Pay Dearly: Unfit Parents Should Take Heed," *Virginia Beach Beacon,* November 11, 1994, 7; Richard Grenier, "Susan Smith: For Want of a Government Program," *Washington Times,* November 4, 1994.

42. Douglas and Michaels, 10; Feldstein, 7–9. Linda Kerber defines the concept of "republican motherhood" in *Women of the Republic.*

CHAPTER FIVE

1. Charles M. Sennott, "Smith Case Reveals Dark Side of Union," *Boston Globe,* January 1, 1995. When I asked *Union Daily Times* reporter Anna Brown about the depiction of Union by the national media, she replied bluntly: "We were made to look like *Peyton Place.*" She characterized outside reporters as "vultures" who were often "completely wrong" (interview, September 21, 2005).

2. *NBC Evening News,* November 4, 1994; Chris Burritt, "Mother Charged with Murder: The unraveling life of Susan Smith; She felt world disintegrating," *Atlanta Journal Constitution,* November 6, 1994; Bragg, "Life of a Mother"; Gibbs and Booth, "Death and Deceit."

3. Tamara Jones, "From the Smith Trial, a Town's Secrets Emerge," *Washington Post,* July 30, 1995.

4. Adler and Carroll, "Innocents Lost"; Peyser and Carroll, "Southern Gothic on Trial."

5. Hal Crowther, "Cathedrals of Kudzu," *Oxford American,* October–November 1996, 12; Fred Hobson, "The History of the Southern Gothic Sensibility," *Oxford American,* October–November 1996, 16–17.

6. Crowther, "Cathedrals of Kudzu," 12–13; Cobb, 256.

7. Adler and Carroll, "Innocents Lost"; Patricia Yaeger, *Dirt and Desire: Reconstructing Southern Women's Writing, 1930–1990* (Chicago: University of Chicago Press, 2000), 70.

8. Cobb, 231, 322; Florence King, "In the Dark."

9. *Hee Haw* was a popular television show in the 1970s that featured people dressed up as southern farmers, in overalls and exaggerated accents, telling corny jokes and singing bad songs (*Hee Haw,* created by Frank Peppiatt, 1969–92).

10. Ellen Douglas, *Can't Quit You, Baby* (New York: Penguin Books, 1989), 130; Patricia Yaeger, "Beyond the Hummingbird: Southern Women Writers and the Southern Gargantua," in *Haunted Bodies: Gender and Southern Texts,* ed. Anne Goodwyn Jones and Susan V. Donaldson (Charlottesville: University of Virginia Press, 1997), 294. Scholars have long lamented the continued existence of the "Southern Lady" icon. See, for example, Mary Frederickson, "'Sassing Fate': Women Workers in the Twentieth Century South," in *Taking Off the White Gloves: Southern*

Women and Women Historians, ed. Michele Gillespie and Catherine Clinton (Columbia: University of Missouri Press, 1998).

11. Anna Brown, "Smith Book Hits Newsstands," *Union Daily Times,* January 19, 1994; Peyser, 2, 4, 12.

12. Peyser, 14–15, 19.

13. Herbert Ross, director, *Steel Magnolias,* Rastar Films, 1989; Robert Zemeckis, director, *Forrest Gump,* Paramount Pictures, 1994; John Boorman, *Deliverance,* Warner Bros. Pictures, 1972; Martin Scorsese, *Cape Fear,* Amblin Entertainment, 1991; Peyser, 16, 83.

14. Price; "Author Missed the Real Union," *Union Daily Times,* March 9, 1995. Criminologists have largely rejected the idea of the "Southern subculture of violence" (Mann, 52).

15. Charles, *The Narrative History of Union County, SC,* x, 298–306.

16. Ibid., 302; Minchin. Although some mills hired African Americans, throughout the Textile Belt, generally speaking, the industry was a "white domain," and the worst work in the mills went to black men (Hall et al., 66). This scar remained in Union until the end of the century; a large part of the community play "Turn the Washpot Down," which was based on oral history and written and performed by locals at the end of the twentieth century, featured the integration of the textile mills in Union County (Jules Corriere, "Turn the Washpot Down," Community Performance, Inc., 2002).

17. Hall et al., xvi; Cash, 204; Morland, ix; Conway, 15; Hall et al., 164; Morland, 99, 69, 80; Simon, 3.

18. Charles, *The Narrative History of Union County, SC,* 312. Historian David Carlton recounts one such incident in 1900 in the mill village surrounding Union Cotton. Fears of new medical science led local mill workers to resist smallpox vaccination administered by the town's doctor. Some workers were arrested for refusing the vaccine, and others soon formed a mob who expressed "fear for their lives" as well as protests against the incarceration of resisters. The town eventually gave up, and smallpox raged on. The local doctor lamented, "We hope to stamp it out if the people will allow us to vaccinate them" (156–57).

19. Charles, *The Narrative History of Union County, SC,* 427, 433. The neighboring counties of Chester and York had dropped to 82 percent and 72 percent textile-dependent, respectively, by 1970 (434).

20. Ibid., 435–36. Torance Inman of the Union Chamber of Commerce downplayed the extent of the economic depression caused by the closings of the mills, arguing that it was part of the "national recession" and that the 1990s were actually much harder on the county's economy (Inman, interview).

21. Inman, interview; Roberts, interview. The job losses were as follows: Buffalo Mills (500 people), Union Mills (425), and Conso (number unavailable). The total number of jobs lost in a decade was 2068 (Inman, interview).

22. "Union County, South Carolina, Business Data," www.city-data.com/business2/econ-Union_County-SC.html (accessed February 20, 2011).

23. Inman, interview.

24. Paul Harvey, "Religion, Race, and the Right in the South, 1945–1990," in Feldman, ed., *Politics and Religion in the White South,* 101.

25. Ted Ownby, "Donald Wildmon, the American Family Association and the Theology of

Media Activism," in Feldman, ed., *Politics and Religion in the White South,* 237; James L. Guth, "Southern Baptist Clergy, the Christian Right, and Political Activism in the South," in Feldman, ed., *Politics and Religion in the White South,* 194; Mark J. Rozell and Clyde Wilcox, "The Christian Right in Virginia Politics," in Feldman, ed., *Politics and Religion in the White South,* 259; Samuel S. Hill and Dennis E. Owen, *The New Religious Political Right in America* (Nashville: Abingdon Press, 1982), 18; Feldman, "The Status Quo Society," 323.

26. Executive Order 10925, "Establishing the President's Committee on Equal Employment Opportunity," www.eeoc.gov/eeoc/history/35th/thelaw/eo-10925.html (accessed July 5, 2011); Executive Order 11246, "Equal Employment Opportunity," www.archives.gov/federal-register/codification/executive-order/11246.html (accessed July 5, 2011).

27. Quoted in Edsall and Edsall, 221.

28. Quoted in Lamis, 8.

29. Edsall and Edsall, 198.

30. Njeri Jackson, "Fathering Injustice: Racial Patriarchy and the Dismantling of Affirmative Action," *Western Journal of Black Studies* 27 (2003): 51–56.

31. Howard Fineman and Andrew Murr, "Race and Rage," *Newsweek,* April 3, 1995. In an in-depth analysis and comparison of election returns, Grant Reeher and Joseph Cammarano debunked the idea of the "angry white male" ("In Search of the Angry White Male: Gender, Race, and Issues in the 1994 Elections," in *Midterm: The Elections of 1994 in Context,* ed. Philip A. Klinkner [Boulder, CO: Westview Press, 1996], 125–36). Like the question of whether the South is truly "Gothic," however, the question of whether 1994 really was the year of "angry white males" is moot; there was clearly a pervasive cultural belief in this trend, no matter the reality.

32. Charles S. Bullock III and Mark C. Smith, "The Religious Right and Electoral Politics in the South," in Feldman, ed., *Politics and Religion in the White South,* 222; Charles L. Warner, "Union County Voters Could Determine S.C.'s Political Future," *Union Daily Times,* January 14, 1995. Warner argued that Union County was more than just reflective; it was, in fact, proactive: "Within the next two years Union County will find itself positioned to not only help determine who controls the S.C. Senate but also whether the Republican Party will continue to dominate South Carolina." The county was "ground zero" of this realignment.

33. Glen T. Broach and Lee Bandy, "South Carolina: A Decade of Rapid Republican Ascent," in Lamis, ed., 71

34. Thom White, interview; Hobbs, interview.

35. Inman, interview.

36. Hobbs, interview; *Union Daily Times,* May 5, 1995. Ann Currie explained that the people who took refreshments to the media "weren't trying to get interviewed," it was just that the journalists were all "so hot and sweaty, and they wanted them to feel welcome" (interview, Carthage, NC, July 11, 2005).

37. Brackett, interview; Charles, interview; Kingsmore, interview; Eftimiades, 240–41.

38. Reverend Allen Raines, interview, August 12, 2005; Anna Brown, "Forum Planned for Citizens to Voice Feelings on Case," *Union Daily Times,* November 5, 1994. The meetings were held at different churches over the months, and they drew a "tremendous crowd." Reverend Brackett said he had "never seen the community in [his] years here come together as it did for this situation" (interview).

39. Anna Brown, "Mother Charged," *Union Daily Times*, November 4, 1994. In her confession on November 3, 1994, Smith wrote: "My children, Michael and Alex, are with our Heavenly Father now, and I know that they will never be hurt again. As a mom, that means more than words could ever say" (the full text of the confession is available in Henderson, *Nine Days in Union*, 117–18).

40. One of the poems written from the boys' perspective began: "Hello, God, I'm Michael Smith and Alex here's my brother. / We've come home to you Dear Father, because we have no mother" ("Many Share Their Feelings," *Union Daily Times*, November 8, 1994); Another woman wrote: "I say to the families that it's a tragic loss, but the one thing that will help me and you too is knowing that they are with the Lord. Yes, two perfect, precious little angels and they are surely in a better place than we are" ("Many Share Their Feelings," *Union Daily Times*, November 7, 1994); "Many Share Their Feelings," *Union Daily Times*, November 12, 1994.

41. Charles, *The Narrative History of Union County, SC,* xi; Inman, interview.

42. Beth Barton Schweiger, "Max Weber in Mount Airy; or, Revivals and Social Theory in the Early South," in Schweiger and Matthews, 32; Wade Clark Roof, "Southern Protestantism: New Challenges, New Possibilities," in *The Changing Shape of Protestantism in the South,* ed. Marion D. Aldridge and Kevin Lewis (Macon, GA: Mercer University Press, 1996), 11–12; William H. Willimon, "On Being a Southerner and a Christian at the Same Time," in Aldridge and Lewis, 33, 32.

43. Paul Harvey, "Religion," in *The South,* ed. Rebecca Mark and Rob Vaughan (Westport, CT: Greenwood Press, 2004), 413–14.

44. Samuel S. Hill Jr., ed., *Religion and the Solid South* (Nashville: Abingdon Press, 1972), 20; Notes from "A Community Service to Help Us Experience God's Healing," from the personal papers of Reverend Tom Currie, Carthage, NC.

45. Nancy Hardesty, "From Religion to Spirituality: Southern Women In and Out of Church," in Aldridge and Lewis, 70.

46. Notes from sermon, Sunday, November 6, 1995, from the personal papers of Reverend Tom Currie.

47. Susan Smith and her family actually came to Cato's home for counseling and to escape the media a week into the investigation. There were so many people that they ran out of chairs. Susan sat on the floor, "rocking back and forth" and "crying out, 'Where are my babies?'" Cato had a premonition that night that Susan knew more than she was telling. "Nobody knows what happened that night in my living room," he told me. "That night, before I went to bed, I said, 'Honey, something's not right'" (interview).

48. Eftimiades, 220–21; Cato, interview. Rev. Cato received calls from as far away as Australia and many from within the United States.

49. "Many Share Their Feelings," *Union Daily Times*, November 8, 1994; Brackett, interview.

50. Anna Brown, "Union Minister Stays Calm Under National Spotlight," *Union Daily Times*, March 25, 1995; Raines, interview; Eftimiades, 240.

51. Anna Brown, "Linda Russell Says She Never Suspected Daughter," *Union Daily Times,* January 26, 1994; Bruck, interview.

52. "Report: Susan Smith Reported Stepfather for Sexual Molestation," *Union Daily Times*, November 28, 1994.

53. Russell, 43–44.

54. Ibid., 51–53.

55. Ibid., 55–57.

56. Ibid., 62–65.

57. Ibid., 61–65; 69–70. Although a few locals told the *Union Daily Times* that there had been rumors of Russell's abuse while Susan was in high school, for the most part, only her immediate family and her counselors, including Reverend Tom Currie, knew the details. In fact, the confidential knowledge posed something of a problem for Currie later on when Beverly Russell was proposed for Rotary Club membership: "When he was proposed for membership, I was in a quandary, because I had known about some of the problems at home, but I knew it in confidence and was not able to share that and really just had to sit on my hands and hope all that had gotten straightened out. And then, I couldn't stand up and say, you know, I think don't think we ought to receive him into membership, and they said why, and I said because you know he had at least in the past molested his stepdaughter" (interview).

58. Smith, 40; Anna Brown, "Abuse Allegations Surprise Friends," *Union Daily Times*, February 21, 1995. Apparently, Russell was molesting Susan the entire time he was campaigning for Robertson (Anna Brown, "Report Details Molestation Allegations," *Union Daily Times*, April 1, 1995; Smith, 40).

59. Anna Brown, "Court Records Show Russell Abused Smith," *Union Daily Times*, February 20, 1995; Anna Brown, "Report Details Molestation Allegations," *Union Daily Times*, April 1, 1995. Pat Robertson was the head of the Christian Coalition who ran unsuccessfully for the Republican nomination in 1988; a *Time* magazine poll showed that only 26 percent of Republican voters supported him at the height of his campaign (Steve Bruce, *The Rise and Fall of the New Christian Right: Conservative Protestant Politics in America, 1978–1988* [New York: Oxford University Press, 1993], vii).

60. "Smith Court Documents Sealed," *Union Daily Times*, December 1, 1994. The "case of the missing file" prompted an inconclusive State Law Enforcement Division (SLED) investigation (Brown, "Report Details Molestation Allegations"; Associated Press, "Probe of Missing Susan Smith Files Finds 'Nothing Remarkable,'" *Union Daily Times*, June 20, 1995; "Where is the File?" *Union Daily Times*, July 25, 1995). Russell resigned from his position on the executive committee of the Union County Republican Party before Smith's murder trial (Charles L. Warner, "GOP To Pick Russell Replacement," *Union Daily Times*, May 15, 1994); Russell, 66; Associated Press, "Report: Smith, Stepfather Had Affair Through Last Year," *Union Daily Times*, April 24, 1995.

61. Cato, interview; Thom White, interview.

62. Anna Brown, "Deposition Detailed Pair's Relationship," *Union Daily Times*, May 5, 1995; Anna Brown, "Report: Defense May Claim Smith Sexually Abused by Husband," *Union Daily Times*, May 19, 1995; Anna Brown, "David Smith Will Promote Book on Summer Television Interviews," *Union Daily Times*, June 14, 1995; Anna Brown, "Book, Movie Deals Focus of Defense," *Union Daily Times*, June 20, 1995. David Smith's editor released a statement in late June saying that the grieving father wrote the book for healing, not profit ("Editor: David Smith Writing Book to 'Heal Himself,'" *Union Daily Times*, June 23, 1995).

63. Bragg, "A Killer's Only Confidant," *New York Times*, August 4, 1995. Thom White, interview. Some locals believe that the investigation and the media coverage would have been drastically different had Wells's opponent won the election (Tom Currie, interview; Inman, interview). Torance Inman of the Union Chamber of Commerce explained: "The world wanted to see a little

podunk town, but that's not what they got. And Howard had only been sheriff for a short time. Had his opponent won, it would've been a different story" (interview).

64. Anna Brown, "Unwanted Spotlight," *Union Daily Times,* February 6, 1995; Anna Brown, "Sheriff Getting Mountains of Mail Concerning Case," *Union Daily Times,* November 17, 1994; "Many Share Their Feelings," *Union Daily Times,* November 7–8, 1994; Wells reportedly signed the exclusive contract for a story of his life and his role in the case to "insure that Union County benefits from any movie that is made about the Susan Smith case and to insure that it does not show the community in a bad light" (Charles L. Warner, "Wells Signs Contract with Movie Producer," *Union Daily Times,* August 3, 1995).

65. Russell, 13.

66. "Smith Trial Will Lay Waste to Time, Money and Justice," *Union Daily Times,* May 23, 1995; "Let's Get Smith Trial Over with as Soon as Possible," *Union Daily Times,* May 30, 1995. Rev. Brackett wrote one of these letters, as did his friend Jesse Jackson. It was not that he did not think that Smith should be punished, he told me: "We did not ask Tommy Pope not to seek justice, but we asked him not to seek the death penalty" (interview). Pope saw the anti–death penalty letters as a strategy of Smith's defense team: "The defense used that as a tactic really to keep me extremely busy, because they amped up the letter-writing campaign, and the calls, that kind of thing. Because, to the best of my ability, kind of like when you wrote me, I'm a public servant, I'll make time for the public, you know. And I'm going to return all my phone calls, and anyway so. . . . man, they swamped me with them. You had people calling and—oh, I got threatening letters, and it was really you know worldwide, really, you know, stuff from all over the board." Then he compared his decision to a "Far Side" cartoon in which the devil is poking a man with a pitchfork yelling at him to choose one of two doors, which are labeled "Damned if you do" and "Damned if you don't." Although the ultimate decision rested with him, Pope told me that, if David Smith had not supported the death penalty, it might not have been a capital case (interview). David Bruck, who opposes the death penalty altogether, said he understood why Pope might leave such a decision up to a jury, rather than make it "unilaterally" on his own in a case in which there was so much "outrage and public uproar" (interview). A few locals speculated to me that Pope's decision may have been political, perhaps motivated by connections to conservative politicians at the state level (Tom Currie, interview; Kingsmore, interview). Smith offered to plead guilty in exchange for life imprisonment, the exact sentence that she received at trial (Bruck, interview).

67. The judge eventually decided, after lengthy discussions with other court officials and requests from the defense team, to ban cameras in the courtroom (Anna Brown, "Court Officials to Discuss Media Coverage of Smith Trial," *Union Daily Times,* February 14, 1995; Anna Brown, "Lawyers Ask Judge to Ban TV Cameras," *Union Daily Times,* June 8, 1995; Anna Brown, "Judge Bars Cameras from Smith Trial," *Union Daily Times,* July 1, 1995). The major television networks relied on sketch artists. Betty Wells, who had worked on other high-profile cases such as those of John Hinckley and Manuel Noriega, drew for NBC. She told the *Union Daily Times* that she enjoyed her time in town: "The prosecutors have fabulous faces, good angles, good hair," and "Susan [was] easy to draw" (Anna Brown, "With Cameras Banned, Sketch Artists Provide Courtroom Scenes for TV," *Union Daily Times,* July 15, 1995).

68. Anna Brown, "Community to Discuss Problems of Smith Trial," *Union Daily Times,* May 31, 1995; Carolyn Farr, "OSAP Meeting Prepares Community for Smith Trial," *Union Daily Times,*

June 30, 1995. By mid-February, most of the motel rooms were already booked, and reporters were scouring the upstate for "homes, trailers, and other structures to rent" (Anna Brown, "Booked Up," *Union Daily Times,* January 14, 1995). Some enterprising locals rented out their homes to the "media horde," reportedly for as much as $3,000 per week ("Union Homeowners Plan to Cash in on Media Horde," *Union Daily Times,* June 15, 1995). Others planned to "make big bucks" by selling concessions like hot dogs, coffee, and "cold cokes" (Jesse J. Holland, "Union Residents Ready to Make Big Bucks Off Trial," *Union Daily Times,* July 6, 1995). Reporters from as far as Germany and Japan came to Union to cover the trial (Anna Brown, "World Media Preparing to Descend on Union," *Union Daily Times,* June 13, 1994).

69. Farr, "OSAP Meeting"; Ann Currie, interview; Tom Currie, interview.

70. "Union County Will Be Tested in Weeks Ahead," *Union Daily Times,* July 8, 1995.

71. Anna Brown, "Smith Ruled Competent for Trial," *Union Daily Times,* July 11, 1995; Associated Press, "Minister: Smith is Forgiven," *Charleston Post & Courier* (SC), July 10, 1995; Anna Brown, "Jury Selection Begins in Smith Case," *Union Daily Times,* July 10, 1995; Jesse J. Holland, "Ms. Smith Ready to Die, Pastor Says," *Union Daily Times,* July 10, 1995; Charles L. Warner, "Union Churches Plan Monday Night Services," *Union Daily Times,* July 10, 1995; Anna Brown, "Media Takes Over Main Street," *Union Daily Times,* July 10, 1995. In late May, the defense team filed a motion for dismissal of the state's notice of intent to seek the death penalty and a continuance of the trial, alleging that Pope had violated the gag order imposed by the judge (Graham Williams, "Smith Lawyers Cite Leaks to the Media," *Union Daily Times,* May 23, 1995; Anna Brown, "Smith's Lawyers May Ask for Delay," *Union Daily Times,* May 26, 1995). The motion was not granted ("Let's Get Smith Trial Over with as Soon as Possible," *Union Daily Times,* May 30, 1995; Melinda Waldrop, "Supreme Court Again Threatens Reporter with Jail," *Union Daily Times,* July 13, 1995).

72. Locally, the trial was also known as "O.J. East" (Brown, "Media takes over Main Street").

CHAPTER SIX

1. *NBC Evening News,* July 9, 1995.

2. Elayne Rapping, "The Movie of the Week: Law, Narrativity, and Gender in Prime Time," in *Feminism, Media, and the Law,* ed. Martha Fineman and Martha T. McCluskey (New York: Oxford University Press, 1997), 94.

3. Bill Hewitt and Gail Cameron Westcott, "Tears of Hate, Tears of Pity," *People,* March 13, 1995; *NBC Evening News,* July 15, 1995; Rick Bragg, "Judge Rules Susan Smith is Fit for Trial on Murder Charges," *New York Times,* July 12, 1995. The evil, Medea image of Susan—"the most famous murderess since Lizzie Borden"—still beckoned from the tabloid racks of grocery store aisles across the nation. Technicolor, multi-page exposés entitled "Sex, Betrayal, and Murder" and "Baby Killer Smith's X-Rated Secret Life" offered a crazed, sexualized version of Smith's life and crime (Elizabeth Gleick and Lisa H. Towle, "Sex, Betrayal, and Murder," *Time,* July 17, 1995; Associated Press, "Tabloids Having a Field Day," *Charleston Post and Courier* (SC), July 18, 1995; Bill Hewitt and Gail Cameron Wescott, "Tears of Hate, Tears of Pity," *People,* March 13, 1995; Rheta Grimsley Johnson, "Considering and Crossing Thin Lines in Union, SC," *Atlanta Journal-Constitution,* July 30, 1995).

4. Jonathan Harr, *A Civil Action* (New York: Vintage Books, 1995), 236; Barbara Ann Barnett, "Medea in the Media: A Narrative Analysis of Print News Coverage of Women Who Kill Their Children," Ph.D. diss., University of North Carolina–Chapel Hill, 2003, 18; *NBC Evening News*, July 18, 1995.

5. Rick Bragg, "A Small Town in the South Prepares to Try a Neighbor," *New York Times*, July 17, 1995.

6. Anna Brown, "Susan Smith Case May Be Biggest Challenge of Pope's Career," *Union Daily Times*, July 6, 1995; Pope was so unfamiliar with the families of Union that, when he tried to visit David Smith the weekend after Susan's arrest to introduce himself as the prosecutor, he went to Russell's house mistakenly. It was an awkward moment in which Russell had to give the self-described "potential executioner" directions across town to David's apartment (Pope, interview).

7. Anna Brown and Charles L. Warner, "David Smith Testifies for Prosecution," *Union Daily Times*, July 25, 1995. Rapping identifies the figure of the paternal lawyer, the "white, middle-class, straight male authority" that "declaws" his criminal client, as a stock character of television movies ("The Movie of the Week," 99). Rapping analyzes the movie "The Burning Bed," about Francine Hughes, who murdered her husband and claimed "battered wives' syndrome." An alternative example is the prosecutor in the Diane Downs's case (discussed in chapter 2); in this case, he was the protector of her living children rather than the wayward woman. In fact, he adopted the children after she was sentenced to life in prison—the ultimate fulfillment of the "paternal lawyer" role (Rule).

8. Bruck knew insanity might be a stretch, and the State Mental Health Department's evaluation of Smith confirmed that, while she was severely depressed, she was not legally insane. When this news went public, reactions were mixed. Obviously, Smith's legal competency to stand trial had the potential to harm a mentally ill defense; on the other hand, the state doctors argued that Smith's "severe depression . . . could have played a role in causing her" to commit the murders. This diagnosis, according to one Columbia attorney, could spell trouble for the state's case because "the people at the state hospital are notoriously conservative" ("Report: Susan Smith Not Insane," *Union Daily Times*, May 25, 1995). The concept of "guilty but mentally ill" was adopted after a jury found John Hinckley insane after shooting Ronald Reagan; a key difference between this defense and insanity is that the jury can still mete out harsh sentences, like lengthy imprisonment or death, as opposed to the hospitalization required by an insanity verdict ("Definitions of Legal Terms in Smith Case," *Union Daily Times*, July 11, 1995). The Mental Health Department's report, which Judge Howard originally ordered sealed, leaked to the *State*'s Twila Decker in late May, causing a sideshow drama to the actual trial as the South Carolina judges, including the state Supreme Court, debated the state's "shield law" protecting confidential sources. Judge Howard found Decker in contempt of court and ordered her jailed, although he delayed her incarceration and eventually rescinded the order. Decker never revealed her source; the prosecution, the defense attorneys, law enforcement authorities, and State Department of Mental Health officials all contend that they did not leak the information (Anna Brown, "Judge Rules Smith's Evaluation Results Closed," *Union Daily Times*, May 17, 1995; Robert Tanner, "Smith Case May Also Be First Test of State's Shield Law," *Union Daily Times*, May 27, 1995; Anna Brown, "Pre-trial Publicity Cited by Attorney," *Union Daily Times*, May 27, 1995; Jesse J. Holland, "Reporter Asks Supreme Court to Reconsider," *Union Daily Times*, July 8, 1995).

9. Bruck, interview. Those signs that Bruck saw immediately as evidence of mental illness alternatively served as proof for Tommy Pope that Smith was cool, calm, and calculating. To this day, Pope believes Smith rationally orchestrated her own defense. He argues that she could cry on command in the courtroom, which she only did in the presence of the jury, and that she has been known to be sexually coercive in prison (Pope, interview).

10. *NBC Evening News*, July 15, 1995; Bragg, "Prayers and Tears for 2 Carolina Boys," November 7, 1994; Bragg, "Keeping Mother's Trial in Hometown Could Be Crucial," *New York Times*, July 13, 1995. By the third day of jury selection, Bragg reported that "over half" of the potential jury pool said "either that they could not put anyone to death or that they would have a hard time living with it if they did" (Bragg, "Smith Trial Stalls on Questions about Book Deal," *New York Times*, July 14, 1995). A reporter for the *Union Daily Times* wondered if the proposed county tax increase to cover the looming deficit in the annual budget caused by the trial might result in some "animosity" on the part of potential jurors (Anna Brown, "How Will Tax Increase Affect Potential Jurors in Smith Trial?" *Union Daily Times*, June 9, 1995).

11. Jesse J. Holland, "Mothers, Young and Old, Perfect Jurors for Smith Trial, Lawyers Say," *Union Daily Times*, June 7, 1995; *NBC Evening News*, July 22, 1995; Bruck, interview. The men and women who were to gauge the weight of Smith's crimes included three white women, one of whom had been sexually abused as a teenager. Another had worked at the day care that young Susan attended as a child. There were five white men on the jury; one was a Rush Limbaugh fan, one used to work with David Smith, another used to date Linda Russell (Susan Smith's mother), and yet another had a brother who had been found not guilty of murder by reason of insanity. Four African American men served on the jury. Each said he could be impartial despite Smith's racist lie, although one reported fearing that, as a black man, he might "be accused" during the investigation ("Jurors Selected for Susan Smith Trial," *Union Daily Times*, July 18, 1995).

12. Bragg, "A Small Town in the South Prepares to Try a Neighbor"; Brackett, interview; Hobbs, interview; Bruck, interview. This division of phases was a result of the 1972 Supreme Court decision that the death penalty was "cruel and arbitrary." Juries could no longer convict and sentence simultaneously; the penalty phase "allowed the defense to admit evidence that was relevant to the punishment but irrelevant to the question of guilt, such as drug use or childhood abuse." This second phase is now used in all states with capital punishment (Arlene Levinson, "Penalty Phase of Susan Smith Trial Reflects '70s Death Penalty Revisions," *Union Daily Times*, July 28, 1995).

13. The South experienced record heat that July. Reporters covering the trial had to "battle the heat" with cold drinks, shade, sunscreen, and canopies draped over the scaffolding they had set up on Main Street. Others had lawn chairs with attached umbrellas and "makeshift 'Arab-style' headdresses" to protect themselves from the sun. Cliff LeBlanc of the *State* was raised in Panama, but he had never experienced such heat: "I'm not used to this, this really consistent heat with no break, no clouds, no nothing, and you've got to be outside almost the entire time, it just drains you" (Charles L. Warner, "Media Battling Heat," *Union Daily Times*, July 13, 1995).

14. It should be noted that Susan Smith did not invent this method of criminal cover-up. Criminology studies indicate that infanticidal parents often initially report their children's disappearance as a kidnapping. Parents are, in fact, the most likely perpetrators in any crime involving a child (Wilczynski, 32).

15. South Carolina v. Smith, 2387; *NBC Evening News,* July 18, 1995; South Carolina v. Smith, 2394; Helen Birch, "If Looks Could Kill: Myra Hindley and the Iconography of Evil," in Birch, ed., *Moving Targets,* 34.

16. South Carolina v. Smith, 2401.

17. Ibid., 2400–2401.

18. Ibid., 2402–4.

19. Pope, interview; South Carolina v. Smith, 2504–5.

20. South Carolina v. Smith, 2519, 2516.

21. Bragg, "A Killer's Only Confidant."

22. The "sexy" details, which anyone familiar with the media coverage may remember, included the allegations that Susan had said in the past that she wished she had "waited to have a family," that she was charged with adultery because of their relationship (even though David had had a serious girlfriend of several months at the time of their separation), and that she had attended hot tub parties featuring drunkenness, nudity, and adultery on the grounds of Findlay's father's mansion (South Carolina v. Smith, 2665–71). Pope also implied that Smith frequented a local bar (the only one in town) and slept around. Evidence of Smith's sordid sexual history included the fact Smith had told Findlay the day of the murders that she had also slept with his father, who was her boss, although she also told him later that day that she had "made up the entire story" about Cary Findlay (South Carolina v. Smith, 2697–99).

23. South Carolina v. Smith, 2738–47; Jesse J. Holland, "Susan Smith Trial Its Own Soap Opera," *Union Daily Times,* July 24, 1995.

24. South Carolina v. Smith, 2896.

25. Anna Brown, "Smith Defense Building Case," *Union Daily Times,* July 21, 1995. Judge Howard did not allow Pope to show the court pictures of the bodies after the car was pulled from the lake, and he did not allow testimony about the extent of their decay because "the images were so terrible they would be prejudicial" (Rick Bragg, "Mother Was Remorseful, Witness Says," *New York Times,* July 21, 1995). The defense team, obviously taken aback, did not even have all of their witnesses at the courthouse yet, and Bruck made a halfhearted move for acquittal on the grounds that the State had not proven Smith's "malice" to a sufficient degree. The move was denied (South Carolina v. Smith, 2907).

26. Two Southern Bell employees testified later that day; Susan had indeed requested a check for a tap on her phone on October 24, 1994, the day before the murders. No tap was found (South Carolina v. Smith, 3010–19, 2994–97).

27. Brown, "Smith Defense Building Case."

28. South Carolina v. Smith, 3038.

29. Ibid., 3096.

30. Ibid., 3105, 3128–29, 3136. In fact, Pope's overzealous attack on the seriousness of Smith's previous suicide attempts led to an unexpected move for mistrial from David Bruck on the morning of July 21, 1995. In his questioning of Dr. Andrews, Pope quoted a former counselor as saying that Susan was not really suicidal or depressed, and that "you can't kill yourself taking Aspirin." Bruck argued that the prosecution had withheld information from interviews because he had not been informed of this statement, which would be grounds for a mistrial. Judge Howard denied the motion but allowed Bruck to bring in a new witness, the former counselor in question.

Under oath, the counselor flatly denied questioning the seriousness of Susan's overdose attempts, characterizing them as "a cry for help" from a very "troubled" girl (South Carolina v. Smith, 3134, 3229–31).

31. South Carolina v. Smith, 3289; 3292; 3297. The entire text of Smith's confession can be found in the trial transcripts (2544) and in Henderson, *Nine Days in Union,* 117–18.

32. South Carolina v. Smith, 3299, 3301–2, 3304, 3313; Anna Brown, "Jury Could Get Smith Case Today," *Union Daily Times,* July 22, 1995.

33. South Carolina v. Smith, 3315, 3321.

34. Ibid., 3322–23, 3330.

35. Ibid., 3336, 3340.

36. Ibid., 3342–43, 3346, 3349.

37. Ibid., 3383–86.

38. Ibid., 3436–37.

39. These witnesses were Iris Rogers, who knew Smith as a small child, and Debbie Green, Smith's high-school English teacher (South Carolina v. Smith, 3450–90).

40. *NBC Evening News,* July 21, 1995.

41. Rick Bragg, "Focus on Smith's Lies and a Smile," *New York Times,* July 25, 1995; *CBS Evening News,* July 23, 1995. There was, however, something of a surprise for the defense team at the end of this phase of the trial. Because the prosecution had proceeded with questions regarding Smith's mental state, they "created an opening" for the defense to present their mental health evidence during the guilt phase, although they had planned on using it during the sentencing phase. This turn of events, and especially the focus on Smith's suicidality, led the judge to instruct the jury that they could consider involuntary manslaughter (i.e., involuntary death at Smith's hands in the course of a suicide attempt) in their deliberations. Such a verdict would entail a maximum of ten years in prison (Bruck, interview; Howard, interview; Anna Brown, "Jury Deliberated Only 2 1/2 Hours Before Reaching Guilty Verdict," *Union Daily Times,* July 24, 1995). Reverend Toni White, Susan Smith's friend and counselor, says that she believes that the jury almost felt as if they had a "mandate" to convict Smith of murder because of her lie (interview). Smith's attorneys are now well-known anti-death penalty experts. David Bruck devoted his career to saving his clients' lives for over two decades in South Carolina before moving to Virginia to run the Capital Case Clearinghouse at Washington and Lee University ("Defending a Killer's Life on Principle," *MacLean's,* July 24, 1995; Bruck, interview). His co-counsel Judy Clarke has been involved in almost every high-profile capital case in the United States in the past two decades, including September 11 co-conspirator Zacarias Moussaoui, "Unabomer" Ted Kaczynski, Atlanta Olympics bomber Eric Rudolph, and most recently, the "Tucson Shooter" Jared Lee Loughner (Korva Coleman, "Experienced Public Defender to Assist Accused Tucson Shooter," National Public Radio, January 10, 2011). Susan Smith's was the first infanticide case either attorney had ever handled. Rick Bragg said it was clear to the reporters in Union that Smith's defense attorneys were "true believers," opponents of the death penalty: "They battled against the death penalty. And all along it was mostly whether or not there was going to be a death penalty, not whether or not there was going to be a conviction. It was whether or not there will be a death penalty. I thought her lawyers did a wonderful job of saving her life." The defense attorneys were just doing their job, but Bragg was very clear in his interview that he did not buy

their "Susan": "I think that if the defense's justification for the murders of the babies is indeed just, then we would be covered up in dead babies. We would not be able to walk down the street for dead babies. If you put anything in that attached to my name: we would not be able to move for the dead children" (interview).

42. Bragg, interview.

43. Rick Bragg, "Union, SC, is a Town Torn Asunder," *New York Times*, July 24, 1995; Bragg, interview.

44. South Carolina v. Smith, 3964.

45. Ibid., 3966; 3974; 3968.

46. Ibid., 3979–80.

47. Ibid., 4047; Rapping, *Law and Justice*, 236.

48. Elizabeth Gleick and Lisa H. Towle, "No Casting of Stones," *Time*, August 7, 1995; Anna Brown, "State Rests Case After Emotional Day," *Union Daily Times*, July 26, 1995; *NBC Evening News*, July 25, 1995; "Notes from Union," *Spartanburg Herald-Journal* (SC), July 27, 1995.

49. Anna Brown, "State Rests After Emotional Day," *Union Daily Times*, July 26, 1995; Bragg, "Father Testifies in Penalty Part of Smith Trial," *New York Times, July 25, 1995. CBS Evening News,* July 25, 1995; Christopher Sullivan, "Hometown Residents Eager to Read David Smith's Story," *Union Daily Times*, July 26, 1995.

50. Bruck, interview.

51. Jesse J. Holland, "Final Days of Smith Trial Get Crowded," *Union Daily Times*, July 28, 1995.

52. South Carolina v. Smith, 4858–86.

53. Anna Brown, "Jury Spares Smith's Life," *Union Daily Times*, July 29, 1995.

54. Anna Brown, "Jury to Decide Smith's Fate Today," *Union Daily Times*, July 28, 1995.

55. South Carolina v. Smith, 4812.

56. Ibid., 4826, 4835.

57. Ibid., 4913–17.

58. Ibid., 5018–19.

59. Near the outset of his statement, Bruck told the jury about the difficulty of his job: "And I'm going to sit down and I'm going to think, oh, I forgot to tell them that. I forgot to tell them this. And I have to tell you that if Susan should be sentenced to death, I will carry that with me for—"; the judge interrupted him: "No, counsel, that's not appropriate argument, sir" (South Carolina v. Smith, 5031, 5037, 5072).

60. South Carolina v. Smith, 5081–86, 5093. Although Bruck himself downplays his use of Christian language in the trial, Tommy Pope does not; in his next capital case, he filed a motion to suppress the use of biblical references in the courtroom (Pope, interview).

CHAPTER SEVEN

1. John Heilprin, "Smith Gets Life in Prison; Jurors Explain Verdict," *Charleston Post and Courier* (SC), July 29, 1995; Robert Gearty, Paul Schwartzman, and Helen Kennedy, *Daily News* (NY), July 29, 1995; Anna Brown, "Jury Spares Smith's Life," *Union Daily Times*, July 29, 1995. Although she was found guilty, the sentence of life in prison can be seen as a "win" for the defense because they successfully avoided the death penalty (Bruck, interview; Pope).

2. South Carolina v. Smith, 5137–38.

3. Anna Brown, "Jury Spares Smith's Life," *Union Daily Times*, July 28, 1995. Even those observers in the courtroom who did not agree with the sentence were relieved that the trial was over. It was an intense trial during a summer of record heat. Rick Bragg, who generally believed the prosecution's "boyfriend motive," although he did not necessarily support capital punishment, said that covering the trial on location in Union was one of the hardest assignments he's ever taken: "You know, I covered atrocities in Haiti and militant Islamic fundamentalists in central Asia. I covered the bombing of the Oklahoma City Murrow Building. You know, all I did was cover sadness for a very long time. So much so that I'll never do it again. That was the single most concentrated, methodical, manipulated sadness I'd ever been a part of." He returned to this theme, unprompted, later in our conversation: "I'm no expert on trials, court; I've covered a lot of them, covered a lot of sadness. That's the saddest one I've ever sat through. That's the saddest thing that I've ever sat through on a day-to-day methodical basis. I was in Haiti for a few months during the time when they were trying to bring Aristide back into the country, and they were killing people every day. And, as sad as that was, and the amount of killing that was, it wasn't, there was a distance still, even though you're there. With the Susan Smith trial, every detail of the crime was played out in front of you. And it just made you sick" (Bragg, interview).

4. Charles L. Warner, "Onlookers Not Surprised by Jury's Decision," *Union Daily Times*, July 29, 1995; Howard, interview; Bruck, interview; Anna Brown, "Smith Trial Was 'Union's Case,'" Solicitor Says," *Union Daily Times*, August 12, 1995; Associated Press, "Jurors spare Smith because of tragic life," *Rock Hill Herald* (SC), July 30, 1995; Lucy Howard and Carla Koehl, "Who's News," *ABA Journal*, October 1995, 38.

5. Roberts, interview; Heilprin, "Smith Gets Life in Prison"; Inman, interview; "Smith's Mental State Next Issue," *Charleston Post and Courier*, July 24, 1995. This was not just a local view. CBS producer Amy Birnbaum said that she disagreed with reporter Randall Pinkston, with whom she worked closely on the Smith coverage; he believed the "boyfriend motive," but to her, that story seemed "forced." She believed Smith was "psychotic" or mentally ill, probably because she didn't receive appropriate counseling in that small town" (interview).

6. Tom Morganthau, Vern E. Smith, "Condemned to Life," *Newsweek*, August 7, 1995; Jesse J. Holland, "Union Prays for Strength to Forgive," *Rock Hill Herald*, July 31, 1995.

7. Wells told Smith that the intersection where Smith had allegedly been carjacked had actually been under police surveillance; the carjacking thus could not have occurred as Smith had reported. Rick Bragg, "Sheriff Says Prayer and a Lie Led Susan Smith to Confess," *New York Times*, July 18, 1995.

8. Bragg, "A Killer's Only Confidant."

9. Bragg, "Life of a Mother"; Charles L. Warner, "Sheriff looks back at Smith investigation," *Union Daily Times*, August 3, 1995.

10. *NBC Evening News*, July 28, 1995, July 31, 1995.

11. Otto Pollack, *The Criminality of Women* (Philadelphia: University of Pennsylvania Press, 1950); Ann Jones, 9.

12. Wilczynski, 115; Concetta C. Culliver, "Women and Crime: An Overview," in *Women and Criminality: The State of the Art*, ed. Concetta Culliver (New York: Garland Publishing, 1993), 10; Malcolm, 42; Chesney-Lind, 4. This idea surfaced repeatedly in discussions of the Andrea Yates

verdict. Some observers lamented that Smith's life sentence dictated that infanticidal mothers would never get the death penalty—a truly offensive failure of the cautionary tale (these observers obviously ignored the Darlie Routier trial—she is now on Death Row in Texas for killing her two sons in 1997).

13. Meyer and Oberman, 69. The extreme disparity in the sentences of infanticidal·women—ranging from outpatient psychological care to capital punishment—is most likely related to the women's performance of "appropriate" gender roles.

14. Rapping, "The Movie of the Week," 96.

15. Rapping, *Law and Justice,* 228.

16. Christopher Sullivan, "'Why-dunnit': Challenges for Defense in Smith Case," *Union Daily Times,* July 17, 1995. The defense team was well aware of how carefully they had to handle the abuse in Smith's past. According to David Bruck, "The moment the press started reporting leaks from law enforcement about her history of molestation by her stepfather, Alan Dershowitz was pounding the airwaves about the abuse excuse." He continued: "I knew that this was a very loaded—that almost anything having to do with her background had to be handled very carefully so as not to fall into that stereotype, sort of hostile, victim-blaming. She'd been so demonized, and almost any mitigating factor would turn into dross if it wasn't very carefully and very honestly investigated and presented" (interview).

17. Rapping, *Law and Justice,* 9, 239, 243; "About *Law & Order,*" www.nbc.com/Law_and_Order/about/ (accessed July 5, 2011).

18. Gillespie and Schellhas, 37–41.

19. Giola Dillberto, "A Violent Death, a Haunted Life," *People,* October 8, 1984.

20. Internet Movie Database, "The Burning Bed," www.imdb.com/title/tt0087010/ (accessed July 5, 2011); Rapping, "The Movie of the Week," 99.

21. Chan, 91.

22. At least three infanticidal mothers before the Smith case were found to be insane in courts of law and received lesser punishments: Ann Green of New York (Ronald Sullivan, "Jury, Citing Mother's Condition, Absolves Her in 2 Babies' Deaths," *New York Times,* October 1, 1988), Sheryl Massip of California (Reuters, "Woman Clear in Son's Killing," *New York Times,* December 24, 1988), and Lucrezia Gentile of New York (Leonard Buder, "Judge Accepts Insanity Plea in '88 Drowning of Infant," *New York Times,* November 10, 1989). These mothers did not receive the same kind of overwhelming press attention that Smith and Yates did.

23. Snitow, 32–51.

24. *Feminist Studies* 20, no. 1 (Spring 1994).

25. "Murderous Mom Susan Smith Still Enthralls Nation," *Atlanta Journal Constitution,* March 2, 2000; Tom Turnipseed, "Continuing Saga of Sex, Murder, and Racism: Susan Smith Still Scheming in Prison," *Common Dreams,* September 14, 2000; "Pregnant Inmate Vows to Kill Herself—And Her Unborn Twins!" *Weekly World News,* November 14, 2000; "Online Personal Ad Features Child Killer Susan Smith," *USA Today,* July 11, 2003; Jordan Rodack and Dawna Kaufmann, "Outrage! Keep These Monsters Caged," *Globe,* October 24, 2011.

26. In 1996, psychologist Diane Eyer exposed the scapegoating of mothers for a host of perceived social problems, including the welfare system, the day care crisis, and the "epidemic" of single motherhood. The various authors in *"Bad Mothers": The Politics of Blame in Twentieth-*

Century America picked up where Eyer left off, revealing the fault lines of race, class, and politics within the label of "bad mother." In 1996, sociologist Sharon Hays deconstructed the "cultural contradictions" within the ideology of "intensive mothering," arguing that the enormous amounts of energy that women expended trying to live up to impossible ideals gained them no power and in fact supported traditional gendered and economic modes of domination. The following year, in 1997, English professor Elaine Tuttle Hansen argued that the vibrant critique of pronatalism that characterized the feminism of the 1970s was crippled by the backlash, but that contemporary fiction picked up where feminism left off, offering some resolutions to conflicts within the maternal discourse. That same year, historian Lauri Umansky offered motherhood as the "organizing metaphor" of the second wave of feminism, arguing that it could still serve as a rallying point for the embattled women's movement. (Eyer; Ladd-Taylor and Umansky; Sharon Hayes, The Cultural Contradictions of Motherhood [New Haven, CT: Yale University Press, 1996], x, 165; Elaine Tuttle Hansen, Mother Without Child: Contemporary Fiction and the Crisis of Motherhood [Berkeley: University of California Press, 1997]; Lauri Umansky, Motherhood Reconceived: Feminisms and the Legacies of the Sixties [New York: New York University Press, 1996].)

27. Ann Jones, 12–14. Other criminologists chimed in in the late 1990s, as well, including Chesney-Lind and Mann. The ideas that the female violent crime rate rose with organized feminism and that women were getting away with their crimes is attributed to Freda Adler's Sisters in Crime: The Rise of the New Female Criminal (New York: McGraw-Hill Book Co., 1975). In 1996, Coramae Richie Mann published a statistical analysis of female crime that finally debunked the backlash hypothesis that women were getting away with murder; according to her findings, the "chivalry hypothesis," or the idea that women are treated more leniently by the justice system, was a false generalization.

28. Wilczynski, 65.

29. Ibid., 93. Criminologists in the 1970s developed a typology of motive that included "altruism" along with "acutely psychotic," "unwanted child," "accidental," and "spouse revenge." See Meyer and Oberman, 20, for an extended explanation of this typology. Toni Morrison made altruistic infanticide famous in her award-winning Beloved; she modeled the infanticidal mother Sethe after Margaret Garner, the escaped slave who murdered her child rather than see her returned to slavery. Sethe explains her crime in terms of her daughter's best interests: "I didn't have time to explain before because it had to be done quick. She had to be safe, and I put her where she would be." See Morrison's Beloved (New York: Alfred A. Knopf, 1987), 100.

30. The full text of Smith's confession is available in Henderson, Nine Days in Union, 117–18. In fact, Smith was typical of female murderers in general. Infanticide is the "most common and prevalent" violent crime committed by women (Lita Linzer Schwartz and Natalie K. Isser. Endangered Children: Neonaticide, Infanticide, and Filicide [Boca Raton, FL: CRC Press, 2000], 2). Most mothers who kill their children are young, and a study of mothers who committed fatal child abuse in Georgia revealed a mean age of twenty-three—Smith's age when she committed her crime (Mann, 74). Filicidal mothers tend to choose less aggressive methods of murder (Mann, 63). About 39 percent of filicidal mothers with diagnosed depression kill more than one child, and of those crimes, over half were "attempted or successful murder-suicides" (Meyer and Oberman, 86). Another study found that approximately 80 percent of filicidal mothers had a diagnosable personality disorder (Schwartz and Isser, 95). Ania Wilczynski found that, in her

sample of filicidal mothers, three-fifths had depressive disorders and one-third had previously attempted suicide (82).

31. Meyer and Oberman, 72.

32. Pam Easton, "Woman Tells Police of Methodically Killing Children," Associated Press State and Local Wire, June 22, 2001; Cary Clack, "What Could Drive a Loving Mother to Kill Her Own Children?" *San Antonio Express-News,* June 23, 2001.

33. Zondra Hughes, "Depression After Delivery: Black Mothers and the Postpartum Crisis," *Ebony,* October 2001. Medical professionals distinguish between three types of depression following childbirth: the "baby blues," which are comparatively mild mood disturbances; "postpartum depression," which shares the symptoms of other depressive disorders and is characterized only by the timing of its onset; and "postpartum psychosis," which is a much more severe form of depressive disorder combined with psychotic symptoms like hallucinations and delusions (Nunacs). Andrea Yates, who reported hearing voices and believed that the devil was directing her actions, clearly had postpartum psychosis and not just depression. Some media accounts acknowledged this important distinction between postpartum depression, which affects about 10 percent of new mothers ("Lowering the Rate of Postpartum Depression," *Psychiatry* 523 [23 May 2002]), and postpartum psychosis, which affects only about one to four of every 1000 births and "can lead to suicide or infanticide" (Connell, 145). Ignorance on the subject of postpartum mental disturbances, however, meant that the subsequent "definitional creep," or the unofficial widening of the relatively narrow definition of postpartum depression, went virtually unnoticed (Margaret Talbot discusses the process of "definitional creep" in diagnoses of Munchausen Syndrome by Proxy in "The Bad Mother," *The New Yorker,* August 9, 2004). For information about the legal treatment of postpartum depression, see March, 247.

34. The violent details were publicized widely; journalists did not mince words, spare details, or review the murders delicately. Few readers could forget that Yates systematically drowned all five of her children, or that she had to chase her oldest son, Noah, seven, and carry him to the bathtub. This detail is so horrifying and so unforgettable that journalists often offered it as the only detail from the crime scene. See, for example, Easton, "Mother Tells Police of Methodically Killing Children."

35. Marianne Szegedy-Maszak, "Mothers and Murder," *U.S. News and World Report,* March 18, 2002.

36. The few unsympathetic observers, like a spokeswoman for a Texas victims' rights group who argued that Yates's status as the children's mother should further enrage people (because "mothers are the protectors of our children") rather than serve as a basis for sympathy, were in the minority in their references to the rapidly dying Good Mother discourse of just a few years before (Juan A. Lozano, "Many Supportive of Woman Accused of Drowning Her Five Children," Associated Press State and Local Wire, June 23, 2001). Unlike the Susan Smith case, in which the dominant journalistic tone was one of sensationalist condemnation if not outright anger, journalists seemed to be trying to understand Andrea Yates. This widespread sympathy made Ann Coulter's attempt to connect Yates's crimes with feminism by using an abortion metaphor—she called the Yates children "choices," and Yates the "late-term abortion" provider—seem half-cocked at best, and Coulter's opinion, for once, enjoyed little press (Ann Coulter, "Stop Persecuting Andrea Yates!" *National Review,* September 6, 2001).

37. Anne Belli Gesalman, "A Dark State of Mind," *Newsweek,* March 4, 2002.

38. Anne Belli Gesalman and Lynette Clemetson, "A Crazy System," *Newsweek,* March 25, 2002; Mary Alice Altorfer, "Letters," *Houston Chronicle,* January 7, 2005; Rene Karpas, "Letters," *Houston Chronicle,* January 7, 2005. Dr. Park Dietz, a well-known psychiatrist who has testified in various high-profile trials, described on the stand an episode of the popular television show *Law & Order* on which a mother drowned her children and won her case with an insanity plea, implying that this was the script for Yates's crime. The judge overturned Yates's conviction because this episode does not exist. Dietz's testimony had enormous influence on the outcome of the trial; one juror wrote the judge a letter stating he was ready to vote not guilty by reason of insanity before Dietz's testimony (George Flynn, "Judging Andrea," *Houston Chronicle,* January 20, 2005). Dietz was actually hired by the prosecuting team in Smith's case as well, but he never took the stand (Pope, interview; Anna Brown, "Psychiatrist to Assist Smith Prosecution," *Union Daily Times,* March 18, 1995). Dietz is something of a "star" expert witness in infanticide trials because he so adamantly believes that filicidal mothers are pure evil. He has argued: "no amount of stress alone can account for women killing their children. . . . It doesn't come from who you hang out with, what your opportunities in life are or how much money you have. It comes from something being wrong with the person" (quoted in Margaret Spinelli, ed., *Infanticide: Psychosocial and Legal Perspectives on Women Who Kill* [Washington, DC: American Psychiatric Publishing, Inc., 2003], 10).

39. "Her Private Hell," *People,* August 9, 2004; Dirk Johnson and Carol Rust, "Who's Babysitting the Kids?" *Newsweek,* January 17, 2005; Anne Belli Gesalman, "Andrea Yates Still Battling Her Demons—And Her Past," *Newsweek,* October 20, 2003.

40. AP Wire, "Suburbia Sizzles in 'Housewives,'" September 30, 2004, www.msnbc.msn .com/id/6133690/ (accessed February 20, 2011). If there was a feminist message about motherhood on *Desperate Housewives,* it was offered in the character of Lynette, who, according to one columnist, showed viewers "you can be fiercely in love with your children and long to pack up the minivan and drive off" (Ellen Goodman, "Desperate Housewives, Indeed," *Boston Globe,* November 21, 2004).

41. Marie Osmond, *Behind the Smile: My Journey Out of Postpartum Depression* (New York: Warner Books, 2001); Brooke Shields, *Down Came the Rain: My Journey Through Postpartum Depression* (New York: Hyperion, 2005); *The Oprah Winfrey Show,* June 20, 2005; Jane Brody, "Don't Let Your Baby Blues Go Code Red," *New York Times,* June 7, 2005. The *New York Times* even printed Shields's response to Cruise's "rant" as an opinion piece (Brooke Shields, "War of Words," *New York Times,* July 1, 2005). Cox-Arquette spoke of her experiences on CNN's *Larry King Live,* July 22, 2005, transcripts.cnn.com/TRANSCRIPTS/0507/22/sbt.01.html (accessed February 20, 2011). Carnie Wilson's admissions preceded Cox-Arquette by one day ("Carnie Supports Brooke After Revealing Her Own Post-Birth Blues," www.contactmusic.com/new/xmlfeed.nsf/story/ carnie-supports-brooke-after-revealing-her-own-postbirth-blues [accessed February 20, 2011]).

42. Shoshana S. Bennett and Mary Jo Codey, *Postpartum Depression for Dummies* (New York: For Dummies, 2007); Laura J. Miller, "Postpartum Depression," *JAMA* 287 (2002): 762–65; Katherine L. Wisner, Christina Chambers, and Dorothy K.Y. Sit, "Postpartum Depression: A Major Public Health Problem," *JAMA* 296 (2006): 2616–18; Douglas and Michaels.

43. Judith Warner, "Mommy Madness," *Newsweek,* February 21, 2005. The New Jersey

bill passed in April 2006 (American Public Health Association, "Postpartum Depression Bill Signed!" press release available online at www.apha.org/membergroups/newsletters/section-newsletters/matern/summer06/2774.htm [accessed February 20, 2011]). The Texas bill did not pass (www.postpartumprogress.com/weblog/2009/03/postpartum-depression-psychosis-texas-could-be-first-state-with-infanticide-law.html [accessed April 25, 2011]).

44. Dale Lezon, Peggy O'Hare, and Rosanna Ruiz, "Jury Finds Yates Insane, Not Guilty," *Houston Chronicle*, July 26, 2006; Peggy O'Hare and Dale Lezon, "Second Jury is Taking Longer to Reach Verdict on Yates," *Houston Chronicle*, July 26, 2006; Maria Newman, "Yates Found Not Guilty by Reason of Insanity," *New York Times*, July 26, 2006; Dale Lezon, Peggy O'Hare, and Rosanna Ruiz, "Yates Found Insane, Not Guilty," *Houston Chronicle*, July 26, 2006. The media saturation of the Yates case and the subsequent spotlight on postpartum depression seem to have made similar stories unnewsworthy. When Deanna Laney of east Texas stoned her three sons, killing two of them, because she "'had to' for religious reasons," she barely made the national news (Anne Belli Gesalman, "Andrea Yates Redux," *Newsweek*, May 17, 2003).

45. Sally Satel, "The Newest Feminist Icon: A Killer Mom," *Wall Street Journal*, September 11, 2001.

46. Toni Morrison, *Beloved*; Mark Reinhardt, *Who Speaks for Margaret Garner? The True Story that Inspired Toni Morrison's* Beloved (Minneapolis: University of Minnesota Press, 2010). For information on the medicalization of normal female biology, see: Barbara Ehrenreich and Deirdre English, *Complaints and Disorders: The Sexual Politics of Sickness* (New York: Feminist Press, 1973), and *For Her Own Good: 150 Years of Experts' Advice to Women* (New York: Doubleday, 1978); and Rachel Maines, *The Technology of Orgasm: "Hysteria," the Vibrator, and Women's Sexual Satisfaction* (Baltimore: Johns Hopkins University Press, 1999).

47. Morris and Wilczynski, 215.

48. Meyer and Oberman, 10. The British statute reads: "Where a woman by any willful act or omission causes the death of her child being under the age of twelve months, but at the time of the act or omission the balance of her mind was disturbed by reason of her not having fully recovered from the effect of giving birth to the child . . . then, notwithstanding that the circumstances were such that but for this Act the offense would have amounted to murder she shall be guilty of felony, to wit infanticide, and may for such offense be dealt with and punished as if she had been guilty of the offense of manslaughter of the child" (Jessica Butterfield, "Blue Mourning: Postpartum Psychosis and the Criminal Insanity Defense: Waking to the Reality of Women Who Kill Their Children," *John Marshall Law Review* 39 [2006]: 536).

49. Wilczynski, 164; Jacob M. Appel, "When Infanticide Isn't Murder," *Huffington Post*, September 8, 2009.

50. There is, in fact, a long history to this defense, as seen in the earlier discussion of the scorned and desperate Medea. Ann Jones traces it to an 1872 case in which an attorney argued that a seduction by an older man traumatized his homicidal female client at the tender age of fifteen (164).

51. "Low Income Urban Mothers Have High Rate of Postpartum Depression," University of Rochester Medical Center News Room, www.urmc.rochester.edu/news/story/index.cfm?id=2760 (accessed July 5, 2011); Zondra Hughes, "Depression After Delivery: Black Mothers and the Postpartum Crisis," *Ebony*, October 2001; Segre et al., 316–21.

52. Postpartum depression is not a new problem by any means; maternity wards used to be called "weeping wards" because of the emotional new mothers they served (Nunacs, 127).

53. Chan, 181–82; Connell, 143–69; Dobson and Sales, 1098, 1102.

54. Wolf, *The Beauty Myth: How Images of Beauty Are Used Against Women* (New York: Anchor Books, 1991), 198. Melissa Benn posits the same thing about premenstrual tension/syndrome when she quotes a feminist scholar's argument that PMT is "at its root a political construct—a part of patriarchal ideology. Many feminists have supported the idea of PMT and have promoted its acceptance by the medical profession but have feared that it might be 'used against women'" (Benn, "Body Talk: The Sexual Politics of PMT," in Birch, ed., *Moving Targets*, 158).

55. Chesney-Lind, 97.

56. Laura Briggs, "The Race of Hysteria: 'Overcivilization' and the 'Savage' Woman in Late Nineteenth-Century Obstetrics and Gynecology," *American Quarterly* 52, no. 2 (2000): 246–73; E.A. Howell, P.A. Mora, M.D. DiBonaventura, and H. Leventhal, "Modifiable Factors Associated with Changes in Postpartum Depressive Symptoms," *Archives of Women's Mental Health* 12 (April 2009).

57. Wilczynski, 25; Ann Jones, 14.

58. "David Smith on Casey Anthony Case," June 16, 2011, drdrew.blogs.cnn.com/2011/06/16/david-smith-on-casey-anthony-case/ (accessed August 15, 2011).

EPILOGUE

1. Howard, interview. Even those that knew Smith well commented upon her general lack of affect during the trial; Kevin Kingsmore, who testified on her behalf as a character witness, said her "poker face" and "blank stare" were very strange and unlike her (interview). A major exception to this lack of emotions came when Smith cried openly during David Smith's testimony (Brown, "State Rests Case"). This kind of dissociated state is consistent with symptoms of trauma and depression, and Smith was certainly on heavy doses of Prozac throughout the trial (Brown, "Smith Ruled Competent"; "Psychiatrists Say Smith Needs Suicide Watch While in Treatment," *Union Daily Times*, July 17, 1995).

2. Susan Smith, letters to author, July 22, 2005; August 28, 2005; October 10, 2005.

3. The ad itself is very childlike. Beneath a photo of Smith smiling in prison-issue sweats, the ad read: "I am 31 years old. My birthday is September 26. I am looking to meet new people and, hopefully, become friends. During my spare time, I enjoy reading, working puzzles, and writing. I love rainbows, Mickey Mouse, the beach, the mountains, and waterfalls. My favorite color is navy blue and my favorite flower is the daisy. I am a Christian and I enjoy attending church. I consider myself to be sensitive, caring, and kind-hearted. I'm currently serving a life sentence on the charge of murder. I have grown and matured alot since my incarceration, but I will always hurt for the pain I've caused so many, especially my children. I hope to receive letters from those who are not judgmental and who are sincere. I look forward to hearing from new people and, hopefully, finding new friends. May God bless each one of you!" Although the ad has since been removed from the site, it is available online at www.thesmokinggun.com/file/murderous-mommy-seeks-pen-pals (accessed July 5, 2011).

4. "Smith Moved to Prison General Population," *Union Daily Times*, September 28, 1995;

Susan Smith, letter to author, August 28, 2005; Tom Currie, interview; Kingsmore, interview; Toni White, interview; Reverend Toni White told me that "all these creeps, all these guys from all over the country write" Smith (interview); Susan Smith, letter to author, December 18, 2006.

5. Cato, interview; Toni White, interview.

6. Pope, interview. Pope argued that the many experts who interviewed Smith during the trial preparations were actually "training" her for an insanity or mentally ill defense: "It has been close to three months, and I am aware of at least two experts Bruck has allowed to meet with Mrs. Smith. . . . She has spent three months in insanity training, in insanity school" (Anna Brown, "Smith Trained by Experts, Pope Says," *Union Daily Times,* January 28, 1994).

7. Adrienne Rich, *Of Woman Born: Motherhood as Experience and Institution* (New York: W. W. Norton and Co., 1976), 1.

8. From Smith's written confession, rpt. in Henderson, *Nine Days in Union,* 117. The full text of her written confession can be found online: www.teleplex.net/shj/smith/ninedays/ssconf .html.

9. Rich, 4–5. In this passage, Rich is referring to the 1974 case of Joanne Michulski, a mother of eight who killed her two youngest children.

10. Donna Schaper, "Having a child is not a picnic, Susan Smith case reminds us," *National Catholic Reporter,* December 2, 1994.

11. Marouf Hasian Jr. and Lisa A. Flores, "Mass Mediated Representations of the Susan Smith Trial," *Howard Journal of Communication* 11 (2000): 172; "Lives of Quiet Desperation," *Time,* December 5, 1994; Lynn Smith, "Moms with Urges to Kill Give Their Side of the Story," *Los Angeles Times,* November 30, 1994; Diane Erwin, "Drowning of Sons Wounds Myth of Motherhood," *Sacramento Bee,* November 8, 1994.

12. Anna Quindlen, "Playing God On No Sleep," *Newsweek,* July 2, 2001.

13. "Mail Call," *Newsweek,* July 23, 2001.

14. Susan Faludi, *The Terror Dream: Fear and Fantasy in Post-9/11 America* (New York: Metropolitan Books, 2007); John Leonard, "Macho Security State," *New York Times,* October 14, 2007; Gail Collins and Stacy Schiff, "Of Mama Grizzly Born?" *New York Times,* August 18, 2010; Jodi Jacobson, "Was Asking Bachman About 'Submission' a Sexist Question?" RHRealityCheck.com, www.rhrealitycheck.org/blog/2011/08/12/asking-bachmann-about-submissionsexist-question (August 12, 2011); "Rosen's Words about Romney Fuel 'Mommy Wars,'" *Tell Me More, National Public Radio,* April 17, 2012, www.npr.org/2012/04/17/150803660/rosens-words-about-ann-romney-fuel-mommy-wars (accessed July 31, 2012)."

BIBLIOGRAPHY

PRIMARY SOURCES

Films

B., Beth, director. *Two Small Bodies*, VHS. Germany: Daniel Zuta Filmproduktion, 1993.

Boorman, John. *Deliverance*. DVD. USA: Warner Brothers Pictures, 1972.

Butler, Robert, director. *A Question of Guilt*, VHS. USA: Lorimar Productions, 1978.

Greene, David, director. *Small Sacrifices*. VHS. USA: Anchor Bay Entertainment, Inc., 1989.

Malmuth, Bruce, director. *Where Are the Children?* DVD. USA: Braun Entertainment Group, Inc., 1986.

Parker, Alan. *Mississippi Burning*. DVD. USA: Orion Pictures Corporation, 1989.

Ross, Herbert, director. *Steel Magnolias*. DVD. USA: Rastar Films, 1989.

Roth, Joe, director. *Freedomland*. USA: Revolution Studios, 2006.

Scorsese, Martin, director. *Cape Fear*. DVD. USA: Amblin Entertainment, 1991.

Zemeckis, Robert, director. *Forrest Gump*. DVD. USA: Paramount Pictures, 1994.

Government Documents

State of South Carolina, County of Union, in the Court of General Sessions. *State of South Carolina vs. Susan Vaughan Smith.*

U.S. Census Bureau. "Fertility of American Women, 1994." Available online: www.census.gov/hhes/fertility/data/cps/1994.html (accessed August 1, 2011).

———. "Fertility of American Women, 2002: Population Characteristics." Available online: www.census.gov/prod/2003pubs/p20–548.pdf (accessed August 1, 2011).

U.S. Department of Health and Human Services. "Poverty Guidelines." *Federal Register* 59, no. 28 (February 10, 1994): 6277–78.

———. Administration for Children and Families. "Survey Shows Dramatic Increase in Child Abuse and Neglect, 1986–1993." Press Release, September 18, 1996. Available online: www.prevent-abuse-now.com/stats.htm#Increase (accessed July 5, 2011).

U.S. Department of Justice. "National Crime Victimization Survey: Carjacking, 1993–2002." Available online: bjs.ojp.usdoj.gov/content/pub/ascii/co2.txt (accessed August 15, 2011).

U.S. Equal Employment Opportunity Commission. "A 'Toothless Tiger' Helps Shape the Law and Educate the Public." Available online: www.eeoc.gov/eeoc/history/35th/1965-71/index.html (accessed July 5, 2011).

U.S. Executive Order 10925. "Establishing the President's Committee on Equal Employment Opportunity." Available online: www.eeoc.gov/eeoc/history/35th/thelaw/eo-10925.html (accessed July 5, 2011).

U.S. Executive Order 11246. "Equal Employment Opportunity." Available online: www.archives.gov/federal-register/codification/executive-order/11246.html (accessed July 5, 2011).

Interviews

Birnbaum, Amy. Interview by author. Interview by email. October 3, 2007, transcripts in author's possession.

Brackette, A. L. Interview by author. Union, SC. July 20, 2005, tape recording in author's possession.

Bragg, Rick. Interview by author. New Orleans. July 27, 2005, tape recording in author's possession.

Brown, Anna. Interview by author. Email interview. September 21, 2005, transcripts in author's possession.

Bruck, David. Interview by author. Phone interview, tape recording. July 29, 2005, tape recording in author's possession.

Cato, Bob. Interview by author. Laurens, SC. January 11, 2006, transcripts in author's possession.

Charles, Allan D. Interview by author. Union, SC. November 2, 2006, tape recording in author's possession.

Corriere, Jules. Interview by author. Email interview. April 14, 2005, transcripts in author's possession.

Currie, Ann. Interview by author. Carthage, NC. July 11, 2005 tape recording in author's possession.

Currie, Tom. Interview by author. Carthage, NC. July 11, 2005, tape recording in author's possession.

———. Personal Papers, 1994–1995, photocopies in author's possession.

Decker-Davis, Twila. Interview by author. Email interview. July 24 2006, transcripts in author's possession.

Dotson, Bob. Interview by author. Phone interview. November 4, 2006, transcripts in author's possession.

Henderson, Gary. Interview by author. Spartanburg, SC, November 3, 2006, transcripts in author's possession.

Hobbs, Phil. Interview by author. Email interview. November 16, 2006, transcripts in author's possession.

Howard, Bill. Interview by author. Charleston, SC. June 14, 2007, tape recording in author's possession.

Hughes, McElroy. Interview by author. Union, SC. July 16, 2006, tape recording in author's possession.

Inman, Torance. Interview by author. Union, SC. June 18, 2007, transcripts in author's possession.

Kingsmore, Kevin. Interview by author. Moore, SC. November 3, 2006, tape recording in author's possession.

Pope, Tommy. Interview by author. York, SC. July 19, 2005, tape recording in author's possession.

Raines, Allen. Interview by author. Interview by letter. August 12, 2005, transcripts in author's possession.

Roberts, Michael. Interview by author. Buffalo, SC, November 4, 2006, transcripts in author's possession.

White, Thom. Interview by author. Union, SC. July 19, 2005 tape·recording in author's possession.

White, Toni. Interview by author. Columbia, SC. July 15, 2005, tape recording in author's possession.

Magazines

Ebony.
The Economist.
Ms.
The Nation.
National Bureau of Economic Research Digest.
The National Review.
Newsweek.
The Oxford American.
People.
Time.
What is Enlightenment?
U.S. News and World Report.
Weekly World News.

Newspapers

Arkansas Democrat-Gazette.
Associated Press State and Local Wire.
Atlanta Journal Constitution.
Augusta Chronicle (GA).
Austin American-Statesman (TX).

Boston Globe.
Charleston Gazette (WV).
Charleston Post & Courier (SC).
Charlotte Observer (NC).
Chicago Tribune.
Christian Science Monitor.
Columbia State (SC).
Daily News (NY).
Greenville News (SC).
Greensboro News & Record (NC).
Houston Chronicle.
Knoxville News-Sentinel (TN).
New Orleans Times-Picayune.
New York Times.
Peoria Journal-Star (IL).
Portland Tribune (OR).
Roanoke Times (VA).
Rock Hill Herald (SC).
Sacramento Bee (CA).
San Antonio News-Express (TX).
Spartanburg Herald-Journal (SC).
St. Petersburg Times (FL).
Tampa Tribune.
Union Daily Times (SC).
USA Today.
Virginia Beach Beacon (VA).
Virginian Pilot (VA).
Washington Post.
Washington Times.

Television Shows

A Current Affair, Fox.
Desperate Housewives, ABC.
Evening News, ABC.
Evening News, CBS.
Evening News, NBC.
Hee Haw, CBS.
Nightline, ABC.
TalkBack Live, CNN.

The Oprah Winfrey Show, ABC.

Today Show, NBC.

SECONDARY SOURCES

Adler, Freda. *Sisters in Crime: The Rise of the New Female Criminal*. New York: McGraw Hill Book Company, 1975.

Aldridge, Marion D., and Kevin Lewis, eds. *The Changing Shape of Protestantism in the South*. Macon, GA: Mercer University Press, 1996.

Allison, Dorothy. *Bastard Out of Carolina*. New York: Penguin Books, 1992.

———. *Skin: Talking About Sex, Class, and Literature*. Ithaca, NY: Firebrand Books, 1994.

———. *Two or Three Things I Know for Sure*. New York: Dutton Books, 1995.

Ansell, Amy. *New Right, New Racism: Race and Reaction in the United States and Britain*. New York: New York University Press, 1997.

Applebome, Peter. *Dixie Rising: How the South Is Shaping American Values, Politics, and Culture*. New York: Times Books, 1996.

Asen, Robert. "Women, Work, Welfare: A Rhetorical History of Images of Poor Women in Welfare Policy Debates." *Rhetoric and Public Affairs* 6, no. 2 (2003): 285–312.

Bacote, Clarence A. "Negro Prescriptions, Protests, and Proposed Solutions." In *The Negro in the South Since 1865*, ed. Charles Wynes. University: Alabama University Press, 1965. 471–98.

Barnett, Barbara Ann. "Medea in the Media: Narrative and Myth in Print Media Coverage of Women Who Kill Their Children." Ph.D. diss., University of North Carolina–Chapel Hill, 2004.

Bass, Jack, and Jack Nelson. *The Orangeburg Massacre*. Macon, GA: Mercer University Press, 1996.

Bederman, Gail. *Manliness and Civilization*. Chicago: University of Chicago Press, 1995.

Benn, Melissa. "Body Talk: The Sexual Politics of PMT." In *Moving Targets*, ed. Birch, 152–71.

Birch, Helen. "If Looks Could Kill: Myra Hindley and the Iconography of Evil." In *Moving Targets*, ed. Birch, 32–61.

———. "Introduction." In *Moving Targets*, ed. Birch, 1–6.

———, ed. *Moving Targets: Women, Murder, and Representation*. Berkeley: University of California Press, 1994.

Boydston, Jeanne. *Home and Work: Housework, Wages, and the Ideology of Labor in the Early Republic*. New York: Oxford University Press, 1994.

Boylan, Jeanne. *Portraits of Guilt: The Woman Who Profiles the Faces of America's Deadliest Criminals*. New York: Pocket Books, 2000.

Bragg, Rick. *All Over But the Shoutin'*. New York: Pantheon Books, 1997.

Brandon, Craig. *Murder in the Adirondacks: An American Tragedy Revisited.* Utica, NY: North Country Books, 1986.

Briggs, Laura. "The Race of Hysteria: 'Overcivilization' and the 'Savage' Woman in Late Nineteenth-Century Obstetrics and Gynecology." *American Quarterly* 52, no. 2 (2000): 246–73.

Broach, Glen T., and Lee Bandy. "South Carolina: A Decade of Rapid Republican Ascent." In *Southern Politics in the 1990s*, ed. Alexander P. Lamis. Baton Rouge: Louisiana State University Press, 1999. 50–80.

Brooks, Peter, and Paul Gerwitz. *Law's Stories: Narrative and Rhetoric in the Law.* New Haven, CT: Yale University Press, 1996.

Bruce, Steve. *The Rise and Fall of the New Christian Right: Conservative Protestant Politics in America, 1978–1988.* New York: Oxford University Press, 1990.

Brundage, Fitzhugh. *Lynching in the New South: Georgia and Virginia, 1880–1930.* Urbana: University of Illinois Press, 1993.

Bullock, Charles S. III, and Mark C. Smith, "The Religious Right and Electoral Politics in the South." In *Politics and Religion in the White South*, ed. Feldman, 215–30.

Butterfield, Fox. *All God's Children: The Bosket Family and the American Tradition of Violence.* New York: Harper Perennial, 1995.

Butterfield, Jessica. "Blue Mourning: Postpartum Psychosis and the Criminal Insanity Defense: Waking to the Reality of Women Who Kill Their Children." *John Marshall Law Review* 39 (2006).

Campbell, Nancy D. "States of Secrecy: Women's Crimes and the Practices of Everyday Life." *Journal of Women's History* 10, no. 3 (Autumn 1998): 204–14.

Capozi, George. *Ordeal By Trial.* New York: Walker & Co., 1972.

Carcasson, Martin. "'Ending Welfare as We Know It': President Clinton and the Rhetorical Transformation of the Anti-Welfare Culture." *Rhetoric & Public Affairs* 9, no. 4 (Winter 2006): 655–92.

Carlton, David. *Mill and Town in South Carolina, 1880–1920.* Baton Rouge: Louisiana State University Press, 1982.

Cash, Wilbur J. *The Mind of the South.* New York: Vintage Books, 1941.

Chan, Wendy. *Women, Murder, and Justice.* New York: Palgrave, 2001.

Charles, Allan D. *The Narrative History of Union County, SC.* 3rd ed. Greenville, SC: A PRESS Printing Co., 1997.

Chesney-Lind, Meda. *The Female Offender: Girls, Women, and Crime.* Thousand Oaks, CA: SAGE Publications, 1997.

Christensen, Ron. *Political Trials: Gordian Knots in the Law.* New Brunswick, NJ: Transaction Books, 1986;

Clark, Mary Higgins. *Where Are the Children?* New York: Mass Market Paperbacks, 1992.

Cleaver, Eldridge. *Soul on Ice.* New York: Mass Market Paperbacks, 1970.

Clinton, William J. "Remarks to the Governor's Leadership Conference in New York City," October 19, 1994: www.presidency.ucsb.edu/ws/?pid=49326#axzz1hmkyILoj.

Cobb, James. *Away Down South: A History of Southern Identity.* New York: Oxford University Press, 2005.

Collins, Patricia Hill. *Black Feminist Thought: Knowledge, Consciousness, and the Politics of Empowerment.* New York: Routledge, 2000.

Connell, Michelle. "The Postpartum Defense and Feminism: More or Less Justice for Women?" *Case Western Law Review* 53 (2002): 143–69.

Conway, Mimi. *Rise Gonna Rise: A Portrait of Southern Textile Workers.* Garden City, NY: Anchor Press, 1979.

Corriere, Jules. "Turn the Washpot Down." Community Performances, Inc., 2002.

Crawford, Allan. *Thunder on the Right: The 'New Right' and the Politics of Resentment.* New York: Pantheon Books, 1980.

Culliver, Concetta. "Women and Crime: An Overview." In *Women and Criminality: The State of the Art,* ed. Concetta Culliver. New York: Garland Publishing, 1993. 3–21.

Degler, Carl N. *Place Over Time: The Continuity of Southern Distinctiveness.* Athens: University of Georgia Press, 1997.

Denno, Deborah. "Who Is Andrea Yates? A Short Story about Insanity." *Duke Journal of Gender Law and Policy* 10, no. 1 (Summer 2003): www.law.duke.edu/shell/cite.pl?1 0+Duke+J.+Gender+L.+&+Pol'y+1 (accessed October 20, 2011).

Dobson, Velma, and Bruce Sales. "The Science of Infanticide and Mental Illness." *Psychology, Public Policy, and Law* 6 (2000): 1098–1112.

Donovan, Nancy McIlvaine. "Susan Smith: An 'American Tragedy' Narrative Retold." *Dreiser Studies* 34, no. 1 (Summer 2003): 58–65.

Douglas, Ellen. *Can't Quit You, Baby.* New York: Penguin, 1989.

Douglas, Susan, and Meredith Michaels. *The Mommy Myth: The Idealization of Motherhood and How It Has Undermined All Women.* New York: Free Press, 2004.

Downing, John, Ali Mohammadi, and Annabelle Sreberny-Mohammadi, eds. *Questioning the Media: A Critical Introduction.* London: Sage Publications, 1990.

Dreiser, Theodore. *An American Tragedy.* New York: Signet Classics, 1964.

Duster, Alfreda, ed. *Crusade for Justice.* Chicago: University of Chicago Press, 1970.

Eady, Cornelius. *Brutal Imagination.* New York: G. P. Putnam's Sons, 2001.

Edsall, Thomas Byrne, and Mary D. Edsall. *Chain Reaction: The Impact of Race, Rights, and Taxes on American Politics.* New York: W. W. Norton & Co., 1991.

Eftimiades, Maria. *Sins of the Mother: The Heartbreaking True Story Behind the Susan Smith Murder Case.* New York: St. Martin's, 1995.

Egerton, John. *The Americanization of Dixie: The Southernization of America.* New York: Harper & Row, 1974.

Euripides. *Medea and Other Plays.* New York: Penguin Books, 1963.

Eyer, Diane. *Motherguilt: How Our Culture Blames Mothers for What's Wrong with Society.* New York: Times Books, 1996.

Faludi, Susan. *Backlash: The Undeclared War Against American Women.* New York: Crown Publishers, 1991.

———. *The Terror Dream: Fear and Fantasy in Post-9/11 America.* New York: Metropolitan Books, 2007.

Fass, Paula. *Kidnapped: Child Abduction in America.* New York: Oxford University Press, 1997.

Feimster, Crystal. *Southern Horrors: Women and the Politics of Rape and Lynching.* Cambridge, MA: Harvard University Press, 2009.

Feldman, Glenn. "The Status Quo Society, the Rope of Religion, and the New Racism." In *Politics and Religion in the White South,* ed. Feldman, 287–352.

———, ed. *Politics and Religion in the White South.* Lexington: University of Kentucky Press, 2005.

Feldstein, Ruth. *Motherhood in Black and White: Race and Sex in American Liberalism, 1930–1965.* Ithaca, NY: Cornell University Press, 2000.

Fineman, Martha A., and Isabel Karpin, eds. *Mothers in Law: Feminist Theory and the Legal Regulation of Motherhood.* New York: Columbia University Press, 1995.

Fineman, Martha A., and Martha T. McCluskey, eds. *Feminism, Media, and the Law.* New York: Oxford University Press, 1997.

Fiske, John. *Media Matters: Everyday Culture and Political Change.* Minneapolis: University of Minnesota Press, 1994.

Flamming, Douglas. *Creating the Modern South: Millhands and Managers in Dalton, Georgia, 1884–1984.* Chapel Hill: University of North Carolina Press, 1992.

Flavin, Jeanne. *Our Bodies, Our Crimes: The Policing of Women's Reproduction in America.* New York: New York University Press, 2009.

Fost, Dan. "The Lost Art of Fatherhood." *American Demographics,* March 1996, findarticles.com/p/articles/mi_m4021/is_n3_v18/ai_18056285/ (accessed July 5, 2011).

Fraiman, Susan. "Geometries of Race and Gender: Eve Sedgwick, Spike Lee, and Charlayne Hunter-Gault." *Feminist Studies* 20, no. 1 (March 1994): 67–84.

Francis, David R. "Changing Behavior of Married Working Women." *National Bureau of Economic Research Digest,* November 2005, www.nber.org/digest/nov05/w11230 .html (accessed August 1, 2011).

Frederickson, Mary. "'Sassing Fate': Women Workers in the Twentieth-Century South." In *Taking Off the White Gloves: Southern Women and Women Historians,* ed. Michelle Gillespie and Catherine Clinton. Columbia: University of Missouri Press, 1997. 15–27.

Genevie, Louis, and Eva Margolies. *The Motherhood Report: How Women Feel About Being Mothers.* New York: Macmillan Publishing Co., 1987.

Gillespie, Ed, and Bob Schellhas, eds. *Contract with America: The Bold Plan by Rep. Newt Gingrich, Rep. Dick Armey, and the House Republicans to Change the Nation.* New York: Times Books, 1994.

Gilmore, Glenda. *Gender and Jim Crow: Women and the Politics of White Supremacy in North Carolina, 1896–1920.* Chapel Hill: University of North Carolina Press, 1996.

———. "Murder, Memory, and the Flight of the Incubus." In *Democracy Betrayed: The Wilmington Race Riot of 1898 and Its Legacy,* ed. David S. Cecelski and Timothy B. Tyson. Chapel Hill: University of North Carolina Press, 1998. 73–94.

Ginzburg, Ralph, ed. *One Hundred Years of Lynchings.* Baltimore: Black Classic Press, 1962.

Gladwell, Malcolm. *The Tipping Point: How Little Things Can Make a Big Difference.* New York: Little, Brown, and Co., 2000.

Glaser, James M. *Race, Campaign Politics, and the Realignment in the South.* New Haven, CT: Yale University Press, 1996.

Glassner, Barry. *The Culture of Fear: Why Americans Are Afraid of the Wrong Things.* New York: Basic Books, 1999.

Goodman, James. *Stories of Scottsboro.* New York: Vintage Books, 1995.

Gordon, Linda. *Heroes of Their Own Lives: The Politics and History of Family Violence.* New York: Viking Press, 1988.

———. *Pitied But Not Entitled: Single Mothers and the History of Welfare, 1890–1935.* Cambridge, MA: Harvard University Press, 1998.

Gross, Kenneth. *The Alice Crimmins Case.* New York: Alfred A. Knopf, 1975.

Gruneau, Richard, and Robert A. Hackett. "The Production of Television News." In *Questioning the Media,* ed. Downing et al., 281–95.

Guare, John. *The Landscape of the Body.* New York: Grove Press, 1977.

Guth, James L. "Southern Baptist Clergy, the Christian Right, and Political Activism in the South." In *Politics and Religion in the White South,* ed. Feldman, 187–213.

Haag, Pamela. *Consent: Sexual Rights and the Transformation of American Liberalism.* Ithaca, NY: Cornell University Press, 1999.

Hall, Jacquelyn Dowd. "'The Mind That Burns in Each Body': Women, Rape, and Racial Violence." In *Powers of Desire: The Politics of Sexuality,* ed. Ann Snitow, Christine Stansell, and Sharon Thompson. New York: Monthly Review Press, 1983. 328–49.

———. *Revolt Against Chivalry: Jessie Daniel Ames and the Women's Campaign Against Lynching.* New York: Columbia University Press, 1993.

———, James Leloudis, Robert Korstad, Mary Murphy, Lu Ann Jones, and Christopher B. Daly. *Like a Family: The Making of a Southern Cotton Mill World.* Chapel Hill: University of North Carolina Press, 1987.

Hansen, Elaine Tuttle. *Mother Without Child: Contemporary Fiction and the Crisis of Motherhood.* Berkeley: University of California Press, 1997.

Hardesty, Nancy. "From Religion to Spirituality: Southern Women In and Out of Church." In *The Changing Shape of Protestantism in the South,* ed. Aldridge and Lewis. 70–78.

Harr, Jonathan. *A Civil Action.* New York: Vintage International, 1995.

Harvey, Paul. "Gods and Negroes and Jesus and Sin and Salvation: Racism, Racial

Interchange, and Interracialism in Southern Religious History." In *Religion in the American South: Politics and Others in History and Culture,* ed. Beth Barton Schweiger and Donald G. Mathews. Chapel Hill: University of North Carolina Press, 2004. 283–91.

———. "Religion." In *The South,* ed. Rebecca Mark and Rob Vaughan. Westport, CT: Greenwood Press, 2004. 413–14.

———. "Religion, Race, and the Right in the South, 1945–1990." In *Politics and Religion in the White South,* ed. Feldman, 101–23.

Hasian, Marouf Jr., and Lisa A. Flores. "Mass Mediated Representations of the Susan Smith Trial." *Howard Journal of Communication* 11 (2000): 163–78.

Hayes, Sharon. *The Cultural Contradictions of Motherhood.* New Haven, CT: Yale University Press, 1996.

Heinzelman, Susan Sage. "Women's Petty Treason: Feminism, Narrative, and the Law." *Journal of Narrative Technique* 20, no. 2 (Spring 1990): 89–106.

Henderson, Gary. *Nine Days in Union: The Search for Michael and Alex Smith.* Spartanburg, SC: Honoribus Press, 1995.

Hill, Samuel S. "Religion and Politics in the South." In *Religion in the South,* ed. Charles Reagan Wilson. Jackson: University Press of Mississippi, 1983. 139–53.

———. *Religion and the Solid South.* Nashville: Abingdon Press, 1972.

———, and Dennis E. Owen, *The New Religious Political Right in America.* Nashville: Abingdon Press, 1982.

Hobson, Fred. *Tell About the South: The Southern Rage to Explain.* Baton Rouge: Louisiana State University Press, 1983.

Hodes, Martha. *White Women, Black Men: Illicit Sex in the Nineteenth-Century South.* New Haven, CT: Yale University Press, 1997.

Howard, Lucy and Carla Koehl. "Who's News." *ABA Journal* (October 1995): 38.

Howell, E.A., P.A. Mora, M.D. DiBonaventura, and H. Leventhal, "Modifiable Factors Associated with Changes in Postpartum Depressive Symptoms." *Archives of Women's Mental Health,* 12 (April 2009).

Huang, Connie. "It's a Hormonal Thing: Premenstrual Syndrome and Postpartum Psychosis as Criminal Defense." *Southern California Review of Law and Women's Studies* (Spring 2002): litigation-essentials.lexisnexis.com/webcd/app?action=Document Display&crawlid=1&doctype=cite&docid=11+S.+Cal.+Rev.+L.+%26+Women's+ Stud.+345&srctype=smi&srcid=3B15&key=53ce376217d38aaa0c87ab8d25392e9e (accessed October 20, 2011.

Huckerby, Jayne. "Women Who Kill Their Children: Case Study and Conclusions Concerning the Differences in the Fall from Maternal Grace by Khoua Her and Andrea Yates." *Duke Journal of Gender and Law Policy* 10, no. 147 (2003): 149–72.

Hughes, Zondra. "Depression After Delivery: Black Mothers and the Postpartum Crisis." *Ebony,* October 2001.

Hunter, Tera. *To 'Joy My Freedom: Southern Black Women's Lives and Labors.* Cambridge, MA: Harvard University Press, 1997.

Hurwitz, John, and Mark Peffley. "Public Perceptions of Race and Crime: The Role of Racial Stereotypes." *American Journal of Political Science* 41, no. 2 (April 1997): 375–401.

Jackson, Njeri. "Fathering Injustice: Racial Patriarchy and the Dismantling of Affirmative Action." *Western Journal of Black Studies* 27 (2003): 51–56.

Jacobs, Becky L. "PMS: Perpetuating Male Superiority." *Texas Journal of Women and the Law* 14, no. 1 (Fall 2004): papers.ssrn.com/sol3/papers.cfm?abstract_id=962972 (accessed October 20, 2011).

Jacobs, Michelle S. "Requiring Battered Women Die: Murder Liability for Mothers Under Failure to Protect Statutes." *Journal of Criminal Law and Criminology* 88, no. 2 (Winter 1998): 579–660.

Jagger, Gill, and Caroline Wright, eds. *Changing Family Values.* New York: Routledge, 1999.

Jones, Ann. *Women Who Kill.* Boston: Beacon Press, 1996.

Jones, Jacqueline. *Labor of Love, Labor of Sorrow: Black Women, Work, and the Family, from Slavery to the Present.* New York: Basic Books, 1985.

Kantrowitz, Stephen. *Ben Tillman and the Reconstruction of White Supremacy.* Chapel Hill: University of North Carolina Press, 2000.

Karst, Kenneth L. *Law's Promises, Law's Expression: Visions of Power in the Politics of Race, Gender, and Religion.* New Haven, CT: Yale University Press, 1993.

Kerber, Linda K. *Women of the Republic: Intellect and Ideology in Revolutionary America.* Chapel Hill: University of North Carolina Press, 1980.

Klinenberg, Eric. *Heat Wave: A Social Autopsy of Disaster in Chicago.* Chicago: University of Illinois Press, 2002.

Kozol, Wendy. "Fracturing Domesticity: Media, Nationalism, and the Question of Feminist Influence." *Signs* (Spring 1995): 646–67.

Kruse, Kevin. *White Flight: Atlanta and the Making of Modern Conservatism.* Princeton, NJ: Princeton University Press, 2005.

Ladd-Taylor, Molly, and Lauri Umansky, eds. *"Bad Mothers": The Politics of Blame in Twentieth-Century America.* New York: New York University Press, 1998.

Lamis, Alexander P. "The Two-Party South: From the 1960s to the 1990s." In *Southern Politics in the 1990s,* ed. Alexander P. Lamis. Baton Rouge: Louisiana State University Press, 1999. 1–49.

Lassiter, Matthew D. "Inventing Family Values." In *Rightward Bound: Making America Conservative in the 1970s,* ed. Bruce J. Shulman and Julian E. Zelizer, 13–28. Cambridge, MA: Harvard University Press, 2008.

———. *The Silent Majority: Suburban Politics in the Sunbelt South.* Princeton, NJ: Princeton University Press, 2006.

———, and Joseph Crespino, eds. *The Myth of Southern Exceptionalism*. New York: Oxford University Press, 2010.

Lefkowitz, Bernard. *Our Guys: The Glen Ridge Rape and the Secret Life of the Perfect Suburb*. Berkeley: University of California Press, 1997.

Lindquist-Dorr, Linda. *White Women, Rape, and the Power of Race in Virginia, 1900–1960*. Chapel Hill: University of North Carolina Press, 2004.

Luker, Kristen. *Abortion and the Politics of Motherhood*. Berkeley: University of California Press, 1984.

Malcolm, Janet. *The Journalist and the Murderer*. New York: Alfred A. Knopf, 1990.

Mann, Coramae Richey. *When Women Kill*. Albany: State University of New York Press, 1996.

March, Christie L. "The Conflicted Treatment of Postpartum Depression Under Criminal Law." *William Mitchell Law Review* 32, no. 1 (November 2005): www.wmitchell.edu/lawreview/Volume32/Issue1/7March.pdf (accessed October 20, 2011).

Maschke, Karen J., ed. *Feminist Legal Theories*. New York: Garland Publishing, Inc., 1997.

May, Elaine Tyler. *Homeward Bound: American Families in the Cold War Era*. New York: Basic Books, 1988.

McGovern, James. *Anatomy of a Lynching*. Baton Rouge: Louisiana State University Press, 1982.

Mendelberg, Tali. "Executing Hortons: Racial Crime in the 1988 Presidential Campaign." *Public Opinion Quarterly* 61, no. 1 (Spring 1997): 134–57.

Metalious, Grace. *Peyton Place*. New York: Julian Messner, Inc., 1956.

Meyer, Cheryl, and Michelle Oberman. *Mothers Who Kill Their Children: Understanding the Acts of Moms from Susan Smith to the "Prom Mom."* New York: NYU Press, 2001.

Miller, Laura J. "Postpartum Depression." *Journal of the American Medical Association* 287 (2002): 762–65.

Minchin, Timothy. *Hiring the Black Worker: The Racial Integration of the Southern Textile Industry, 1960–1980*. Chapel Hill: University of North Carolina Press, 1999.

Mink, Gwendolyn. "Violating Women: Rights Abuses in the Welfare Police State." *Annals of the American Academy of Political and Social Science,* 577 (September 2001): 79-93.

Morland, J. K. *Millways of Kent*. Chapel Hill: University of North Carolina Press, 1958.

Morris, Allison, and Anna Wilczynski. "Rocking the Cradle: Mothers Who Kill Their Children." In *Moving Targets*, ed. Birch, 198–217.

Morrison, Toni. *Beloved*. New York: Alfred A. Knopf, 1987.

Murray, Charles. *The Bell Curve: Intelligence and Class Structure in American Life*. New York: Simon & Schuster, 1994.

Newitz, Annalee. "Murdering Mothers." In *"Bad Mothers,"* ed. Ladd-Taylor and Umansky, 334–55.

Nunacs, Rita. *A Deeper Shade of Blue: A Woman's Guide to Recognizing and Treating Depression in Her Childbearing Years.* New York: Simon & Schuster, 2006.

O'Connor, Alan. "Culture and Communication." In Downing et al., 27–41.

O'Connor, Flannery. "Some Aspects of the Grotesque in Southern Fiction." 1960. www.en.utexas.edu/amlit/amlitprivate/scans/grotesque.html (accessed October 20, 2011).

O'Malley, Suzanne. *Are You There Alone? The Unspeakable Crime of Andrea Yates* New York: Pocket Star Books, 2004.

Osmond, Marie. *Behind the Smile: My Journey Out of Postpartum Depression.* New York: Warner Books, 2001.

Ott, Brian L., and Eric Aoki. "The Politics of Negotiating Public Tragedy: Media Framing of the Matthew Shepard Murder." *Rhetoric and Public Affairs* 5, no. 3 (2002): 483–505.

Ownby, Ted. "Donald Wildmon, the American Family Association and the Theology of Media Activism." In *Politics and Religion in the White South,* ed. Feldman, 231–55.

Page, Helan E. "Black Male Imagery and Media Containment of African-American Men." *American Anthropologist* 99, no. 1 (March 1997): 99–111.

Pearson, Patricia. *When She Was Bad: Violent Women and the Myth of Innocence.* New York: Viking Press, 1997.

Perlin, Michael L. "She Breaks Just Like a Little Girl: Neonaticide, the Insanity Defense, and the Irrelevance of 'Ordinary Common Sense.'" *William and Mary Journal of Women and the Law* 10, no. 1 (Fall 2003): scholarship.law.wm.edu/wmjowl/vol10/iss1/2 (accessed October 20, 2011).

Perry, Lindsey C. "A Mystery of Motherhood: The Legal Consequences of Insufficient Research on Postpartum Illness." *Georgia Law Review* 42 (Fall 2007): 193–226.

Peyser, Andrea. *Mother Love, Deadly Love: The Susan Smith Murders.* New York: HarperCollins, 1995.

Pollack, Otto. *The Criminality of Women.* Philadelphia: University of Pennsylvania Press, 1950.

Poovey, Mary. *Uneven Developments: The Ideological Work of Gender in Mid-Victorian England.* Chicago: University of Chicago Press, 1988.

Price, Richard. *Freedomland.* New York: Random House, 1998.

Rabinowitz, Dorothy. *No Crueler Tyrannies: Accusation, False Witness, and Other Terrors of Our Times.* New York: Free Press, 2003.

Raper, Arthur. *The Tragedy of Lynching.* Chapel Hill: University of North Carolina Press, 1933.

Rapping, Elayne. *Law and Justice as Seen on Television.* New York: New York University Press, 2003.

———. "The Movie of the Week: Law, Narrativity, and Gender in Prime Time." In *Feminism Media, and the Law,* ed. Fineman and McCluskey. 91–103.

Reeher, Grant, and Joseph Cammarano. "In Search of the Angry White Male: Gender, Race, and Issues in the 1994 Elections." In *Midterm: The Elections of 1994 in Context*, ed. Philip A. Klinkner. Boulder, CO: Westview Press, 1996. 125–36.

Rekers, George. *Susan Smith: Victim or Murderer?* Lakewood, CO: Glenbridge Publishing Company, 1996.

Rhodes, Deborah L. "Media Images/Feminist Issues." In *Feminism, Media, and the Law*, ed. Fineman and McCluskey. 8–21.

Rich, Adrienne. *Of Woman Born: Motherhood as Experience and Institution*. New York: W. W. Norton and Co., 1976.

Roof, Wade Clark. "Southern Protestantism: New Challenges, New Possibilities." In *The Changing Shape of Protestantism in the South*, ed. Aldridge and Lewis. 11–34.

Royster, Jacqueline Jones, ed. *Southern Horrors and Other Writings*. Boston: Bedford Books, 1997.

Rozell, Mark J., and Clyde Wilcox. "The Christian Right in Virginia Politics." In *Politics and Religion in the White South*, ed. Feldman, 255–70.

Rule, Ann. *Small Sacrifices*. New York: TimeWarner Paperbacks, 2004.

Russell, Linda (with Shirley Stephens). *My Daughter, Susan Smith*. Brentwood, TN: Authors' Book Nook, 2000.

Saletan, William. *Bearing Right: How Conservatives Won the Abortion War*. Berkeley: University of California Press, 2003.

Schernitzski, Rebecca Ann. "What Kind of Mother Are You? The Relationship Between Motherhood, Battered Woman Syndrome and Missouri Law." *Journal of the Missouri Bar* 56, no. 1 (January–February 2000): www.mobar.org/journal/2000/janfeb/scher.htm (accessed October 20, 2011).

Schulman, Bruce J., and Julian E. Zelizer, eds. *Rightward Bound: Making America Conservative in the 1970s*. Cambridge, MA: Harvard University Press, 2008.

Schwartz, Lita Linzer, and Natalie K. Isser. *Endangered Children: Neonaticide, Infanticide, and Filicide*. Boca Raton, FL: CRC Press, 2000.

Schweiger, Beth Barton. "Max Weber in Mount Airy; or, Revivals and Social Theory in the Early South." In *Religion in the American South: Politics and Others in History and Culture*, ed. Beth Barton Schweiger and Donald G. Mathews. Chapel Hill: University of North Carolina Press, 2004. 31–66.

Shields, Brooke. *Down Came the Rain: My Journey Through Postpartum Depression*. New York: Hyperion, 2005.

Segre, Lisa S., Michael W. O'Hara, Stephan Arndt, and Scott Stuart. "The Prevalence of Postpartum Depression: The Relative Significance of Three Social Status Indices." *Social Psychiatry and Psychiatric Epidemiology* 42, no. 4 (2007): 316–21.

Sharabi, Hisham. *Neopatriarchy: A Theory of Distorted Change in Arab Society*. New York: Oxford University Press, 1988.

Simon, Bryant. *A Fabric of Defeat: The Politics of South Carolina Millhands, 1910–1948*.

Chapel Hill: University of North Carolina Press, 1998.

Skolnick, Arlene. "Talking about Family Values After 'Family Values,'" *Dissent* 57, no. 4 (Fall 2010): 96–102.

Smith, David (with Carol Calef). *Beyond All Reason: My Life with Susan Smith*. New York: Pinnacle Books, 1995.

Snitow, Ann. "Feminism and Motherhood: An American Reading." *Feminist Review* 40 (Spring 1992): 32–51.

Southern Commission on the Study of Lynching. *Lynchings and What They Mean*. Atlanta: Southern Commission on the Study of Lynching, 1931.

Spinelli, Margaret, ed. *Infanticide: Psychosocial and Legal Perspectives on Women Who Kill*. Washington, DC: American Psychiatric Publishing, Inc., 2003.

Spruill, Marjorie J. "Gender and America's Right Turn." In *Rightward Bound: Making American Conservative in the 1970s*, ed. Bruce J. Shulman and Julian E. Zelizer, 71–89. Cambridge, MA: Harvard University Press, 2008.

Stacey, Judith. *In the Name of the Family: Rethinking Family Values in the Postmodern Age*. Boston: Beacon Press, 1996.

State of South Carolina v. Susan Vaughan Smith

Tanenbaum, Leora. *Slut! Growing Up Female with a Bad Reputation*. New York: Seven Stories Press, 1999.

Taylor, George H. "Transcending the Debate on Legal Narrative." *University of Pittsburgh School of Law Working Paper* 11 (April 2005): law.bepress.com/pittlwps/papers/art11 (accessed August 15, 2011).

Thernstrom, Abigail, and Henry D. Felter. "From Scottsboro to Simpson." *Public Interest* 122 (January 1, 1996): available online through Academic Search Premier.

Thomas, Sari. "Myths In and About Television." In Downing et al., 330–44.

Thomas, Susan. "From the Culture of Poverty to the Culture of Single Motherhood: The New Poverty Paradigm." *Women & Politics* 14, no. 2 (September 1994): 65–97.

Timbs, Larry. "To Print or Not to Print an Alleged Victim's Claims." *Editor and Publisher* 127, no. 51 (December 17, 1994): list.msu.edu/cgi-bin/wa?A2=ind9910a&L=aejmc&P=6167 (accessed October 20, 2011).

Uhnak, Dorothy. *The Investigation*. New York: Pocket Books, 1978.

Umansky, Lauri. *Motherhood Reconceived: Feminisms and the Legacies of the Sixties*. New York: New York University Press, 1996.

Waldrep, George. *Southern Workers and the Search for Community*. Urbana: University of Illinois Press, 2000.

Wattenberg, Ben J. *The Birth Dearth*. New York: Pharos, 1989.

Weaver, R. Kent, Robert Y. Shapiro, and Lawrence R. Jacobs. "The Polls—Trends: Welfare." *Public Opinion Quarterly* 59 (1995): 606–27.

Whitfield, Stephen J. *A Death in the Delta: The Story of Emmett Till*. Baltimore: Johns Hopkins University Press.

Wilczynski, Ania. *Child Homicide.* London: Greenwich Medical Media Ltd., 1997.

Williams, Patricia. *The Alchemy of Race and Rights: Diary of a Mad Law Professor.* Cambridge, MA: Harvard University Press, 1991.

Williamson, Joel. *The Crucible of Race: Black-White Relations in the American South Since Emancipation.* New York: Oxford University Press, 1984.

Willimon, William H. "On Being a Southerner and a Christian at the Same Time." In *The Changing Shape of Protestantism in the South,* ed. Aldridge and Lewis, 29-36.

Willis, Ellen. "Abortion: Is a Woman a Person?" In *Powers of Desire: The Politics of Sexuality,* ed. Ann Snitow, Christine Stansell, and Sharon Thompson. New York: Monthly Review Press, 1983. 471–76.

Wolf, Naomi. *The Beauty Myth: How Images of Beauty Are Used Against Women.* New York: Anchor Books, 1991.

Wolfe, Tom. *The Bonfire of the Vanities.* New York: Bantam Books, 1988.

Wright, Richard. *Native Son.* New York: Harper & Row Publishers, 1940.

Wurtzel, Elizabeth. *Bitch: In Praise of Difficult Women.* New York: Random House, 1998.

Wylie, Philip. *Generation of Vipers.* Normal, IL: Dalkey Archive Press, 1942.

Yaeger, Patricia. "Beyond the Hummingbird: Southern Women Writers and the Southern Gargantua." In *Haunted Bodies: Gender and Southern Texts,* ed. Anne Goodwyn Jones and Susan V. Donaldson. Charlottesville: University of Virginia Press, 1997.

———. *Dirt and Desire: Reconstructing Southern Women's Writing, 1930–1990.* Chicago: University of Chicago Press, 2000.

Yang, Vue. "Postpartum Depression and the Insanity Defense: A Poor Mother's Two Worst Nightmares." *Wisconsin Journal of Law, Gender, and Society* 24, no. 229 (Spring 2009): hosted.law.wisc.edu/wjlgs/issues/2009-spring/yang.pdf (accessed October 20, 2011).

INDEX